As an editor of a pastoral books written to help Christian growth, yet, *A Wonder-Filled Life* by Joshua A. McClure primarily offers encouragement toward life transformation. Written for people who may identify as Christians, this book raises key questions about whether they live a "normal Christian life, a life filled with wonder."

McClure asserts that Jesus offers abundant life—and that the Christian life is to be a life filled with wonders. Throughout the book, he shares many of his encounters with Jesus that led to that realization. McClure reminds us that life with Jesus, when active and centered on the Gospel, becomes a life filled with His wonders—a manifestation of God's wonderful love story.

McClure asserts that many people who simply attend church experience disappointment and frustration because they are living out of their false selves. They fulfill their standards of morality when they do not know their true selves in Christ. One can come to know their true self by encountering the God who created them and the Son who redeemed them. They will only be their true self and live a life of wonder when they come to know God, His amazing love, and Jesus's great redemption.

No Jesus, No Wonder.

Know Jesus, Know Wonder.

Because they do not have personal knowledge of Jesus, they also don't know the true self that God created and which Jesus redeemed.

While reminding us about the difference between cognitive knowledge and "personal experiential knowing," McClure guides the readers to go to the Scripture to know the truth of who Jesus is and what he has done, and to surrender to the power of the Holy Spirit. As readers deepen their understanding and learn to walk with the Spirit through practices of surrendering, self-denying, obedience, they can begin to experience this wonder. Ultimately, this book follows the thoughts and understandings of someone who knows what it means to see life as it should be. Readers will be encouraged to deepen their roots in Jesus and join him in a *wonder-full* adventure.

Stephen Cha, PhD
Lead Pastor, Onnuri English Ministry
Seoul, South Korea

Joshua McClure's book *A Wonder-Filled Life* is remarkable and fascinating in that it keeps one reading with anticipation, page after page. The reader will be challenged or inspired to look closer at who God is! It will also cause the reader to consider who he or she is (our identity), and who we are in Christ.

A Wonder-Filled Life causes us to take a closer look at our faith walk. Are we able, as Joshua McClure says, to define the "wonders" we have experienced in our life with Jesus Christ? One thing that is made clear through his testimony in the book is that the movement of the Holy Spirit is real in the lives of His people.

This book should be read by all who profess a relationship with Jesus Christ, and even by those who have not yet made that confession. I believe it could help someone to make a decision.

The Rev. Dr. Vincent L. Thompson, Jr.
Pastor Emeritus, Community Baptist Church, Newport, RI

This book, *A Wonder-Filled Life,* includes insightful wisdom and advice through the lifelong journey of a pastor who has experienced hope and joy as a Christian. The author tells of the benefits of peace and companionship with the Holy Spirit, as well as his story, based on the Scriptures. Undoubtedly, I have sometimes felt difficulty in following the way of a Christian's life. However, the instruction and story of the author gave me comfort, relief, and assurance, derived from the sacrifice of Jesus Christ. In this book, readers will find more guidance than expected.

Prof. John Sanghyun Lee
Soongsil ("Revering God") University
Seoul, South Korea

Are you dissatisfied with your relationship with God? Are you floating on the surface of Christianity instead of being submerged? Are you waiting for the Lord's return, or for Him to take you home so that you can experience the rich and fulfilling life He promised? If you answer yes to any of these questions, Joshua McClure's *A Wonder-Filled Life* turns this entire concept on its head by challenging a belief amongst Christians that the life Christ is referring to is experienced in death. McClure contends that if we embrace the walk of God with childlike faith, we can experience kingdom living and its application here on earth, rather than in heaven.

In *A Wonder-Filled Life,* Joshua McClure offers interesting insights by the use of sound doctrine and solid biblical teaching. He paints a clear picture of the cross and describes the experience of Jesus Christ, bringing his pain to life. McClure shares his own struggles, including the lack of fulfillment he felt going through the motions of being an active church participant, but not living the abundant life.

A Wonder-Filled Life is heart-wrenching and serves as a bold, no-nonsense, straightforward approach, calling for action from pastors and congregants alike. Joshua McClure assesses the issues that exist in the church and identifies that we are in an era of tradition and religion, rather than a sincere and intimate relationship with Christ. Through his wise counsel, by the end of this book as said about Peter and John in Acts 4:13, when people see you, they should view "an ordinary man or woman with no training that has been with Jesus."

Juanita Hadley, attorney
Founder and CEO, changingcases.org;
and author, *CYKAS: Can You Keep a Secret?*

Here in your latest book *A Wonder-FILLED Life*, I can certainly tell by their might and clarity that these thoughts and convictions were certainly allowed by the Lord God to mature and strengthen for forty years(!) in your mind, heart, and soul for a definitive purpose. In the past week I have reread this fine work and purposely took notes in the process to indicate what was most profoundly speaking to me through your wise pen.

I have to say, I believe this book may be among my favorites of all you have written. It seems to me to be a kind of magnum opus of your distinguished life of service and authorship. Each section works very effectively as a separate unit but then simultaneously all come together in a wonderful collective unity. Your life's experience in the Lord and the plethora of wisdom you have accrued in His service come through with each sentence. Well done. What an amazing "second" career (vocation!) the Triune God has given you in the proficiency of your mind and pen!

The Rev. Mark R. Galloway, BA, ThM, MA, STM (retired)
Bishop, The Church of The Apostles (Evangelical Anglican)
Coventry, RI

*Debbie,
Abundant Blessings*

A WONDER FILLED LIFE

Galatians 2:20

Joshua A. McClure

A Wonder-Filled Life
Copyright © 2022 Joshua A. McClure

Published by Deep River Books
Sisters, Oregon
www.deepriverbooks.com

All rights reserved. No part of this book may be reproduced or transmitted in any form or by any means, electronic or mechanical, including photocopying and recording, or by any information storage and retrieval system, without permission in writing from the publisher.

All Scripture quotations, unless otherwise noted, are taken from the *Holy Bible*, New Living Translation, Copyright © 1996, 2004, 2015 by Tyndale House Foundation. Used by permission of Tyndale House Publishers, Inc. Carol Stream, Illinois 60188. All rights reserved.

Scripture quotations marked KJV are taken from the King James Version. Public domain.

Scripture quotations marked TLB are taken from The Living Bible copyright © 1971 by Tyndale House Foundation. Used by permission of Tyndale House Publishers Inc., Carol Stream, Illinois 60188. All rights reserved.

Scripture quotations marked NIV are taken from the Holy Bible, New International Version®, NIV® Copyright ©1973, 1978, 1984, 2011 by Biblica, Inc.® Used by permission. All rights reserved worldwide.

Cover design by Joe Bailen, Contajus Designs

ISBN—13: 9781632695888
Library of Congress Control Number: 2022905557

Printed in the USA
2022—First Edition
31 30 29 28 27 26 25 24 23 22   10 9 8 7 6 5 4 3 2 1

Dedicated to
the sick, afflicted, and hurting at Briarcliffe
Hear Jesus say,
"Stand up, pick up your mat, and walk!"
(John 5:8)

CONTENTS

Foreword 11

Preface 13

Introduction 21

Section I **27**

    One: Not of the World 29

    Two: Falling Stones 43

    Three: The Crucified Life 59

    Four: Life Exchange 75

    Five: Restored Image 91

    Six: Fan Or Follower 105

    Seven: Life Centering 121

    Eight: The Name of Jesus 135

    Nine: The New Life 149

    Ten: Kingdom Life 163

Section II **177**

    Eleven: Life In The Body 179

Twelve: Living Roots 193

Thirteen: Spirit Life 207

Fourteen: River of Life 221

Fifteen: Wonder-Filled Life 235

Sixteen: Life Promise 247

Seventeen: Living Faith 261

Eighteen: The Love Life 277

Nineteen: Indwelling Presence 293

Twenty: Beholding 307

Endnotes 323

FOREWORD

Right from the start of my reading of *A Wonder-Filled Life,* Joshua A. McClure grabbed my mind to *think* about Galatians 2:20. I have read it many times, quoted it, taught it, and even preached it. But this exposition of this text gave me fresh insight. As we study God's Word, we are all progressive learners—because the Christian life is a journey toward maturity, as we yield ourselves to the Holy Spirit. God is giving us new insight into His Word as we grow. However, we also can learn from well-seasoned, mature believers like Joshua A. McClure.

He has given us a wealth of wisdom from the solid research of notable scholars. He has also been biblical in his reference, along with down-to-earth stories and illustrations. As I read this book, I kept thinking that this should be read by all new believers as they begin their discipleship process. Each chapter takes you deeper to discover and question, as it did with me, am I missing something? Once I started reading, it was hard to put down. The thoughts in this well-thought-through book just stay with you, like a good perfume or cologne!

Dr. Charles R. Leslie Jr.
Mission Mobilizer
Mission Global Fellowship

PREFACE

This book has been a long time coming! I have penned these words over and over in my mind since the fall of 1977, after I returned from a conference on the Holy Spirit at the Green Lake Conference Center/American Baptist Assembly in Oshkosh, Wisconsin. The general information communicated at this gathering was more than worthwhile, but none was as stimulating and all-embracing as the day I was introduced to a new concept in my faith journey called "Kingdom Living."

After spending more than four decades in the gospel narratives, I now realize why Paul's words in Galatians 2:20 so captured my heart that they are with me every waking moment of my life: "My old self has been crucified with Christ. It is no longer I who live, but Christ lives in me. So I live in this earthly body by trusting in the Son of God, who loved me and gave himself for me." Little did I realize at the time that this exposition on "Living in the Kingdom of God" would ignite the flame to fire my passion for living in God's presence under the lordship of Jesus Christ, in the power for daily living supplied by the Holy Spirit.

To say that this was my "aha" moment in comprehending the Scripture passage I had embraced as my lifelong goal would be a huge understatement. Like many believers, I had viewed the Christian life as "work hard, be a good citizen, take care of my family, read my

Bible, attend church, and pray." I thought that because of my relationship with Christ, my life would get better and somewhat easier and I would find the comfort, peace, joy, and satisfaction promised in the Scriptures. But I must confess, I found more disappointment than fulfillment and at times it caused me to question my walk with the Lord. I often found myself asking, "Why is it so difficult to live a joyous Christian life? Why can't I stop doing some of the things I did before I came to Christ?" I thought things would be different. I imagined it would be easier, but it had been a struggle. And yet each day I maintained a hope that things would change.

I was uncertain that one could live out the life that Jesus came into the world, suffered, and died for. I now know that it is not only possible but that it is very near to us. However, the Scriptures explain why it is so challenging:

> The sinful nature wants to do evil, which is just the opposite of what the Spirit wants. And the Spirit gives us desires that are the opposite of what the sinful nature desires. These two forces are constantly fighting each other, so you are not free to carry out your good intentions. (Galatians 5:17)

However, we are encouraged by Paul's words:

> But you are not controlled by your sinful nature. You are controlled by the Spirit if you have the Spirit of God living in you. (And remember that those who do not have the Spirit of Christ living in them do not belong to him at all.) And Christ lives within you, so even though your body will die because of sin, the Spirit gives you life because you have been made right with God. (Romans 8:9–10)

I then realized that the life I sought did not have to be so elusive—that the life I was most accustomed to maintaining in this world was not, in reality, the life God intended for me. Since "My old self has been crucified with Christ. It is no longer I who live, but Christ lives in me" (Galatians 2:20). The Holy Spirit who lives in my mortal body was the guarantee that I would realize what God had planned the Christian life to be. Thus, crucifixion would unlock the real life hidden in Christ Jesus.

I was aware of the well-to-do and successful people who commonly state who we are in terms of *what we have*, and measure our peace and happiness by how well we achieve our goal. And yet, at the same time no one needs to be reminded that in our present life we have seemingly failed to produce anything that exceeds our forefathers to give us satisfaction and fullness in our living. Today we possess great learning as computers, science, and artificial intelligence have opened our minds to a world of possibility; and medicine with its modern procedures and wonder drugs have prolonged life. However, with a profusion of leisure time we exhaust ourselves running to and fro, following pursuits that stimulate our minds but not our hearts. The fact is, we continue searching for that peace, joy, and comfort, more often than not frustrated by the lack of capability to fulfill our longing. I am reminded of the experience of the wise man Solomon, granted immeasurable perception and wisdom by God, who appears to give support to the futility of seeking peace and comfort in material gain:

> I came to hate all my hard work here on earth, for I must leave to others everything I have earned. And who can tell whether my successors will be wise or foolish? Yet they will control everything I have gained by my skill and hard work under the sun. How meaningless! So I gave up in despair, questioning the value of all my hard work in this world. (Ecclesiastes 2:18–20)

16   A Wonder-Filled Life

After Solomon's general observances of life, he concludes that life in the world is meaningless. Is Solomon then suggesting that satisfaction in the earthly realm is a lost cause? That living a good life is not worth the effort? That hard work is foolishness? I think not. The point is, hard work bears no fruit for those who work solely to earn money and gain possessions. Not only will everything be left behind at death, but it may be left to those who have done nothing to earn it. Remember that God has given us work to do, and that you will become dissatisfied if you lose the sense of purpose God intended for your work. Your ability to find satisfaction in your work depends to a large extent upon your attitude and relationship to God.

Because we are created in God's image, we have a spiritual thirst. God has "planted eternity in the human heart" (Ecclesiastes 3:11). We can never be completely satisfied with earthly pleasures and pursuits. Nothing but the eternal God can truly satisfy us. God has built in us a restless yearning for the kind of perfect world that can only be found in his perfect rule. He has given us a glimpse of the perfection of his creation. But it is only a glimpse; we cannot see into the future or comprehend everything. We must trust God now and do his work on earth.

Thus, amid our everyday struggles, we hear the words of Scripture concerning Jesus. John, in his gospel (1:14), records, "So the Word became human and lived here on earth among us." Consequently, many have queried, "Why did Jesus come into the world? What was the purpose of it all?" Jesus himself replies in John's gospel (10:10), "My purpose is to give them a rich and satisfying life." Here Jesus supplies the missing link to all of our queries. It is obvious that since the fall, Satan's mission in the world has been to kill and destroy any semblance of happiness, joy, and peace in those who image God. By contrast, Jesus gave his life to fulfill our quest for "a rich and satisfying life."

That being the case, the question arises: Where and how do we find this rewarding life avowed by Jesus? And how, then, must this rich and satisfying life be lived out? Jesus's purpose is clear. However, what I believe to be the key to our stumbling block is found in Jesus's words, "At that time Jesus prayed this prayer: 'O Father, Lord of heaven and earth, thank you for hiding these things from those who think themselves wise and clever, and for revealing them to the childlike'" (Matthew 11:25). Here Jesus mentions two kinds of people: the "wise and clever"—arrogant in their knowledge; and the "childlike"—humbly open to receive the truth of God's Word. I often wonder if, when we insist on bringing our worldly experiences in interpreting and understanding the Word of God, if we are not indeed among the arrogant in knowledge—veiling the truth of God. Thus there is a need to be empty of "self," to receive the Word of God with a childlike attitude. Facts do not produce life, nor do they bring belief. It is through the Spirit's revelation that we can know God intimately. Once "knowing" comes, we enter into God's presence and we move closer to his heart—to be centered in him.

In comparison, John the Baptist, the forerunner of Jesus, began preaching in the Judean wilderness proclaiming the good news of God, urging, "Repent of [turn from] your sins and turn to God, for the Kingdom of Heaven is near" (Matthew 3:2). John was announcing that the Kingdom of Heaven, the reign and rule of God, was at hand. That was the whole purpose of Jesus coming into the world. He was to be the physical embodiment, incarnation, expression of the Kingdom of God. In Jesus's life, we see the perfect example, a model of what we are to become. He shows us how to live, where to live, and gives us the power to live "a rich and satisfying life." This is what the "good news," the gospel, it is about—God inaugurating his spiritual rule and reign in the heart and the world, seeking to reconcile all things to himself, to reverse the sentence of the first Adam, and to establish a people in the likeness of the second Adam, Jesus Christ. That was the game plan of Jesus. It's a breathtaking story of a fulfilling and fulfilled purpose, and the truly marvelous news is that we are all invited to share and to serve this purpose of God in Christ Jesus.

People like you and me are called to repent and believe the gospel, to lose ourselves in Christ. Therefore, this good news is no longer a dream; the Kingdom of God is at hand. *Here, upon, within, near, available, now*—these are the terms Jesus uses. However, most believers today simply absorb these terms into our everyday language and fail to view them as a new motif for living. We fail to understand that the life we are now living on this earth is not the life Jesus came to bring us; hence, we are ignorant or simply do not care that there is another life at hand. This new life is available to be lived out here and now, but many still view "real" spirituality not as earthly but as "heavenly"; therefore, the life we now live can only be a future reality. Our old self (sin nature), which previously occupied our bodies in this fallen world, cannot view the present reality of the kingdom in the world.

Over the years I have heard people speak openly about their disappointment, frustration, and dismay at being plagued by the same problems as experienced before: "I don't feel a whole lot different. When I first came to Christ I felt great; however, I don't seem to have that feeling anymore." They are still struggling with the old life of sin.

I suspect many have failed to make the transition from the old physical life to the new life in Christ. What happened on the inside has not yet manifested itself on the outside. Change, renewal, and transformation have not surfaced, even though they try to live a new and improved life. Their effort to be better persons has been thwarted because the heart has changed but the residence has not.

They try to live simply hoping to do better, not realizing that Jesus left the world to go back to the Father. Consequently, their old place of residence has to be abandoned as well. A new way of living as a new creature in Christ—in a new home in the Kingdom of God, under the lordship of the King—must take place.

At the moment of conversion, we do not merely turn over a new leaf; we begin a new life under a new master. The Spirit of Christ living in our mortal bodies now sits on the right hand of the Father in heaven. One of the most important and helpful passages of transition about living the new life is found in Colossians 3:1–2, where Paul urges us to change our way of thinking—to put heaven's priorities into daily practice, and to concentrate on the eternal rather than on the temporal. If we understand that our real home is where Christ lives, it will give us a different perspective of our life here on earth. Instead of looking at the obstacles and difficulties we encounter daily, we will now look to God's promise of supply. We will look at life from God's perspective and seek what he desires, and not measure our success or failure by the world's standards. The more we regard the world around us as God does, the more we live in harmony with him.

In the final analysis, we are all dependent on God. He is the source of all things, including us. He is the power who sustains and rules the world that we live in, and he alone deserves our praise. God does not want us to continue to frustrate ourselves by trying to change our own lives, and then cry out to him only when we are in trouble. He wants us to live daily in his presence, avoiding the anxiety and disappointments of the old life apart from him. He wants us to learn of him; he wants us to grow in him; and he desires intimacy that can only come from spending time in his presence. Therefore, Jesus's purpose in coming into a fallen world was to provide a place of happiness, joy, peace, and eternal fellowship with God: "My purpose is to give them a rich and satisfying life."

INTRODUCTION

In this exploration of *A Wonder-Filled Life*, I have chosen twenty quotes from the narrative and insights on kingdom living that stood out to me most powerfully and will tell of how they speak to me personally.

Joshua McClure writes, *"Like many believers, I had [at one time] viewed the Christian life as hard work."* How true this has been for me far too often in my Christian journey (even as a so-called "mature" believer). Even now, when I find myself falling back into this trap and wrong-headed thinking, I must make sincere and overt efforts to get myself out of this false mindset.

"I must confess, that I found more disappointment than fulfillment [in the Christian life and ordained ministry] and at times [this] caused me to question my walk with the Lord." Joshua, I greatly admire your honesty and vulnerability in this statement. This is so utterly true about my own life in Christ and especially in my nearly thirty years of work in the ordained ministry. I find this to be particularly the case as I (in "retirement") reflect upon the decades and thousands upon thousands of hours that I put forward in the work of ministry—that in many (most certainly most) cases and situations yielded (from a worldly standard) little results.

"Nothing but the eternal God can truly satisfy us." Absolutely. And I am ashamed to say that I cannot count how many times I

absolutely lost track or simply ignored this most obvious fact in human endeavor. As I struggle along in life with Parkinson's and become more and more removed from the "lime-light" of active full-time leadership in the church, this biblical truth is constantly knocking on my conscience and soul, reminding me of the ultimate eternal truth— the Triune God is real and my soul shall always be restless until it unconditionally rests in Him (St. Augustine of Hippo).

"*. . . a new way of living as a new creature in Christ is a new home in the Kingdom of God under the lordship of the King must take place [in a believer's life if they are to be free].*" I believe much, if not the vast majority, of the church universal (clergy and laity alike) have lost this truth (or have never really believed it or heard it proclaimed).

"*. . . [we need to] put heaven's priorities into daily practice.*" This simple but profound statement is a gem. I know exactly what you mean with this statement, and I admit I have struggled to do it in my own life consistently, never mind effectively transmitting the power of this reality to the thousands of souls that I have pastored through the decades.

"*If we understand that our real home is where Christ lives, it will give us a different perspective of our life here on earth.*" Indeed, we are not citizens of this world but are mere resident aliens, as the apostle Peter says. The more "Christians" believe they can build a utopia on this earth, the more wayward, ineffective (and eventually virtually irrelevant) the church shall become in culture.

"*. . . he [God] alone deserves our praise.*" In a world flooded with the 24/7 narcissism of social media, this ultimate truth is rapidly being lost on most "members" of the Christian church.

"*No man, woman or child, need ever remain the way they are.*" This truth, I am afraid, is no longer believed by many of those who serve in the pastorate of the churches—and their acquiescing to the perversions of sexual immorality, the ignoring of the central necessity of the nuclear family in God's plan for mankind, and the incremental acceptance of the binary and gender fluidity apostasy are tolling the bell on the rapid sunset of the mainline Protestant establishment.

"Materialism often takes over, at the same rate at which our spirituality declines." This is accurate. The rise of the heretical "prosperity gospel" historically coincides precisely with this very real spiritual decline—that leaves even many a full (mega)church but a morbid funeral parlor, the gathering place of the spiritually dead.

". . . do I know what is needed to live out this Christian life?" The answer to the rhetorical question here is NO. The average pew-sitter today does not know. And I put the fault of this pathetic reality at the feet of the clergy of the past fifty years in the church universal.

"Every person who claims or purports to be a believer in Jesus Christ should have a vision of God that transcends every earthly thing." How often have I met and worked with people in various modes of church leadership (lay and ordained) who just can never quite get there— grasping the vision of kingdom living"? So very many people I know have bailed on their vocations in both the lay and ordained ministry in just the past few years because of their unwillingness to accept the immutable truth articulated with the above-quoted statement.

"Why have we not become the light of the world? Why have we not done more to change the world? Why is it so hard for us to break the stranglehold of the world in our lives?" These are amongst the most perplexing questions I have asked of myself on many occasions: as a baptized and confirmed member of the church universal, as an ordained deacon and priest, and as a consecrated bishop. Why is the church (the bride of Christ himself) so anemic and ineffective when she is empowered with the infinite grace and love of

the supreme Sovereign and Creator? Why? Because (in reality) she rarely dares to embrace kingdom living.

". . . the whole purpose in [one's] life was to speak boldly for Christ and to become more like him." This statement struck a very deep measure within me. In reflection upon my fifty-seven years thus far lived upon this earth this truth reaches out (more literally, claws) at my conscience as being the essence of what my being should always be about—no matter the worldly cost.

"Christ is never strong in us until we are weak." Time and again I have had to learn this supreme lesson the hard way. How foolish and blatantly prideful I have far too often been in my life—in the process always increasing the pain of my steps on the pilgrim's way.

"Shying away from the [Holy] Spirit leaves us empty, powerless, and inadequate to cope with everyday living." This irrefutable biblical fact is the real pandemic in the contemporary church—far more spiritually deadly than COVID-19 could ever be physically.

"What do the Scriptures mean when they say that our body belongs to God?" I used this quote in some recent teaching I have done when speaking about the blight and evil of abortion, transgenderism, bodily mutilation, and the massive scourge of addiction to pornography in our culture. Indeed, we do not belong to ourselves—we were bought with an incalculable price—the body is the temple of the Holy Spirit.

"I thought I could keep it together by myself, but I could not." This statement articulates what I so deeply admire about Joshua McClure. His transparent honesty and vulnerability in assessing composite pieces of his life are an inspiration to me to emulate my dear friend. Oh, how many times I believed I could keep it all together by thinking I could do it by myself!

"One of the great tragedies of the church in this age, and the source of God's greatest heartache, is that so many believers fail to love." The

COVID-19 pandemic exposed the incredible depth of the soft underbelly of the church in this regard. It amazes me the vitriol which so-called "Christians" (across racial, socioeconomic, and political-ideological lines) are spewing at each other in person and especially on social media. How does a "Christian" ever rationalize simply "canceling" another human being?

"Why do so few believers today manifest the presence of Jesus in their lives?" This is a very important (rhetorical) question put forth here. As we know, many a pew-sitter can babble on with Christian lingo and play their expected social part inside the four walls of the church building without ever being truly regenerated people in their hearts.

"The crowd in heaven . . . praises God, saying that salvation comes from him and the Lamb." I must say, my friend, the "Crowd in heaven" gets more desirable for me every day – absent from this body and the vale of tears and present with the Lord!

Well, there you have it! My dear friend Joshua, it continues to be one of the greatest honors of my life to have you as a spiritual father. My deepest and fondest affection and respect to you in Our Lord Jesus Christ.

> The Rev. Mark R. Galloway, BA, ThM, MA, STM (retired)
> Bishop, The Church of The Apostles (Evangelical Anglican)
> Coventry, RI

SECTION I

My old self has been crucified with Christ.
It is no longer I who live, but Christ lives in me.

SECTION I

ONE

NOT OF THE WORLD

The Spirit of God, who raised Jesus from the dead, lives in you. And just as God raised Christ from the dead, he will give life to your mortal bodies by this same Spirit living within you.

(Romans 8:11)

Somewhere along the way, the words of the Bible or a particular passage of Scripture will have a great impact upon your life. You will sense: this is what your life is all about, this is what you work for. This is why you are here. This is where you will find the ultimate purpose for living. This is the answer to the question, what would God have me do?

Hence my contribution in this book is to tell of one man's experience of that "aha" moment in which God revealed his overwhelming presence, "My old self has been crucified with Christ. It is no longer I who live, but Christ lives in me. So I live in this earthly body by trusting in the Son of God, who loved me and gave himself for me" (Galatians 2:20). To that end, you may find this book

30   A Wonder-Filled Life

unusual, because I am writing not as an observer but as a partaker. Every word, accompanied by every breath I take, is a testimony of the life I now live in this earthly body. It is confirmation that I am living the life that Jesus came into the world to bring us: "My purpose is to give them a rich and satisfying life" (John 10:10b).

Therefore, this book is not a scholarly dissertation, a book for intellectual reasoning, or an instruction manual for dummies. It is not a trial read-through with a return postmark, or a book relegated to my favorite book list. Rather, it is a book to be not merely observed but experienced. It is a book to be lived, a life revealed— no longer our old life, but the life of another: the life of Jesus lived daily under the power and presence of the Holy Spirit. And so, it is the life I now live in this earthly body, trusting in Jesus.

With that in mind, have you ever considered the implications of the commendation of Peter and John by the religious authorities in Acts 4:13? Peter and John were arrested for no other reason than teaching something that conflicted with their beliefs: the resurrection of Jesus Christ. When asked by what authority they spoke Peter went on the offensive, boldly speaking out for God and presenting the good news to these leaders, Scripture records "The members of the council were amazed when they saw the boldness of Peter and John, for they could see that they were ordinary men with no special training in the Scriptures. They also recognized them as men who had been with Jesus."

Similarly, in a book by Brennan Manning, *A Glimpse of Jesus,*[1] there is a story of a blind boy who asks a stranger, "Are you Jesus?" because of the kindness he received at his hands. The man isn't Jesus, of course—but could his actions toward this young boy be recognized as those of Jesus? The point is, each of us who claim to be a follower of Jesus Christ—who clothe ourselves with the name "Christian"—should stop and ask ourselves if the blind boy with two bad eyes sees more than we with our good ones. Is not a follower of Jesus Christ ordained to morph into the kind of living creature that Jesus came into the world to model for us?

"Christ lives in me." That's what this book is about: a life lived daily in the world where the only Jesus people may see is through those of us who walk with him. Whether it is a council of sighted priests, rulers, and elders, or a young blind boy, people should undeniably recognize that we have been with Jesus.

And yet, these things did not have meaning to me until the fall of 1977, when I traveled with members of a church in Greenville, Rhode Island, to the American Baptist Assembly in Green Lake, Wisconsin, to attend the first American Baptist Conference on the Holy Spirit. I was happy to be there, because my years of religious experience in the church had been less than fulfilling, in particular because of my earlier Pentecostal experience. I had previously logged plenty of church time but little understanding and a scant relationship with the Lord—until December of 1976, when I saw a vision of the Lord's heart projected on the wall of my living room and perceived that as my call to leave all and minister to hurting people. I was hungry to experience the deeper things of God. I wanted more of God, and more from God, so my heart was openly seeking him.

Therefore, the Baptist Assembly at Green Lake that following fall proved to be of great consequence, as it was there I heard the words that would alter the course of my Christian experience. It was the first time I had encountered the awesome prospect of "Living in the Kingdom of God." At the time I could not comprehend how life-changing it would be, but it has shaped my ministry to this day. My prior church experience had led me to believe that being born again was the object of my Christian experience, and that once I had been baptized I only had to wait for Jesus's return to take me to heaven. I now know that the new birth is only the beginning of the journey. Our mandate is to live out a

Christ-life in the Kingdom of God, among us, with the power for daily living supplied by the Holy Spirit.

It was in the fall of 1959 that I came to realize that my determination to be my own man had left me with a deep spiritual void. But only when it became clear that my personal goals had been at the expense of my family did I decide to return to my roots. In particular, the price was neglecting my three children, aged one to four years old. I had not been involved in a church, even though my dad had served as an elder in the Pentecostal Holiness Church on Lenox Avenue, New York, which became tantamount to home and family. My drive for independence and to achieve on my own kept me away from the church for a long time. I worked many long weekends, which often precluded my attending church. But in reality, I had fallen away from God and hardly thought of him at all.

The turning point came for me when a man from the local power company in Providence appeared at my job to adjust an electric meter. When he went to remove the glass cover it blew up in his face, and he was severely injured. For the next few moments, I stood there looking at the injured man lying on the floor. While waiting for help to come I saw myself and thought, "That could be me lying there. What would happen to my kids? I need to do something about my life." At that moment I decided to get my family and myself back in church. I asked one of my employees if he knew the churches in the Providence area, and he directed me to a church on the west side of the city. One year later, in 1960, I was baptized and became a member of Pond Street Baptist Church.

My baptism will always linger in my memory because I was afraid of water, due to being forcibly pushed into a pool of deep water during my training at US Navy boot camp several years earlier. The day I heard the pastor's words asking, "Do you believe in Jesus Christ as your Lord and Savior, that he has called you out of darkness into his marvelous light?," I was overjoyed. I do not recall my exact words at the time but I must have said yes or nodded in agreement, for the next thing I remember was being thrust back into cold water and emerging, feeling very wet. But somehow I was not frightened. I had been born again and I thought it was the end of the journey. Praise God, my sin had been forgiven and I was now a member of the church.

Life at Pond Street Baptist Church for the most part began rather innocuously, as the members found me to be just as committed a worker for the Lord as I had been in establishing my own business. I started attending church worship services and Wednesday evening Bible studies. I involved myself in many church functions which, I must confess, seemed rather uneventful. I had never fully understood nor embraced Paul's words in 2 Corinthians 5:17: "This means that anyone who belongs to Christ has become a new person. The old life is gone; a new life has begun!" Living a new life was not on my agenda. My responsibilities before coming to the church thrust me into positions of church leadership, and I soon found myself on many boards and committees. My roles in a leadership position included president of the senior choir, Sunday School teacher, church treasurer, and trustee board; and in 1963, my previous business experience led me to play a key role in the building of a new church on Chester Avenue in South Providence because of a city redevelopment project. At the time I never considered my involvement anything more than a normal church function. However, I came to learn that it was far from God's desire for my life, far from a life of peace and joy in the Holy Spirit. In one of my earlier books, *Almost Persuaded, Now to Believe*, I wrote:

Many people after having life-changing encounters with Jesus Christ vow never to go back to doing the things they did before. And their intentions are pure. However, they soon find themselves drawn irresistibly back into the same old ways. The most prevalent cry is: "I thought I was stronger. I thought God would help me. I'm trying hard to change my ways. I want to do better. What is wrong with me?" I do not think there is anything wrong with this person, nor, do I suggest God let him down. The goal of the Christian is not to be better or simply live better in the place we reside. It is not to be a better person or better citizen in the world, it is not to be free from all pain and distress in daily living. The goal of a Christian is to live life under God in his place of abode. I can continue to struggle where I am in a newly heightened awareness of the things of God or I can simply live each day in peace and freedom under his reign and rule.[2]

The Bible cautions us to be "in" the world but not "of" the world. I did not know exactly what it meant; however, I discovered that this notion was consistent with the teaching of the New Testament. Jesus tells his disciples in John 15:19, "The world would love you as one of its own if you belonged to it, but you are no longer part of the world. I chose you to come out of the world, so it hates you." Further, Jesus prays to the Father:

I have given them your word. And the world hates them because they do not belong to the world, just as I do not belong to the world. I'm not asking you to take them out of the world, but to keep them safe from the evil one. They do not belong to this world any more than I do. (John 17:14–16)

Ever since the resurrection of Jesus our Savior and Lord we are called to a whole new way of living in the world; we can never go back to the way things were. It seems that Jesus understood the tension we would experience, because followers of Christ do not cooperate with the world by joining in their sin; they are living accusations against the world's immorality. The New Testament writers encouraged us to continue our relationships with the world around us but to be careful to live in a way that pleases God, not the culture. Dr. Billy Graham, in a January 28, 2016 article in *Decision Magazine*, "In the World, But Not of It," says we should have a redemptive relationship with society, as Jesus did:

> As we read the New Testament, it is clear that we are not to become entangled with the world. Now at first glance, a new Christian might shrink from this idea. But the question I want to ask today is, "What is the world?" There are at least three meanings attached to the word *world*. First, the Bible says that there is the created world. "God . . . made the world and everything in it" (Acts 17:24). Second, there are the inhabitants of the world, whom God loves and for whom Christ died. "For God so loved the world that He gave His only begotten Son" (John 3:16). Third, there is the cosmos, the world system, which is headed by Satan and based upon self, greed, and pride. This is the world that God warns about, and it is this world system and philosophy that Christians are to shun and remain free from.[3]

However, much confusion remains. What does it mean to be "in" the world, but not "of" the world? Is it how we decide which TV shows to watch, which environments we ought to avoid, or which activities are "out of bounds"? In *Cold-Case Christianity*, a forensic approach to the Scriptures, J. Warner Wallace, a featured cold-case homicide detective, popular national speaker, best-selling author, and adjunct professor of apologetics at Talbot School of Theology (Biola University) and Southern Evangelical Seminary, offers,

Paul was right when he said that we would have to leave the world altogether if we wanted to truly separate ourselves from immoral, "worldly" people. That's not what God is asking us to do. The fact that you might be in a *location* where your Christian worldview is being challenged is not necessarily a bad thing. God may have placed you there so you can have a positive impact on those who don't yet know Jesus, or at least learn more about the culture so you can influence it later.[4]

Dr. Bill McDowell, preacher, writer, and department chair and chancellor at Marshall University, comments:

If the Christian says, "The world is not my true home, I am only passing through" (forgetting sadly, the promise of a renewed earth), the Jew has the saying: "One is as good as the world." The Jewish tradition is tied into a creation-centered spirituality. So should we be? God created the earth and pronounced it Good![5]

Because of sin, the world system is now ruled by Satan. In the words of Jesus, "The world would love you as one of its own if you belonged to it, but you are no longer part of the world" (John 15:19); and "I'm not asking you [Father] to take them out of the world, but to keep them safe from the evil one. They do not belong to this world any more than I do" (John 17:15–16). We may be physically present ("in the world"), but we don't have to be a part of its values. We're set apart from the world's wickedness as we seek the life Jesus came to bring in John 10:10—to live a holy, righteous life. In other words, the world is such a great danger to our souls that it caused Christ, the Son of God, to go to the cross to deliver us from it.

In a moving narrative (John 18:33–37) Jesus is standing before the Roman governor Pilate after the leading priests and elders accused him of encouraging people not to pay taxes, claiming to be a king, and causing riots. They had arrested him for blasphemy (claiming to be God), but that charge would mean nothing to the Romans so they accused him of different crimes.

> "Are you the king of the Jews?" he asked him.
>
> Jesus replied, "Is this your own question, or did others tell you about me?"
>
> "Am I a Jew?" Pilate retorted. "Your own people and their leading priests brought you to me for trial. Why? What have you done?"
>
> Jesus answered, "My Kingdom is not an earthly kingdom. If it were, my followers would fight to keep me from being handed over to the Jewish leaders. But my Kingdom is not of this world."
>
> Pilate said, "So you are a king?"
>
> Jesus responded, "You say I am a king. Actually, I was born and came into the world to testify to the truth. All who love the truth recognize that what I say is true."

Pilate knew what was going on; he knew that the religious leaders hated Jesus, and he did not want to act as their executioner. They could not sentence him to death themselves; permission had to come from a Roman leader. But Pilate initially refused to sentence Jesus without sufficient evidence. Pilate asked Jesus a straightforward question, and Jesus answered clearly: *I am a king, but one whose Kingdom is not of this world.* There seems to have been no question in Pilate's mind that Jesus spoke the truth and that he was innocent of any crime. It also seems apparent that while recognizing the truth, Pilate chose to reject it.

It is a tragedy when we fail to recognize the truth. It is a greater tragedy when we recognize the truth but fail to heed it. If Jesus thought this world was a suitable place to live in, would he have died such a horrible death to prepare another world for us to live in? Therefore, his words "my Kingdom is not of this world" mean that his death gives heightened meaning to his declaration "My purpose is to give them a rich and satisfying life" (John 10:10b). Is it not then folly to think that our goal is to be living persons in a dead and dying world?

Thus, the phrase "in the world but not of it" mandates that our real goal is to live the new life that Christ died to give us, in the place where Christ lives. "So then, since we have a great High Priest who has entered heaven, Jesus the Son of God, let us hold firmly to what we believe" (Hebrews 4:14). Understanding this truth gives us a different perspective on our lives here on earth. Instead of looking at the obstacles and difficulties we encounter, we now look to God's promise of supply. No longer do we measure our success or failure by the world's standard. The Scriptures tell us, "Satan, who is the god of this world, has blinded the minds of those who don't believe. They are unable to see the glorious light of the Good News" (2 Corinthians 4:4). Further, in John 10:10a we are told that the purpose of Satan "is to steal and kill and destroy." Therefore, we are warned, "Don't copy the behavior and customs of this world, but let God transform you into a new person by changing the way you think. Then you will learn to know God's will for you, which is good and pleasing and perfect" (Romans 12:2).

What is revealed here in this text is the distinction between life in the world and living a new life in the presence of God. Believers in Christ may decide that worldly behavior and its standards are off-limits for them, but it must go even deeper than just behavior and customs; it must be firmly planted in our mind to "let God transform you into a new person by changing the way you think." Only when the Holy Spirit renews, reeducates, and redirects our minds are we truly transformed. In Ephesians 4:23–24 we are told, "let the Spirit renew your thoughts and attitudes. Put on your new nature, created to be like God—truly righteous and holy." Our text is clear—"put on your new nature"—but sometimes the hardest thing to do with Scripture is to apply it to our own lives. It's a lot easier to make the application for other people. However, if transformation is to occur in you as God says it must, then you must allow it to take place in your heart. The process only goes as quickly as you give God all your hang-ups and heart troubles. God has only one offer, and that is to change us and to transform us into the likeness of Christ. But it is up to each of us to accept it.

When I came to realize that I was no longer a citizen of this world, I expected things to be different. I desired to change. I needed change. I wanted to live a new and improved life. I tried to be a better person and to stop doing the things I did before. I was not yet aware that the old way of living, the old place of residence, had to be abandoned. I now had to take up a new residence as a new creature in Christ; my home was now in the Kingdom of God under the lordship of the King. At the moment of conversion, we begin a new life under a new master. Paul states in Colossians 2:12b, "And with him, you were raised to a new life because you trusted the mighty power of God, who raised Christ from the dead." This precedes what I believe to be one of the most important and helpful passages of transition from the old to the new:

> Since you have been raised to new life with Christ, set your sights on the realities of heaven, where Christ sits in the place of honor at God's right hand. Think about the things of heaven, not the things of earth. For you died to this life, and your real life is hidden with Christ in God. (Colossians 3:1–3)

What is surprising to me about this passage is the word "since." The word appears to be unassertive and unassuming; however, it is a certainty that carries the weight of the cross. Paul's statement, "Since you have been raised," undeniably points to the fact that something of importance happened in the past, and that this is the result—*since* the cross, you have been raised from death to life; *since* you have been raised from the earthly to the heavenly; *since* you have been raised a natural man to a spiritual man; *since* you have been raised from the earthly kingdom to the heavenly kingdom; *since* you have been brought out of darkness into his marvelous light; *since* you have been united with Christ in his death, our sins are forgiven. We are born again; we are "raised to new life with Christ." The cross is the subject, but the object is being raised by the Holy Spirit into the Kingdom of God. Scripture is clear that God's offer of salvation, originally known to humanity, was revealed when Jesus rose from the dead. His plan, pure and simple, was to redeem his fallen creatures by his unselfish act of dying on the cross.

To not be misunderstood, I offer a disclaimer relative to what I am about to illustrate for easier understanding. Surely being born again has no equal, but I liken its objective to outcomes in sports. The team is three runs behind with the bases loaded in the last inning, and the batter hits a prodigious 451-foot home run. Watching the ball fly out of the park is great but greater still (the object) is winning the game. In double overtime, the football team is two points behind, but they have one last hope with a sixty-one-yard field goal. Both teams hold their breath, watching the high, arching, majestic flight of the ball until the referee, with hands up, signals that the kick is good and the victory won. Again, the object of the game is not the home run nor the skill of the kicker; the object is the change from sure defeat into victory. Sin forgiven. Hope restored. Death into life. A new home in heaven.

This being true, we must rethink the role of the Holy Spirit in our lives, for it is the indwelling of the Holy Spirit in us that identifies us with Christ. Paul writes, "The Spirit of God who raised Jesus from the dead, lives in you. And just as he raised Christ from the dead, he will give life to your mortal body by this same Spirit living within you" (Romans 8:11). The Holy Spirit who raised Jesus from the dead brings his power into our lives, to regenerate us and raise us into our new home. If one was to sum it up, it could be said that the real purpose of this power is to make us more and more like Jesus so that his life is manifest in us. It means, in effect, that the Holy Spirit not only makes us like new, but also keeps us like new.

What I now know to be true is that in my early confession of faith in Jesus Christ at Pond Street Baptist Church I was encouraged to become a good church member. My confessional was sincere and made with the expectation for Jesus to be Lord and Savior of my life. However, I am now aware that the church emphasis was on gaining new members in the body rather than committed disciples of Jesus Christ. My sin was the main focus of teaching and preaching, with little emphasis on the fact that the old way of living, the old place of residence, had to be abandoned. Thus, they failed to teach the single-mindedness of learning to live daily as a new creature in Christ. My initial knowledge of Jesus came from Sunday sermons, traditional Sunday School material, the Bible (much of which I did not fully understand), watching other church members, and "Christian" television programs.

To say the least, when I was introduced to "Kingdom Living" a whole new world opened up to me. I wondered why I had not heard of it before. Why were there so few sermons preached on the Kingdom of God? I had to admit that I was unfamiliar with the Kingdom of God at all. What I was familiar with was life on earth and the promise of a rich and satisfying life after death. I now know that Jesus's declaration in John 10:10 is not just about an afterlife; it is about life, now, and in eternity. From a biblical perspective, it is about how we live on this earth in our cities and countries, jobs, families, and churches. Dr. Bill McDowell, writing in one of his blogs, remarks:

We Christians have viewed "real" spirituality not as earthy but as "heavenly." To imagine the spiritual is to have images of saints with rolled eyes, recluses thin and wan who speak in lovely phrases, and ascetics in whose presence you lower your voice. Far be it from us to consider a 300-pound beer-drinking, back-slapping hulk of a man, who sometimes tells off-colored stories as a saint. Like Martin Luther, G. K. Chesterton, or Thomas Aquinas! But Judaism will have none of this. Rather it is rooted in the sensual, the earthly, the Lord's creation (Isaiah 25:6–8):

> *On the mountain, Yahweh Sabbath will prepare for all peoples a banquet of rich food, a banquet of fine wines, of food rich and juicy, of fine strained wines. On this mountain, he will remove the mourning veil covering all people, and the shroud enwrapping all nations and will destroy Death forever. . . .*

Truly, as Matthew Fox reminds us, "Jewish thinking which is Biblical thinking and which was also Jesus's thinking takes it for granted that the sensual is a blessing and that there is no (spiritual) life without it. . . . To recover a sensual spirituality is to recover a Biblical one."[6]

Thus, rather than seeing the secular (sensual) world—the world we can see and touch—through a sacred lens, we're more apt to look at the sacred (spiritual) through a secular lens. May God help us to see all of life—including our clothes, our humor, our entertainment, our vocation, our relationships, and all the rest—through the eyes of God, as belonging to him, and to give us the resolve to bring them under his lordship.

TWO

FALLING STONES

"So let us come boldly to the throne of our gracious God. There we will receive his mercy, and we will find grace to help us when we need it most."

(Hebrews 4:16)

I do not pretend expertise in writing books, nor do I have a stored wealth of information available to me. Despite this, I never cease to be amazed by the divine promptings when least expected in the wee hours of the morning. While sitting on the side of my bed deliberating what comes next, one of those Holy Spirit moments arrived with emphasis: "Christians do not throw rocks!"

At first, I was startled because it was so loud and clear. And then I recognized their familiarity with Jesus's words to a group of men armed with stones, ready to throw them at a woman caught in the act of adultery: "All right, but let the one who has never sinned throw the first stone.' ... When the leaders heard this, they slipped away one by one, beginning with the oldest, until only Jesus was left in the middle of the crowd with the woman" (John 8:7, 9).

The older men were more aware of their sins than the younger, but whatever our age we must take an honest look at our lives.

I recall that when I was twelve or thirteen years old, one of my favorite pastimes was pretending that one day I would be a major league pitcher. I was short, a bit on the rotund side, shy, out of physical shape, and not heavily into sports, but I couldn't resist pitching rocks at some bottles lined up on a fence behind the apartment house where we lived. Throwing rocks at the bottles was highly satisfying, especially when I hit one. Frequently, I could hear my mother's voice as she peered through the kitchen window, "Josh, stop throwing rocks! Josh, I said, stop throwing rocks!" My rock-throwing and my aspirations for a stellar major league career ended when someone heard the sound of shattering glass and called the police. I ran into the basement, hoping to elude the police and escape involvement in the crime, but that's where the police found me. I confessed straight away, hoping that would help. It didn't. Somehow, I had a penchant for always getting caught whenever I broke the bounds of my parents' disciplines. Rules or not, I did on occasion sever the bonds of parental control, but not without retribution.

After Jesus's resurrection, the disciples understood for the first time many of the prophecies that they had missed along the way. Jesus's words and actions took on new meaning and made more sense. In retrospect, the disciples saw how Jesus had led them into a deeper and better understanding of His truth, maybe none so much as the implications of this story of the woman caught in flagrant adultery. The background of our text in John 8 is one of failure, of abuse, of shame, but also of grace. In the first reading of the narrative, one might think that a woman's sin and shame is the main reason for it to be in the Bible. However, upon reading it over, you discover that its value is not primarily about a woman's adultery and corresponding guilt, nor is it about another man present in simple clothes sitting on the ground, looking into the face of the woman while writing in the sand with his fingers. No, this story is about a group of religious leaders and people, self-appointed custodians of conduct who have come to judge the guilty one and exact the full punishment of the law.

We read in verse 3 that "the teachers of religious law and Pharisees" bring the woman before Jesus and say, "Teacher, this woman was caught in the very act of adultery." The accusation rings off the courtyard walls—in an instant, a woman is yanked from private passion to public spectacle. Heads poke out of windows as the posse drags her through the streets. Dogs bark, neighbors turn, and the city notices her as she clutches the thin robe about her, but nothing can hide her shame. When she goes to the market women will whisper, when she passes heads will turn, when her name is mentioned people will remember. William Shakespeare said in his famous play *Julius Caesar*, "The evil that men do lives after them; the good is oft interred with their bones." This quote is so true; it almost appears that folk can't wait to find one wrong, juicy, negative thing about someone. It outweighs all the good they may have previously done. Moral failures are easy to recall, but the greater travesty, however, can often go unnoticed. Granted, what the woman did is shameful, but what the religious folk did is despicable.

How quick are we to respond when someone is suspected of or caught in sin. Are we among the first to pass judgment? Do we easily point the finger at the accused and condemn him or her? Are we even aware that when we point the finger at someone's failure we are playing God and acting as though we have never sinned? This group of self-righteous folk was there to administer justice. I'm sure at this point this committee of high-ethics folk was feeling pretty smug and cocky. Pretty proud of themselves, these agents of righteousness. This would be a moment they would long remember—the morning they foiled and snagged the mighty Nazarene. As for the woman? Why, she's immaterial. Merely a pawn in their game. Her future? It's unimportant. Her reputation—who cares if it's ruined? She's a necessary yet dispensable part of their plan. But before we condemn her, some questions must be asked.

According to the law, adultery was punishable by death, but only if two people witnessed the act. If there had to be two witnesses, the question is, "How likely are two people to be eyewitnesses to adultery?" What are the chances of two people stumbling upon an early morning flurry of forbidden embraces? Probably unlikely, but if so, odds are it's not a coincidence. And what of the man? Adultery requires two participants. What happened to him? Why was the man not sought out? Is it likely that he could slip out unnoticed? The evidence leaves little doubt that it was a trap for Jesus; the woman would soon realize that she's not the catch—she's only the bait.

She stares at the ground. Her sweaty hair dangles, her tears drip hot with hurt. Her lips are tight, her jaw is clenched. She knows she's been framed. No need to look up—she'll find no kindness. She looks at the stones in their hands, squeezed so tightly that their fingertips turn white. She thinks of running, but where? She could claim mistreatment, but to whom? She could beg for mercy, but these men offer none. She has nowhere to turn except to the lone man, the other figure in simple clothes who seems only slightly interested in her plight.

What does Jesus do about this? Most of us already know, but just for a moment pretend you don't. Pretend you're surprised. Jesus's move is subtle but once again his message is unmistakable. He writes in the sand, and then stoops down and draws in the dirt. The same finger that engraved the warning on Belshazzar's wall, the same finger that etched the words on the tablets of stone at Mt. Sinai, now scribbles on the courtyard floor, and as he writes he speaks these sobering words, "All right, stone her. But let those who have never sinned throw the first stone!"

The men look at each other, the young to the old. The old look in their hearts. They are the first to drop their stones and as they turn to leave, the young who were cocky with borrowed convictions do the same, and the only sound is the thud of rocks and the shuffle of feet. Jesus and the woman are left alone. With the jury gone she stands silent before the judge. She awaits his verdict—then Jesus says to the woman, "Where are your accusers? Didn't even one of them condemn you?" She answers, "No, Lord." Then Jesus says, "Neither do I. Go and sin no more."

This is where most of us leave the story and close the book—where, for most of us, the story ends. It's where we see how God reacts when we fall. However, when I read this text the last time, I realized I had missed the whole point. Rather than the end, this is where the story begins, for the heart of the story begs these questions: What happened to the people who dropped their stones and walked away? Did they ever recognize their need for forgiveness? What happened to the crowds that witnessed the event? Did they recognize their need for Jesus?

Which leads us to the more personal question: What are we going to do with the personal stones we carry into the church? What personal issues are blinding us to our sin? What is keeping us from the riches of God's grace? What is it that causes us to turn the mirror of judgment on other folks as we lurk in the shadows?

On March 11, 2020, COVID-19 was officially declared a pandemic. While the past year-plus has been tremendously challenging, there have been remarkable stories of human resilience, ingenuity, and creativity. While there is the stress of people being confined at home it has been a golden opportunity for innovation: to have a great time with family, for dual-earner couples to spend time with each other, for kids to have more time with parents,

48   A Wonder-Filled Life

chances to learn new skills, time to cherish with friends online, and new opportunities for fellowship and worship.

What I have observed in many cases is that because of the pandemic much has changed, as the church body which was warm and inviting has (not by any fault of its own) experienced physical separation from each other. Recognizing this dilemma, many pastors have done everything they can to halt this splintering by adding virtual worship services, outdoor services, Wednesday evening services, videos, and Bible studies to keep people connected until things return to a semblance of normality. Because many people attend church primarily for fellowship and entertainment, the pandemic has left them feeling isolated and exposed, without the covering of the church body.

It may sound harsh, but I have found that many of our contemporary churches entertain, maintain, and sustain Sunday after Sunday rather than surrender to the worship of Jesus. In some cases, the sign on the outside of the building fails to match with the identity of the people on the inside. Paul writes in Romans 1:16, "For I am not ashamed of this Good News about Christ. It is the power of God at work, saving everyone who believes—the Jew first and also the Gentile." The gospel is the good news of Jesus's death, burial, and resurrection. Thus, one has to wonder how it is possible for people bearing the name of Jesus to have so few conversions, baptisms, convictions, confessions, and acts of repentance if the gospel is preached to the people. Is it any wonder worship is not present? Does that not help explain why many churches today appear dead and dying? The lights may still be on, the AC may be running, people may be sitting in the pews, but the Spirit of God is not present. Would Jesus say to your church, "I never knew you"?

I am reminded of a frightening scene in Ezekiel 8–11 where the glory of the Lord departed the temple because of the people's sins. In 8:3–4, his glory was over the north gate. It then moved to the entrance (9:3), then the south end of the temple (10:3, 4), the east gate (10:18, 19; 11:1), and finally the mountain east of the temple (11:23), probably Mount of Olives. Because of the nation's sins, God's glory had departed. In 8:6, the Lord spoke to the prophet Ezekiel: "do you see what they are doing? Do you see the detestable sins the people of Israel are committing to drive me from my Temple?" Ezekiel had heard about the sins of his countrymen, but now God would show him the sins which had their lodging in Jerusalem and its temple.

I cannot help but think of the parallels with the church today. It is so steeped in doctrines, creeds, and liturgies, so structured with boards, committees, and people who claim to stand in for God. The bottom line is: it is secularized religion, pure and simple, and leaves no place for God. What has happened here is: God has departed the temple. He has withdrawn his presence from among the people and they have yet to notice it. They're still going on with business as usual.

God is getting up and saying, "I've had enough religion; I'm leaving." He is getting up from his throne and moving to the threshold of the temple. He is leaving his church, and no one is trying to stop him. Not one person says, "God is leaving." If the Spirit of God is not in the building, somebody ought to notice. Somebody should stop what they're doing. Somebody ought to get up and say something's wrong here. God is going down the hallway, and yet people are still singing, the organ still playing, while God goes from the Holy of Holies to the doorway, waiting for someone to stop him. From the door of the temple to the Eastern Gate, waiting for someone to stop him. The glory of God now hovers over Mount Zion east of the city waiting for someone to stop him, but the church is still singing and praising, sitting comfortably in their pews without the presence of God. Pure religion, all in vain.

Jesus-less stuff—song without Spirit—liturgy without life—pulpits with an absentee King—pews without power—graceless Christianity—churches void of the Spirit of God. . . .

Beloved, it's not who you are—it's who he is. It's not what you know—it's the Spirit of God dwelling in your heart. It's not how loud you sing—it's the song in your heart. Anything we do void of the Spirit and presence of God is religion. It's in vain. Mike Livingstone, editor of the Explore the Bible series produced by LifeWay, comments,

> I may stand alone, but it grieves me when I see worship services characterized more by props, performances, and pep rally atmospheres than by any sense of divine sacredness; and hallowedness giving way to shallowness. *This is not about worship styles.* The issue is not traditional versus contemporary versus blended worship. It's not about organ versus worship band. That discussion misses the point completely. This is about the heart and focus and intent of worship. . . . *Who or what is the spotlight on?*[1]

Livingstone's point is that the religious experience in the local church is not enough. Fellowship in the local church body is not enough. A certain feeling in the local church body is not enough. The church body must come together to worship the living God. David Joseph Platt, lead pastor at McLean Bible Church, Washington, D.C. and founder of Radical Books, recently asked:

> What if we take away the cool music and the cushioned chairs? What if the screens are gone and the stage is no longer decorated? What if the air-conditioning is off and the comforts are removed? Would His Word still be enough for his people to come together?[2]

Christians are defined as people who are hungry for God. People who have an insatiable thirst for Christ. People who long to be filled with the overflowing presence and power of the Holy Spirit. Nevertheless, we are all part of this world and because of us, God gave his Son as an act of his love according to the essence of his divine nature. Jesus says,

This is my command: Love each other. If the world hates you, remember that it hated me first. The world would love you as one of its own if you belonged to it, but you are no longer part of the world. I chose you to come out of the world, so it hates you. (John 15:17–19)

Therefore, Jesus's counsel to be "in the world, but not of the world" must be seen in the fact that we walk through a lost, sinful, fallen culture, giving it hope only because we remain in conversation with God as we walk through it. Jesus further says, "You are the light of the world." Our light should be relatively indistinguishable from Christ. We are operatives for Christ in the world, but not of the world. Even when we don't feel like talking, it is important we still feel connected.

Sometimes crisis brings out the best in us, but more often than not it depicts the worst in us and reveals who we really are. The fact is that when Christian people form opinions, cement their thoughts, and make conclusions based on personal circumstances or experiences, they still wear the name "Christ." What I have observed during this time of forced separation from the body is that some of our church members have chosen to define themselves by worldly standards. In what may be considered the perfect storm some believers, during a contested presidential election in 2020, decided to turn to social media (Facebook, Twitter, etc.), spewing the same detestable language as those in the world—discharging hate, disparagement, untruths, slander, and dubious attacks upon competing individuals with statements such as, "This is my opinion and I don't care if anyone agrees with me or not."

Certainly everyone is entitled to their opinion, but the words uttered by Jesus's followers cast disparity on the name of Christ. If anyone disagrees with their unyielding declaration, it causes shattered personal relationships and deepening division in the local church body and the body of Christ. But even more, it defines us by the world's standard rather than with Christ's standard. According to the Scriptures, this should not be. Even more, it cannot be the characteristic or attribute of a believer in Christ Jesus.

Remember, we are called to a higher purpose. We are called not to ourselves. Yes, we have grace, but responsibility too! The world does not benefit by our being another voice for evil. The world benefits by hearing the voice of God. Otherwise, Jesus's admonition "Christians do not throw stones" becomes forever obscured.

Lyle Edwin Schaller, American author, workshop leader, speaker, and dean of church consultants, writing in the *New England Baptist Monthly*, stated, "Church members today expect their involvement in a local congregation to transform their lives, not just enrich their lives. . . . Discipleship and ministry, not baptism and active church membership, are the marks of a true Christian."[3] Jesus's greatest desire was that we would become one, as a powerful witness to the reality of God's love. He prayed for unity among believers based on the believer's unity with him and with the Father, in a personal relationship with him through God the Father who sent him to the world: "O righteous Father, the world doesn't know you, but I do; and these disciples know you sent me. And I have revealed you to them and will keep on revealing you. I

will do this so that your love for me may be in them and I in them"
(John 17:25–26).

We must remember in our worship that the cross is the central part of God's plan. The object is God himself. However, the actions of some Christians today make me realize we must have more than a cursory understanding of God's grace. Indeed grace is unmerited favor; however, it is much more than that. I have heard many of the nice church words for grace and I wonder if there is some hidden or unexplainable reason why we do not comprehend, or whether we simply have little understanding of what grace costs God.

Every one of us who bears the name "Christian" has one thing in common: Christ died for our sins. We have received grace which cannot be earned, bought, or stolen. We cannot take credit for it—it is a gift of God freely given. The Scriptures declare, "Salvation is not a reward for the good things we have done, so none of us can boast about it. For we are God's masterpiece. He has created us anew in Christ Jesus so that we can do the good things he has planned for us long ago" (Ephesians 2:9–10). Indeed, grace is unmerited favor. Grace is everything for nothing, to those who don't deserve anything.

The word "grace" has been used in many ways, and we are very familiar with most of those usages because they form a large part of our everyday lives. Most of us say grace before meals; we acknowledge our daily bread as a gift from God. When we are late on a note to the bank or payment on our credit card, there is usually a "grace period." And when we go out to eat or someone does us a service, we usually leave them a tip or gratuity. In all cases, it means receiving something undeserved. Likewise, no one had to plead with Jesus to save us; he came from heaven because he, the Lord Jesus Christ, was full of all grace, and that grace was abounding to us through the redemption he provided in dying for us. It was not our works that saved us but his grace. It was not our character that recommended us to him, but his grace. If he had not been all grace, we would have forever lain in the misery of our broken hopes. But his very name is love. He is gracious. That is why I can know that in him I have new life. He justified me freely, without any cause in me, and all by his grace. And because of Jesus's sacrifice on the cross, "Christians do not throw rocks."

Today there are many pitchers in baseball who at some point in their career realized a dysfunction in their pitching arm and submitted themselves to "Tommy John surgery" to resurrect their career. Few outside of baseball have heard of Tommy John, known as "the bionic man," who pitched for twenty-six seasons for six different major league baseball teams between 1963 and 1989. John was a four-time MLB All-Star and has the second-most wins (288) of any pitcher since 1900 not in the Hall of Fame. In 1974, he suffered what was potentially a career-ending injury when he tore his ulnar collateral ligament; but Los Angeles Dodgers physician Dr. Frank Jobe performed ligament replacement surgery on John later that year. John sat out 1975 recovering from surgery, but became the first pitcher to successfully return to baseball following such surgery. Tommy John surgery has since become a common procedure, with many MLB pitchers receiving it at some point during their careers.[6]

Tommy John reminds me that many believers start out throwing rocks. But a pitcher with dysfunction is no longer of use on the mound. Thus, when our dysfunction (sin) is exposed, God performs transformative surgery on us. When Jesus appears we are resurrected by the grace of God—and seeing Jesus, we drop our rocks and pitch again, emulating his grace.

Philip Yancey, a highly gifted, highly respected Christian writer, in his book *The Jesus I Never Knew* tells one of the most haunting, unforgettable stories of the need for grace. It was the real-life experience of one of the counselors working with the down-and-out in Chicago:

> A prostitute came to me in wretched straits, homeless, sick, unable to buy food for her two-year-old daughter. Through sobs and tears, she told me she had been renting out her daughter—two years old!—to men interested in kinky sex. She made more renting out her daughter for an hour than she could earn on her own in a night. She had to do it, she said, to support her drug habit. I could hardly bear hearing her sordid story. For one thing, it made me legally liable—I'm required to report cases of child abuse. I had no idea what to say to this woman. At last, I asked her if she had ever thought of going to a church for help. I will never forget the look of pure, naïve shock that crossed her face. "Church!" she cried. "Why would I ever go there? I was already feeling terrible about myself. They'd just make me feel worse."

> What struck me about my friend's story is that women, much like this prostitute fled toward Jesus, not away from him. The worse a person felt about herself, the more likely she saw Jesus as a refuge. Has the church lost that gift? Is it indeed true that people stay away from the church because it is condemning? The down-and-out, who flocked to Jesus, when he lived on earth, no longer feel welcome among his followers. What has happened? The more I pondered this question, the more I felt drawn to one word as the key. All that follows uncoils from that one word, "Grace."[5]

In one way or another, this story closely connects with Jesus's description of the woman caught in the act of adultery. Both were judged by appearance. Both were judged by character. Both needed grace and forgiveness. Both exposed the sin of self-righteousness in us. Jesus identifies both of the women not with the sin that brought them to him for judgment but with the pain of embarrassment and suffering. Jesus eventually said, "Let he who is without sin cast the first stone." Therefore, Christians, the embodiment of grace, do not throw stones.

The stated mission of the church is to be a haven of grace in a world of ungrace. The challenge for each one today is to not walk away thinking that this story of Jesus does not apply to you, that it's only about those accusers who picked up their stones. There are no innocent bystanders. We are all part of the cast, we are all guilty, and we all need to hear the same words Jesus uttered to the woman: "Neither do I condemn you, Go and sin no more."

What is most intriguing and worthy of unearthing is the fact Jesus wrote something in the dust on the ground with his finger, but no one knows what he wrote. Many ask, was he listing their sins? Was he writing out the Ten Commandments? We don't know. But we do know that the men who accused the woman were convicted, for when Jesus said, "let the one who has never sinned throw the first stone," both old and young dropped their stones. I for one believe that the Scriptures give us a clue to what Jesus wrote on the ground in plain sight of these men. In Genesis 3, after the fall, every human being ever born (except for Jesus) inherited the sinful nature of Adam and Eve. Paul explains in Romans 5:12–14:

> When Adam sinned, sin entered the world. Adam's sin brought death, so death spread to everyone, for everyone sinned. Yes, people sinned even before the law was given. But it was not counted as sin because there was not yet any

law to break. Still, everyone died—from the time of Adam to the time of Moses—even those who did not disobey an explicit commandment of God, as Adam did.

"Because one person disobeyed God, many people became sinners. But because one person obeyed God, many will be made righteous" (Romans 5:19). Self-righteousness is sin before God. It knows no age barrier, ethnic, language, or cultural barrier. If we think otherwise, then sin has deceived us into thinking we are good and bars us from recognizing our sinful nature. Whatever Jesus wrote on the ground before his announcement, "Let he who is without sin cast the first stone," the men were convicted, because no longer were they the accusers—*they* stood accused by Jesus's words. They looked in the mirror and saw their sin. Paul wrote in Romans 3:10–12, "As the Scriptures say, 'No one is righteous—not even one. No one is truly wise; no one is seeking God. All have turned away; all have become useless. No one does good, not a single one.'" Further, "For everyone has sinned; we all fall short of God's glorious standard" (Romans 3:23).

Countless people have heard the words of Jesus many times over, and dropped their stones and walked away. Choosing not to throw them was the right thing to do; however, it's an admission of guilt and sin. What is lurking ominously beneath this story is the fact that the men in our text, once their sin was exposed, never went back to seek out Jesus, the Savior of sinners. Many people today think that all they have to do is use the name of Christ, go to church, try to be a good person, treat people right, do good deeds, etc. Jesus says, "Indeed, you may have dropped your stones and walked away, but you have never repented of your sins. There is still a big stone lodged in your heart. Its name is sin. You can't drop it, you can't remove it, you can't pay to have it removed, you can't wish it away, and neither can you roll it away. *God alone has to remove it.*"

And the good news is, God already has. He took care of that at Calvary. Jesus did it on the cross. The price has already been paid. "Jesus paid it all / All to him we owe / Sin had left a guilty stain / He washed it white as snow."[6] Because of what Jesus accomplished on the cross for us, Christians do not throw stones.

THREE

THE CRUCIFIED LIFE

"For you know that God paid a ransom to save you from the empty life you inherited from your ancestors. And it was not paid with mere gold or silver, which lose their value. It was the precious blood of Christ, the sinless, spotless Lamb of God."

(1 Peter 1:18–19)

Several years ago at a Bible conference in Dallas, Jamie Buckingham, the internationally renowned best-selling author, columnist, and conference speaker, was sharing his testimony about being healed from cancer. Jamie was the founding pastor of Tabernacle Church in Melbourne, Florida for nearly twenty-five years at a time when he was seeking a deeper relationship with Christ—a search that quickly led him to a fuller understanding of what it means to be truly filled with the Holy Spirit. When Jamie concluded his testimony, he quoted the words of a song of which I was not then familiar: "Mercy there was great and grace was free / Pardon there was multiplied to me / There my burdened soul found liberty / At Calvary."[1]

This song made such an impact on me that from that moment to this very day, each time I hear it or sing it, something happens deep in my spirit. Under the ministering of the Holy Spirit, I feel such an incredible covering of the grace of Christ being poured out upon me so when I think of the cross I hear those very words "Mercy there was great, and grace was free / Pardon there was multiplied to me." It is then that I realize that the cross enacts deep truths in my life that would make no sense apart from it. The cross stands as the death of Christ, in our place, as the greatest symbol of the central fact of Christianity.

But the cross represents only a part of the good news. Yes, Jesus died and was buried—but he rose from the dead. His resurrection means that the cross gives hope when there is no hope. The cross says if you are disqualified, you're qualified. The cross is our strength when we are weak. The very things that make us feel inadequate, the very things that plunder our hope and scuttle our joy, the things that steal our very life, are what God uses to accomplish his work of grace. For proof, look at the cross.

Is it possible to fully describe Jesus Christ's redeeming work on the cross? With as many words as we have in the English language, there are still not enough to adequately describe the character and goodness of Jesus's sacrifice for us. Paul says, "We know that our old sinful selves were crucified with Christ so that sin might lose its power in our lives. We are no longer slaves to sin" (Romans 6:6). To be sure, I am at a loss to try to explain how much God hates sin, but even more than that, as much as God hates sin, he loves the sinner even more. Several Scripture passages state that God had planned in eternity to sacrifice his Son on our behalf:

> Even before he made the world, God loved us and chose us in Christ to be holy and without fault in his eyes. God decided in advance to adopt us into his own family by bringing us to

himself through Jesus Christ. This is what he wanted to do, and it gave him great pleasure. (Ephesians 1:4–5)

Further, Peter writes in his first epistle:

For you know that God paid a ransom to save you from the empty life you inherited from your ancestors. And it was not paid with mere gold or silver, which lose their value. It was the precious blood of Christ, the sinless, spotless Lamb of God. God chose him as your ransom long before the world began, but now in these last days, he has been revealed for your sake. (1 Peter 1:18–20)

So, in eternity, God crafted a plan to redeem his fallen creatures. His plan was centered in Jesus, and it established that when the right time came he would enter this fallen world to save his creations. Because we were utterly helpless to satisfy God's decree for sin and could do nothing about our plight, God's plan called for Jesus to become human to destroy the Devil's power over death.

The death of Jesus was not the result of a panicking sinner's human dilemma. The cross was not a knee-jerk response to a world plummeting toward destruction. It was not a patch job or a stop-gap measure. The death of God's only Son was anything but unexpected peril. No! It was a part of a plan. It was a calculated choice: "But it was the Lord's good plan to crush him and cause him grief" (Isaiah 53:10a). The cross was drawn into the original blueprint. It was written into the script. Revelation 13:8 speaks of the Book of Life, which belongs to the Lamb who was killed before the world was made. The moment the forbidden fruit touched the lips of Eve, the shadow of the cross appeared on the horizon, and between that moment and the moment the spikes were driven through the hands and feet of God, a master plan was fulfilled.

So what does this all mean? It means that God intentionally sent his only Son to die for the likes of you and me. It means that Jesus planned his sacrifice. It means that Jesus willingly placed the iron ore in the heart of the earth from which the nails would be cast. He voluntarily placed Judas in the womb of a woman. He set in motion the political machinery that would send Pilate to Jerusalem. Remember his words to Pilate: "You would have no power over me at all unless it were given you from above" (John 19:11).

Jesus didn't have to do it—but he did. It was no accident. Jesus was born crucified. The cross-shaped shadow could always be seen, and the screams of you and me in hell's prison could always be heard. That is why the ropes used to tie his hands and the soldiers used to lead him to the cross were unnecessary. They were incidental. Had they not been there—had there been no betrayal, no trial, no Pilate, no crowds—the very same crucifixion would have occurred. Had Jesus been forced to nail himself to the cross, he would have done it. It was not the soldiers who killed him, nor the screams of the mob; it was his love and devotion to us. The songwriter says, "While he was on the cross, I was on his mind."

Alfred Edersheim was born on March 7, 1825, in Vienna. He was a Jewish convert to Christianity and a biblical scholar known especially for his book *The Life and Times of Jesus the Messiah* (1883). Edersheim writes:

> The cross was the most disgraceful and one of the cruelest instruments of death ever invented. The Romans, who borrowed it from the Carthaginians, would not allow a Roman citizen to be crucified; but reserved crucifixion for slaves and foreigners or provincials. The Jews customarily used stoning and never crucifixion. It was not only the death of the greatest ignominy but of the most extreme anguish and suffering. . . . The cross of Jesus was probably slightly higher than the

traditional type, in the use of which the feet of the crucified were only a foot or two from the ground. The victim was usually first stripped naked, the garments falling to the lot of the executioners; but in the crucifixion of Jesus, tradition says that a loincloth was used. First, the upright was planted firmly in the ground, and then the victim was laid down with the arms extended on the crossbar, to which they were fastened by cords, and afterward by nails through the palms. Then the transom was raised to its position on the upright and nailed while the body was left to swing or its weight rested on an iron saddle peg driven into the upright. Following this, the feet were nailed through the instep separately, or both together with a single iron spike. There the body was left to hang in agony sometimes two or three days until death from pain and starvation ensued.[2]

I don't know if we truly understand how much God set the agenda of the world around Jesus Christ. I don't know if we understand that in the message of the cross, "a righteousness from God is revealed." For many who do not understand the power of the crucified Christ, the cross is just a physical thing. However, in reality the cross separates me from self. It crucifies me to die with Jesus; it buries my past completely; it removes my fears and erases my failures. The cross gives me a choice: Am I to remain a product of my past—feeling unwanted, unloved, self-pitying—or will I reach out in faith to accept his offer to become the son or daughter of a Father who loves unconditionally?

Max Lucado, author and pastor at Oak Hills Church, San Antonio, in his book *No Wonder They Call Him the Savior*, was asked by a man, "What *really* matters? What counts? Tell me. . . . Tell me the part that matters." After a while, with the question hanging in the air, Max said: "Stop and empathize for a second.

Can you hear his question? Can you taste his frustration? 'Don't give me religion,' he was saying. 'Give me what matters.' What does matter?"

The question still hangs in the air for every man, woman, and child today. What matters to you? What matters in your life? From my observation, many would rather circumvent or simply disregard the question, for the answer may require you to make major changes in your thinking and your lifestyle to know what matters. Lucado confessed that many years later, he knew what he would share with the man.

Think about these words from Paul in 1 Corinthians, chapter 15. For I delivered to you as of *first importance* what I also received, that Christ died for our sins in accordance with the scriptures. "First importance" he says. Read on: that he was buried, that he was raised on the third day in accordance with the scriptures, and that he appeared to Cephas, then to the twelve. There it is. Almost too simple. Jesus was killed, buried, and resurrected. Surprise? The part that matters is the cross. No more and no less. The cross. It rests on the timeline of history like a compelling diamond. Its tragedy summons all sufferers. Its absurdity attracts all cynics. Its hope lures all searchers. And according to Paul, the cross is what counts. My, what a piece of wood! History has idolized it and despised it, gold-plated it and burned it, worn and trashed it. History has done everything to it but ignore it. That's the one option that the cross does not offer. No one can ignore it! You can't ignore a piece of lumber that suspends the greatest claim in history. A crucified carpenter claiming that he is God on earth? Divine? Eternal? The death slayer? No wonder Paul called it the core of the gospel. Its bottom line is sobering: if your account is true, it is history's hinge. Period. If not, it is history's hoax. That's why the cross is what matters. Paul had impressive credentials: upbringing, nationality, family, background, inheritance, orthodoxy, activity, and morality. However, his conversion to faith in Christ was not based on what he had done but on God's grace.[3]

Paul came up with the same conclusion after he considered everything he had accomplished in life. He proclaims in Philippians 3:7–11:

I once thought these things were valuable, but now I consider them worthless because of what Christ has done. Yes, everything else is worthless when compared with the infinite value of knowing Christ Jesus my Lord. For his sake, I have discarded everything else, counting it all as garbage, so that I could gain Christ and become one with him. I no longer count on my own righteousness through obeying the law; rather, I become righteous through faith in Christ. For God's way of making us right with himself depends on faith. I want to know Christ and experience the mighty power that raised him from the dead. I want to suffer with him, sharing in his death, so that one way or another I will experience the resurrection from the dead!

Paul did not merely count his religious pedigree as a loss; he counted all things loss. He counted them worthless because of "the infinite value of knowing Christ Jesus my Lord." It wasn't so much that those things were worthless in themselves, but compared to the greatness of the intimacy of knowing the fullness of Christ, they were nothing.

To gain Christ means to be completely united with him. In him (in Christ), as noted above, points to the closest possible union between Christ and the believer. This truth is beautifully expressed in Paul's declaration, "For to me, living means living for Christ, and dying is even better" (Philippians 1:21); Paul derives all meaning for his life in Christ. The same truth is expressed in his proclamation, "My old self has been crucified with Christ. It is no longer I who live, but Christ lives in me. So I live in this earthly body by trusting in the Son of God, who loved me and gave himself for me" (Galatians 2:20).

Because God's children are human beings, made of flesh and blood, Jesus also became flesh and blood, being born in human form. For only as a human could he die, and only by dying could he break the power of the Devil, who had the power of death. Therefore, it was the act of resurrection that was the undeniable evidence that identified Christ as the Son of God with power. It was the resurrection of Jesus that demonstrated his mighty power that works in all of his children—followers of God in Christ. The resurrection of Jesus raises all who believe in him from spiritual death to a new life in Christ. Consequently, the cross gives forgiveness of sins. But it is the resurrection that broke the power of sin and death that reigns in the mortal body of fallen man, so that all may rise to newness of life in Christ. Such it is that I may know this mighty power of Christ's resurrection, which conquered death and provided the way to know the Lord.

Paul writes in 1 Timothy 1:15, "This is a trustworthy saying, and everyone should accept it: 'Christ Jesus came into the world to save sinners.'" Jesus's purpose in coming to earth was not merely to show us what we looked like, merely to show us how to live a better life, nor to challenge us to be better people. He came to offer us salvation that leads to eternal life. His coming was no afterthought, no accident, but the deliberate plan of God—a plan crafted in eternity. He had to become one like us, but without sin, to accomplish the eternal purpose of God. When God determined the time was right, he sent forth his Word to create a body for Jesus. The eternal God, Christ Jesus, offered himself on the cross as the only acceptable sacrifice for the sin of mankind.

The writer of Hebrews applies to Christ the words of the psalmist in Psalm 40:6–8: "You did not want animal sacrifices or sin offerings. But you have given me a body to offer" (Hebrews 10:5b). Just as the first man, Adam, was given a sinless body, Jesus, as the second Adam, is given a sinless body. Since the Scriptures declare that Jesus alone could become an acceptable sacrifice for us, is it not conceivable that Jesus would be similarly fashioned by God or even in the same way as man? Otherwise, would it not be difficult for us to relate to Jesus as being one of us? We are told: "God formed a man's body from the dust of the ground and breathed into it the breath of life. And the man became a living person" (Genesis 2:7, TLB). From the dust of the ground, God calls forth a lifeless shell of a body, then brings it alive with his own "breath of life." When sin enters, God removes his life-giving breath, and our bodies once again return to dust.

The apostle Paul affirms that Jesus became one like us: "The law of Moses was unable to save us because of the weakness of our sinful nature. So God did what the law could not do. He sent his own Son in a body like the bodies we sinners have" (Romans 8:3). In Old Testament times, animal sacrifices were continually offered at the temple to show the seriousness of sin; blood had to be shed before sins could be pardoned. Because the blood of animals could not remove sin, the sacrifices merely pointed to Jesus's sacrifice, which paid the penalty for all sins. Paul writes: "But God showed his great love for us by sending Christ to die for us while we were still sinners" (Romans 5:8).

The Father sent his own Son—not a son by adoption, but a son who was begotten in the today of eternity. This son existed in the flesh and is, in point of fact, the great "I am who I am"—the God who spoke to Moses on Mt. Horeb. This identification of the Christ with God would seem to be indicated when Paul speaks of Christ as the one who is over all: "And he is God, who rules over everything and is worthy of eternal praise! Amen" (Romans 9:5b). To this Paul adds: "he gave up his divine privileges; he took the humble position of a slave and was born as a human being. When he appeared in human form, he humbled himself in obedience to God and died a criminal's death on a cross" (Philippians 2:7–8). Jesus knew what lay ahead of him and he knew the reason. He reaffirmed his desire to do God's will in the garden of Gethsemane by praying, "I want your will, not mine." His prayer reveals to us that his terrible suffering, his agony was worse than death because he would pay for all sin by being separated from God. The sinless Son of God took our sins upon himself to save us from suffering and separation.

How public was the execution of Jesus? Few events in all of history are as visible, as minutely detailed, and as indelibly recorded in the minds and hearts of people as the last six hours of the life of Jesus on the cross. All of the excruciating pain and suffering of those last hours was recorded. Raw flesh hanging from the scourging of the whips laced with bone chips, blood flowing down from the crown of thorns cruelly thrust down upon his head, the gaping nail holes in his hands and feet, the spear thrust in his side, the mocking of the crowds—the very ones he came to save, the gambling for his garments, all make up the picture of the cross Jesus had to bear for our sins. Even his final words from the cross have been recorded for all eternity. First in a scream of natural agony at the fearful torture, and realizing their complete ignorance of the awful deed, Jesus prayed for his murderers, "Father, forgive them, for they don't know what they are doing" (Luke 23:34).

Next, it is recorded that Jesus had an encounter with two thieves hanging on crosses on either side of him. One of the criminals insulted Christ by challenging him to save himself and themselves. This brought a sharp rebuke and a confession of Christ's innocence from the other criminal: "We deserve to die for our crimes, but this man hasn't done anything wrong." Then he said, "Jesus, remember me when you come into your Kingdom." The Lord's answer to the penitent thief conveyed not only the comfort of answered prayer but also the promise that he would be there in the presence of the blessed: "I assure you, today you will be with me in paradise" (Luke 23:41–43).

A few hours later his beloved disciple John, along with his mother Mary and the faithful women, are standing at his feet. In human thoughtfulness, he commits his mother to the disciple whom he loved. His care for his mother is seen in this his third word from the cross: "'Dear woman, here is your son.' And he said to this disciple, 'Here is your mother'" (John 19:26–27). Immediately, John undertook the sacred deathbed charge and brought Mary, whose soul the sword had pierced, away from the cross to the shelter of his home.

At noonday, beginning the next three hours, when the sun would be at its brightest, a pall of darkness covered the land. It was as if all of nature was cognizant that its Creator was stretched out on a cross, suffering in the throes of death. At that moment Jesus felt the separation from his Father. This was what he dreaded most as he previously prayed with such anguish and distress in the garden. The physical agony was horrible, but even worse was the period of separation from God. Then in the gloom of that Friday afternoon, about three o'clock, Jesus called out with a loud voice, *"Eli, Eli, lema sabachthani?"* which means "My God, my God, why have you abandoned me?" Never before had Jesus felt such loneliness. Never before had he felt the weight of human sin. Never before had the Son of God known separation from the Father. His cry showed the deep expression of the anguish he felt when he took on the sins of the world. He had drank deeply of the cup of sorrow, grief, and pain on our behalf.

70   A Wonder-Filled Life

Those standing around the cross heard Jesus's cry of loneliness and separation, and soon heard him request something to drink. The psalmist (22:15) graphically described the thirst that came from the raging fever that coursed through our Savior's body: "My strength has dried up like sunbaked clay. My tongue sticks to the roof of my mouth. You have laid me in the dust and left me for dead." Now so that the Scripture might be fulfilled, Christ asked for a drink, saying, "'I am thirsty.' A jar of sour wine was sitting there, so they soaked a sponge in it, put it on a hyssop branch, and held it up to his lips. When Jesus had tasted it, he [uttered his final words with a loud triumphant shout], 'It is finished!' Then he bowed his head and gave up his spirit" (John 19:28).

The word "finished" is the same as "paid in full." Jesus had finished God's work of salvation. He had paid the penalty for our sins. The blank check of Calvary had been cashed. Jesus had shed his blood as the sacrificial Lamb of God. It was now time to go back home. The barrier between God and humanity was torn in two so that people could freely approach God once again. Dr. Luke says, "The light from the sun was gone. And suddenly, the curtain in the sanctuary of the Temple was torn down the middle. Then Jesus shouted, "Father, I entrust my spirit into your hands!" And with those words he breathed his last" (Luke 23:45–46). So the Word who became human and lived on earth among us returned home. "We have seen his glory, the glory of the Father's one and only Son" (John 1:14).

May we never take for granted, or take lightly, the cross. May we never fail to remember what it cost God to save us! He reached down to the very depths of human depravity to seek and to save that which was lost. The prophet Isaiah (53:6) exults, "All of us, like sheep, have strayed away. We have left God's paths to follow our own. Yet the Lord laid on him the sins of us all." We are all guilty of sin. And many still wallow in unbelief; many still do not believe why Jesus had to die. My question today is, which of the two thieves hanging next to Jesus are you? Are you still embracing your sin, unwilling to surrender to the power and grace of the cross? Are you still wearing the cross around your necklace as an ornament? Is the cross merely a symbol of a lost life? Or do you see Jesus's suffering and pain as reconciling you to God?

When I contemplate my worldly credentials, and the depth and breadth of my life while confronting the question "What matters?," I have come to the same conclusion as Paul: the cross matters. I was born to the wrong color and ethnicity of parents on the wrong side of the tracks in a town on the wrong side of hope. I was told I was of the wrong lineage. I was forced to live in shoddy housing and attend below-standard schools. During my travels I was exposed to prejudice, bigotry, hatred, name-calling, rejection; was spit at, spit upon, and told to go back to Africa where I belonged. Along the way, I suffered much pain, both spiritual and physical. I was deposed to worship in my "kind" of church. I suffered a ruptured appendix, lumbar stenosis, back pain, surgery, blood clots in both lungs and arm, prostate cancer, weakness, dehydration, congestive heart failure, AFIB, and more. Yet, like Paul, I count all these things loss because they were worthless compared to the greatness of the intimacy of knowing the fullness of Christ. They were nothing. Something greater was always looming before me. The cross! The cross is what matters.

> When he [Jesus] appeared in human form, he humbled himself in obedience to God and died a criminal's death on a cross. Therefore, God elevated him to the place of highest honor and gave him the name above all other names, that at the name of Jesus every knee should bow, in heaven and on earth and under the earth. (Philippians 2:7–10)

For most of us, certain dates are meaningful and forever enshrined in our memories—birthdays, deaths, graduations, holidays, other special events. Certainly the day Jesus Christ, the founder of our faith, died on the cross ought to be one of them. It is a day unlike any other in the life of a Christian. It is even hard for the enemies of Christ to deny the fact that the cross is the symbol of the Christian faith. Every moment from creation on has been leading up to the cross as part of God's eternal plan, and the moment since is lived in light of Jesus's death and resurrection. We recall what the prophet Isaiah wrote:

> And we thought his troubles were a punishment from God, a punishment for his own sins! But he was pierced for our rebellion, crushed for our sins. He was beaten so we could be whole. He was whipped so we could be healed. (Isaiah 53:4–5)

The cross is knowing who the guilty parties are. It's knowing who pierced Jesus's side. It's knowing who wrenched the crown of thorns upon his head. It's knowing because he has exchanged his life for ours. We have been set free from bondage forever.

Please look again. Don't just straighten your tie and clear your throat. Don't allow yourself to descend from Calvary cool and collected. Don't let this be just another day at the office. Those are nails in those hands and feet. That's blood dripping from the thorns piercing His brow. That's raw flesh clinging to the metal spikes of the whip. That's *God on the cross*. It's us who put Him there. He hung in our place. He was the only acceptable substitute.

I don't care how many worship services you attend or good deeds you do. Your goodness is insufficient. You can't be good enough to deserve forgiveness. You can't quench your guilt—no one, not you, not me, not anyone. You can't do it. There's no way. Not with alcohol, not with drugs, not with sex, not even with perfect Sunday School attendance.

And please be aware, it doesn't matter how bad you are, where you have been, or how you got there. You cannot be too bad for the cross. And also know that it doesn't matter how good you are. You can't be good enough for the cross. That's why we need a Savior. That's why Calvary. That's why Jesus exchanged his life for ours. We know that his broken body, in some way beyond telling, has opened the way to wholeness for our brokenness, for "He was beaten so we could be whole. He was whipped so we could be healed." Thus I derive all meaning for my life in Christ because of the cross. This truth is expressed in my undying proclamation that: "My old self has been crucified with Christ. It is no longer I who live, but Christ lives in me. So I live in this earthly body by trusting in the Son of God, who loved me and gave himself for me."

FOUR

LIFE EXCHANGE

"It is no longer I who live, but Christ lives in me."

(Galatians 2:20a)

It has been said that when a man reaches a certain age in life he has earned the privilege of looking back on what has been, to enable him to contemplate what is and optimistically give insight into what may be. Since I believe I have reached that place of dubious distinction I will attempt to share some of the things I have learned which I consider being of grave importance.

Accordingly, there are things in the course of living that touch lives in such profound and lasting ways that they become benchmarks for us in our faith journey. For many years I have known people who stated that after many promptings and urgings of the Holy Spirit that they gave their lives to Jesus Christ. I was one of them until I came to an understanding of Paul's admonition, "give yourselves completely to God, for you were dead, but now you have new life. So use your whole body as an instrument to do what is right for the glory of God" (Romans 6:13). From this I reasoned, "If we are dead to God, how then can we give him our lives?" It stands that the only thing we can offer God is our death. In exchange, because God loves us, he gives us the life of his Son. I ask, is that a fair exchange? Certainly not, but who said that love was fair?

For those who are serious readers of the Bible or even occasional scanners, the opening verses of Matthew 11 present us with a most disturbing situation and an even more disturbing question. John the Baptist was in prison, having been arrested and placed there by Herod. As John sat in prison, he began to have some doubts about whether Jesus was the Messiah. If Jesus was that Messiah, then why was John in prison when he could have been preaching to the crowds, preparing their hearts? Thus he sent his disciples to query Jesus, "Are you really the Messiah we've been waiting for, or should we keep looking for someone else?" Jesus's reply to John's query was even more vexing. There are many explanations as to why John would ask the question, even though he had been the one to herald Jesus, coming as the one spoken of through the prophet Isaiah, "Prepare the way for the Lord" (40:3). Jesus told them,

> Go back to John and tell him what you have heard and seen—the blind see, the lame walk, those with leprosy are cured, the deaf hear, the dead are raised to life, and the Good News is being preached to the poor." And he added, "God blesses those who do not fall away because of me." (Matthew 11:4–6)

This was Jesus's answer to John's agonized query from his prison of doubt. I cannot tell you how John received Jesus's message, but I would like to think he understood. Granted, it was not right for John to be persecuted for something he didn't do, but Jesus knew that better than John. For it wasn't right that people spit into the eyes that had wept for them; it wasn't right that soldiers ripped chunks of flesh out of the back of their God; it wasn't right that spikes pierced the hands that formed the earth; it wasn't right that they mocked the one who had healed the many; it wasn't right that a spear was driven into the side of the one who preached, "if your enemy is hungry feed him"; it wasn't right that the Son of God was forced to hear the silence of his God. It wasn't right—but it happened. For while Jesus was on the cross, God did turn his back and ignore the screams of the innocent. God did nothing while a cry of agony echoed in the black sky, "My God, my God, why have You forsaken Me?" God sat in silence while the sins of the world were placed upon his Son. Was it right? No. Was it fair? No. Was it love? Yes. The prophet Isaiah, in that great passage, affirms:

> Yet it was our weaknesses he carried; it was our sorrows that weighed him down. And we thought his troubles were a punishment from God, a punishment for his own sins! But he was pierced for our rebellion, crushed for our sins. He was beaten so we could be whole. He was whipped so we could be healed. All of us, like sheep, have strayed away. We have left God's paths to follow our own. Yet the Lord laid on him the sins of us all. (Isaiah 53:4–6)

Can one even begin to imagine how much God loved his creations that he would publicly suffer such shame and disgrace, torture, and pain for our sin? I think of those reflective times apart from the public eye when Jesus had to face his coming crucifixion alone. He knew what lay ahead of him, and he knew the reason. He reaffirmed his desire to do God's will in the garden of Gethsemane by praying, "I want your will, not mine." His prayer reveals to us that his terrible suffering, his agony, was worse than death because he would pay for all sin by being separated from God.

78 A Wonder-Filled Life

Sin is real. Sin is serious, and sin is a barrier between ourselves and God. The sinless Son of God took our sins upon himself to save us from suffering and separation. May we never take for granted, or take lightly, the cross. May we never fail to remember what it cost God to save us!

God's eternal plan came into sight when our forefather Adam sinned and, realizing he was naked, tried to hide from God. God asked him, "Who told you that you were naked? . . . Have you eaten from the tree whose fruit I commanded you not to eat?" (Genesis 3:11). Though God had exposed his hiding place, Adam never confessed; he began to make excuses and reverted to blaming Eve for his sin. Is that not like many people today, who when exposed they too blame everyone else for their sin? Like Adam, they accept no responsibility and refuse God's offer for healing. However, in the sickness of sin, they are often found hiding out in the crowd, which becomes a place of estrangement from God.

One of the clearest indications of Jesus's popularity was the fact that wherever he went he was often surrounded by large crowds of people in need of healing. This is confirmed in the Gospels as each of the writers highlights incidents where people who were part of the crowd found healing. In Matthew, we see the following:

> Large crowds followed Jesus as he came down the mountainside. Suddenly, a man with leprosy approached him and knelt before him. "Lord," the man said, "if you are willing, you can heal me and make me clean." Jesus reached out and touched him. "I am willing," he said. "Be healed!" And instantly the leprosy disappeared. (Matthew 8:1–3)

> Jesus traveled through all the towns and villages of that area, teaching in the synagogues and announcing the

Good News about the Kingdom. And he healed every kind of disease and illness. When he saw the crowds, he had compassion on them because they were confused and helpless, like sheep without a shepherd. (Matthew 9:35–36)

Mark, in chapter 2, tells of a paralytic who had to be lowered through a hole in the roof to Jesus because so many people had come to see Him that there was no more room. Luke 8:43–44 records a very familiar narrative: "A woman in the crowd had suffered for twelve years with constant bleeding, and she could find no cure. Coming up behind Jesus, she touched the fringe of his robe. Immediately, the bleeding stopped." And John records in chapter 5, the healing at the pool where a great number of blind, lame, and paralyzed people lay. With these narratives before us, I have observed that the more unsavory and/or the more needy the characters, the more at ease they seemed to feel around Jesus. On the other hand, the more respectable, rich, and influential types usually gave Jesus a chilly response. However, if one would carefully observe the crowds, they would probably find these same rich, pious, respectable naysayers in the very front.

It might help our understanding if you can, for a moment, imagine what happens when a celebrity or grand event comes to your town. The word goes out, people start to gather, crowds begin to form, and people jockey for position, with the stronger folk ending up in front. In the middle of the crowd are the people who either don't know why they came or simply came because they don't want to miss anything; and bringing up the rear are the folk who are the weakest, the rejected and, more often than not, the neediest. This being the case, have you ever paused to ask, "How then do those in the back of the crowd get to Jesus? How do those who come for healing make their way through the mass to touch the Healer?"

And yet, what I deem to be an even more important question is, "Why do people find crowds so appealing?" I have been to many functions where there were large numbers of people, and I have come to realize that crowds are a good place to hide—except for the fact one cannot hide from God. Some people crowded around Jesus because they dared not be there. They didn't believe but they figured if so many other people were here there may be something to it, and if there was they didn't want to miss it. There are also folk in the crowd who are just looking for excitement. They want to be where the action is and don't often care what or who it is about. The excitement is what draws them.

Contrary to these folk, there are people in the crowd who genuinely realize a need for forgiveness and healing and change but often find themselves stifled by those who surround them. The sick, the blind, the lame often ask, "How will God ever notice me amid all these people?" Once in a while, someone may be able to reach out and touch the hem of Jesus's garment when he passes by, like the woman with the issue of blood, but more often than not they lie at the edge of the pool like the paralytic: "One of the men lying there had been sick for thirty-eight years" (John 5:5). The writer says, "Crowds of sick people—blind, lame, or paralyzed—lay on the porches" (v. 3), waiting for someone to come by and stir the water so they could be healed. "When Jesus saw him and knew he had been ill for a long time, he asked him, 'Would you like to get well?'" (v. 6).

When Matthew writes that "Jesus had compassion on the people," he is not saying that Jesus felt casual pity for them. No, the term is far more graphic. Matthew is saying that Jesus felt their hurt in his gut: he felt the limp of the crippled. He felt the isolation of the diseased. He felt the loneliness of the leper. He felt the embarrassment of the sinful. And once he felt their hurts, he couldn't help but heal their hurts. Jesus was so touched by their needs that he forgot his own needs. He was so moved by the people's hurts that he forgot his hurts. Nevertheless, no one would have blamed Jesus had he dismissed the crowds. No one would have criticized him if he had waved away the people. But he didn't. He knew there were people in the crowd who could not get to Him, and so He came to them. Max Lucado tells a story in his book *Gentle Thunder*:

> My friend Kenny and his family had just returned from Disney World. . . . He and his family were inside Cinderella's castle. It was packed with kids and parents. Suddenly all the children rushed to one side. . . . Cinderella had entered. Cinderella. The pristine princess. Kenny said she was perfectly typecast. A gorgeous young girl with each hair in place, flawless skin, and a beaming smile. She stood waist-deep in a garden of kids, each wanting to touch and be touched. For some reason, Kenny turned and looked toward the other side of the castle. It was now vacant except for a boy maybe seven or eight years old. His age was hard to determine because of the disfigurement of his body. Dwarfed in height, face deformed, he stood watching quietly and wistfully, holding the hand of an older brother. . . . She walked quickly across the floor, knelt at eye level with the stunned little boy, and placed a kiss on his face.
>
> Rather than a princess of Disney, we've been considering the Prince of Peace. Rather than a boy in a castle, we've looked at a thief on a cross. In both cases, a gift was given. In both cases, love was shared. In both cases, the lovely one performed a gesture beyond words. But Jesus

did more than Cinderella. . . . Cinderella gave only a kiss. When she stood to leave, she took her beauty with her. The boy was still deformed. What if Cinderella had done what Jesus did? What if she'd assumed his state? What if she had somehow given him her beauty and taken on his disfigurement? That's what Jesus did. . . . Jesus gave more than a kiss—he gave his beauty. He paid more than a visit—he paid for our mistakes. He took more than a minute—he took away our sin.[1]

When I think of how much Jesus gave, I cannot help but think of those awful hours on the cross where Jesus sacrificed his life for ours. Because of this exchange, it is no longer I who live, but Christ lives in me. Here justification takes place, crucifixion happens, a relationship with God begins in unity with Christ, we die to our old life, and daily and regularly we crucify sinful desires that would keep us from following him.

By the time Jesus came into the world, the word "self" had to be reckoned with and put in its place. Self had to be denied, said Jesus. "Crucified," said Paul: "My old self has been crucified with Christ." When Adam was created and God breathed into him the breath of life. Adam became a living being—a living soul. He was a unique "self," created without the ability to cope with guilt. Why? Because he was not made to make mistakes. But sin marred God's creation, and when it did mankind had no way to deal with it. Adam and Eve were unlike yet strangely like their Maker. Each of them was a breath of never-has-been and never-will-be-ever again. They were selves, souls— powerfully free never to be controlled—always their own. Then they disobeyed and ate—and in the eating the illicit "self" remained unique but became excessively greedy. Love died, and it became a sculptured materialism, serving only "self" and giving no root to the purposes of God. Its only concern was: What's in it for me?

On the cross the "selfish self" died and the "selfless self" emerged. That is what Paul means when he says, "It is no longer I who live, but Christ lives in me." At this point one might ask, how can that be? If I have been crucified, how can I now live? God would never ask us to stop being, for if we negate ourselves to the point that we are not there God cannot talk to us at all. He does ask us to stop being self-serving, stop being addicted to our passions, stop being shallow in our adoration—but never to stop being.

The key to understanding Paul's declaration is that a "transition" has taken place. The "I" who no longer lives is the "selfish self." The "me" where Christ now lives is the "selfless self." This gives validity to Paul's words, "Don't be selfish; don't try to impress others. Be humble, thinking of others as better than yourselves. Don't look out only for your own interests, but take an interest in others, too. You must have the same attitude that Christ Jesus had" (Philippians 2:3–5). The life I now live in the body is the life of Jesus; I now simply live the life of the one who now resides in my earthly body.

Jesus said to the crowd, "If any of you wants to be my follower, you must give up your own way, take up your cross daily, and follow me" (Luke 9:23). Though nowhere does Scripture encourage us to become nonexistent, it does teach us to deny ourselves, abdicate our passions, and get rid of those things that claim our lives with petty self-interests. Our call to follow Jesus is to deny self and to allow new appetites to become our focus. More for Christ—and even more the imitation of Christ.

When God pursued Adam to offer help, Adam covered his nakedness and hid in shame. The truth is, we alone cannot deal with our guilt. We cannot deal with our sin. We must have divine help. To forgive ourselves, we must have forgiveness from the one we have offended—yet we are unworthy to even ask God for forgiveness. This is the whole reason for the cross.

The cross did what no other sacrifice could do. It erased our sins not for a year, but for eternity. The cross brought forgiveness and pardon. The cross granted us the right to communicate with, love, and live with God. Even though this happened some two thousand years ago I can never forget what happened on the cross. I can never approach the cross with just my head and not my heart. Calvary is not a mental trip. It's not an intellectual exercise. It's not a divine calculation or a cold theological principle. It's a heart-splitting hour of emotion. It's a transforming of the lost to the found. It's an ear-splitting victory yell from the bowels of Satan's kingdom. It's knowing a great price has been paid.

For many people, the cross is just a physical thing; they do not understand the power of the crucified Christ. When God created Adam he was alive physically and spiritually, but because of Adam's sin and subsequent spiritual death, every person who comes into the world is born physically alive but spiritually dead; a sense of selfishness and rebellion pervades our lives. We tend to insist on doing things our way. We say "I'm in charge; I'll handle it myself; I'll live my life the way I want"—and yet at the first sign of things gone wrong, we blame God. We say, "God, it's your fault this happened to me," for we have no understanding of how much God set the agenda of the world around Jesus Christ. Jesus didn't die on the cross so we could begin thinking better about ourselves; he died so we could quit thinking so much of ourselves and start thinking more of him. The cross gives us the choice to either remain a product of our past—feeling unwanted, rejected, and unloved—or to trust God for our future.

I wonder how many today realize that the cross terrorizes Satan. The cross is Satan's embarrassment. In Colossians 2:14–15 we learn that on the cross Christ was the victor over Satan:

He canceled the record of the charges against us and took it away by nailing it to the cross. In this way, he disarmed the spiritual rulers and authorities. He shamed them publicly by his victory over them on the cross.

It means if you're disqualified, you're qualified. If you're a stranger, alien, or outcast, you're a candidate. If you were excluded before, without hope in the world and without God, don't fret, for, "Once you were far away from God, but now you have been brought near to him through the blood of Christ" (Ephesians 2:13). The mystery of God's secret battle plan is the cross, and the proof is found in 1 Corinthians 2:8: "But the rulers of this world have not understood it; if they had, they would not have crucified our glorious Lord." When Jesus died upon the cross Satan thought it was all over, but what he didn't know was it had just begun, "For God made Christ, who never sinned, to be the offering for our sin, so that we could be made right with God through Christ" (2 Corinthians 5:21). God allowed Jesus to establish a relationship with sin so that the sins of the world—past, present, and future—would fall on him. When Jesus died on the cross our sin was upon him, but when he rose from the grave there was no sin on him. When he ascended to the Father there was no sin on him, and because of the cross we who believe in Jesus Christ as Lord of our lives have also died to sin and are seated in the heavenly realms in Christ Jesus. Bishop Fulton J. Sheen, noted archbishop of the Roman Catholic Church, was once heard to say:

When God created each human heart he kept a small sample of it in heaven and sent the rest of it into the world of time where it would each day learn the lesson that it could never be really happy, never be really wholly in love, and never be really wholehearted until it went back again to the creator to recover the sample which God had kept for it for eternity.[2]

86   A Wonder-Filled Life

The way back to God is the cross. The most terrific thrust of stark realism the world has ever seen—the eternal, dynamic, explosive supercharged answer for sin, God's supreme deed, the dramatic breakthrough of God's grace into this world in time and history—is the cross.

After a mission service, a preacher was hurrying to catch a train. He had just three minutes to catch it when he saw a man running after him. "Sir, "he said breathlessly as he came up, "can you help me? I am very anxious about my salvation. I don't want to die without Christ."

"Well," replied the preacher, "my train is just here and it's the last one, but look up Isaiah 53:6. Go in at the first 'All' and go out at the last 'All.' Good night." When the man arrived home, he took his Bible, and turning to Isaiah 53:6 he read these words: "All of us, like sheep, have strayed away. We have left God's paths to follow our own. Yet the Lord laid on him the sins of us all."[3]

"All of us like sheep have strayed away." I am to go in with that first "All"—I am included in those who have gone astray. And I am to go out with the last "All": "Yet the Lord laid on him the sins of us all." I am to go out free because my sin, my iniquity, has been laid on Christ.

That is the message of the cross: No man, woman, child, need ever remain the way they are. There is no sin too vile, no condition too depraved, no life so worthless. Sin's power has been broken for eternity, and any person's sin laid under the blood of Jesus will be washed clean, changed, and made whole.

I believe the greatest weakness of the church today is that many clergy and laity alike have bought the rotten lie that the best days of the church are behind us. They have more confidence in Satan's ability to deceive us than in the Holy Spirit's ability to lead us. This leads to a further thought that God no longer has power over sin, no longer has power over lust, no longer has the power to change us. He can heal us, but he cannot free us.

The truth of the matter is that the blood of the Lord Jesus Christ has the power to cleanse us and to free us from any bondage to sin. Consequently, "In with the first 'All,' out with the last 'All'" is what we see above everything else in the cross—the pardoning grace of God, taking away the sins that shame us, enslave us, haunt us, terrify us; the sins that bring fear and judgment; the sins that bring the wrath of God, death, and hell. At the cross we see love taking them all away, love canceling the debt, love blotting out the handwriting that was against us, love releasing us from bondage, love's mighty triumph redeeming, restoring, reconciling, renewing, reviving. Love's blank check is the cross.

The news from the cross is what every human heart longs to hear: there is forgiveness of sin, assurance of life eternal, and adoption into the family of God. The good news is that while we were sinners God showed his love, that Christ died for us. The greatest news of all, the hymn writer says, is that "When He Was on the Cross, I Was on His Mind."

But what was probably the pivotal point in Jesus dying on the cross was the incident that took place in John 11, the raising of Lazarus from the dead. In recalling this well-known story of Lazarus and his two sisters Mary and Martha, the tendency is to focus on the "raising of Lazarus from the dead" in deference to the rest of the events. I must tell you that I have been similarly tempted; however, I believe we have missed the point if we do not follow the narrative to its divine conclusion, for there is much more to glean from this encounter. We first learn that Jesus has the power to raise the dead, but we are also shown that Jesus is personally concerned with each one of us as individuals and will go to any length to respond to our needs. He is always thinking about us; he will not

88   A Wonder-Filled Life

forget us nor fail us when we are in danger. So when Lazarus was sick, "the two sisters sent a message to Jesus telling him, 'Lord, your dear friend is very sick'" (v. 3), expecting him to come at once and cure their brother of his affliction.

Jesus's instinct was to hurry to his friend's relief, even though it meant death to himself. But he had a greater mission. Jesus had a whole world to save. Its last hope lay in him. So during those two days of waiting, Jesus was far from forgetting his friends at Bethany or ignoring their sorrow; he was wrestling in prayer uninterruptedly on their behalf, to see if it was God's will whether he should die now, with so little yet accomplished, with so much as it seemed still to do. And certainly once he learned the Father's will he lost himself in prayer for Lazarus. When he arrived at the grave, he gave thanks that God had already heard him, and had granted his request:

> "Father, thank you for hearing me. You always hear me, but I said it out loud for the sake of all these people standing here, so that they will believe you sent me." Then Jesus shouted, "Lazarus, come out!" (vv. 41–43)

Lazarus's sickness and death was the event that led to the fulfillment of the eternal plan of God. It was the fuse that set off the cross of Calvary, the shock that sent ripples throughout all eternity. *God* was saying, "the repercussions of what I am about to do you cannot now know, but I assure you they will be known hereafter for all mankind will be affected."

At the moment of Jesus's call to Lazarus, time stood suspended in space. All sound seemed to have become encased in a steel vault; all movement seemed to have become frozen as if cast in stone. Not only was the physical world watching, but the spiritual world was also watching. Not only were the people around Jesus watching, but the angels in heaven were also watching. Even Satan, who held the keys of death, was sitting on the edge of his seat. Suddenly, here amid Satan's empire—here in the heart of Satan's domain—the Lord Jesus walked into Satan's control room and shouted, "Lazarus, come out!" All the forces of evil shook, all the powers of darkness cringed, for they sensed something was about to happen which was beyond their control. They had heard there was to be a dark Friday afternoon, but now they knew there would also be a resurrection Sunday. They realized the whole universe was soon to witness the glorified Christ. The prison bars were flung open, and he who was once dead now lived. "And Lazarus came—bound up in the grave-cloth, his face muffled in a head swath" (v. 44). And there was great astonishment and wonder among the people.

Most of us would end the narrative here; we think this is where it stops. However, I believe we must go on if we are to be truly set free. *Jesus* doesn't stop there. He completes Lazarus's return from the dead by commanding, "Unwrap him and let him go!" (v. 44).

My point is, many of us are still wearing our "grave clothes." And the only fitting place for grave clothes is the grave. We still hang on to all the old ways, old attitudes, old habits, old prejudices, old sins, and still claim Christ. Yet we're told in 2 Corinthians 5:17, "anyone who belongs to Christ has become a new person. The old life is gone; a new life has begun!" Paul admonishes us in Ephesians 4:22, 24 (NIV), "You were taught with regard to your former way of life, to put off your old self . . . and to put on the new self, created to be like God in true righteousness and holiness." In Christ, you receive new clothes: a new robe, a new walk, a new talk, a new name written down in glory. Therefore, we offer God our death in exchange, because God loves us so much that he gave us the life of his Son.

I ask, is that a fair exchange? Certainly not, but who said that love was fair?

FIVE

RESTORED IMAGE

"And this is the way to have eternal life—to know you, the only true God, and Jesus Christ, the one you sent to earth."

(John 17:3)

The moment I learned about kingdom living, my reading and study of the Bible became more focused on how to live out the new life that Jesus came into the world to make available for us. The reason I believe this to be of such importance is that, along with myself, I have found many believers feeling disappointed and frustrated by their struggle to access the new life promised: "to give them a rich and satisfying life." I also like the KJV version, which says: "that they might have life more abundantly." A rich, satisfying, more abundant life is not only the possibility but the assurance that each believer can expect.

If we rightly understand the message of the cross, Jesus was sent into the world by the Father to restore to his creations the lives lost at the fall. Had Adam and Eve retained their original state, they never would have died; but Eve and then Adam yielded to the serpent's temptation, and death came into the world. Before that moment, they were in a beautiful, pristine state. They existed on a level far above the present condition of the human race until their sin destroyed that relationship, causing God to do a very drastic thing: he cast out his created beings and relegated them to an earthly habitation in the world:

> So the Lord God banished them from the Garden of Eden, and he sent Adam out to cultivate the ground from which he had been made. After sending them out, the Lord God stationed mighty cherubim to the east of the Garden of Eden. And he placed a flaming sword that flashed back and forth to guard the way to the tree of life. (Genesis 3:23–24)

What is clear is that with Adam's sin, humankind had forfeited the right and privilege of living in God's presence and would now be relegated to a life in a world without God. The Scriptures inform us we have been estranged from God and blinded to the divine image; therefore we no longer have a relationship or intimate knowledge of who God is. Therefore God brought forth his divine plan, created in eternity and paid for with the blood of Christ before the world began:

> For you know that God paid a ransom to save you from the empty life you inherited from your ancestors. And it was not paid with mere gold or silver, which lose their value. It was the precious blood of Christ, the sinless, spotless Lamb of God. God chose him as your ransom long before the world began, but now in these last days, he has been revealed for your sake. (1 Peter 1:18–20)

Many today are unaware of the fact that Christ's sacrifice for our sins was not an afterthought. It was not something God decided to do when sin had reached its hands into the divine residence. God's work of salvation had been planned long before the world began. It was God's intention for us at creation to send Jesus to earth to model for us who God is, who we are, what we look like, and how to restore the relationship with God that was damaged by the sin of Adam. Therefore, when Jesus became human and sacrificed himself on the cross, he not only came to die for sin but, more importantly, came to bring us into a right relationship with the Father by giving us a new, never-has-been-and-never-will-be-ever again life to be lived in God's presence, in the place of God's abode, God's kingdom—a life that is abundantly rich and full and eternal and which begins immediately.

In the gospel narratives and other writings, Jesus's sacrifice on the cross provided the only way our daily lives could be inseparably and eternally linked with the Father. He says, "I am the way, the truth, and the life. No one can come to the Father except through me" (John 14:6). This passage in and of itself is clear enough to understand. However, hidden beneath is a greater truth that encompasses the gospel message in its entirety. In John 10:10 Jesus states clearly and with emphasis his real purpose—to bring life where there is death: "The thief's purpose is to steal and kill and destroy. My purpose is to give them a rich and satisfying life." The KJV states: "I have come that they might have life and that they might have it more abundantly." The NIV states: "I have come that they may have life, and have it to the full." All three versions promise a new life that is rich, abundant, full, and satisfying.

This is what first captured my heart when I committed my life to Jesus, and yet disappointment ensued when I struggled so much to find the pathway to such a life. Nevertheless, I never gave up. When I first realized what was happening around me I also became aware of something happening inside of me. Deep within my spirit, I had encountered moments of spiritual dryness, and there remained many unanswered questions in my heart. I knew something was missing. I wanted to know Jesus Christ in a more personal way, and I did not know what to do about it. I wanted to have real peace inside—not just an absence of turmoil but a peace that was real and everlasting. I no longer wanted to do things just because I felt they were right. I desired to know the Lord's will for me and to have the courage to follow His divine direction.

The only thing I knew to do was pray, so I got on my knees and called out to God to give me an understanding of Jesus's words, to "give a rich and satisfying life" or "life more abundantly." From that moment I began to realize that the life Jesus is alluding to can only be lived in the presence of God in his kingdom, under His lordship. All of my human efforts had been thwarted, because I had a changed heart since meeting Jesus but I had not changed my residence. I was in the world, but Jesus had left the world to go back to the Father. I was ignorant of how I could be in two places at the same time—the place where Jesus was and the place I now occupied in the world.

What we learn is that we still live in the world (in a body), but we are not of the world because God reigns and rules in the heart. We take up space in the world because relationally the Kingdom of God occupies space in the world. Though physically we live in the world, we have been transformed into the kingdom. Recall Paul's words, "Don't copy the behavior and customs of this world, but let God transform you into a new person by changing the way you think" (Romans 12:2a). Legally we are crucified to the world, dead to the world. We do not react to the world. We are living life in the body by faith, in a relationship with Christ, meaning that we have entered into a part of Christ's death and resurrection. Again Paul explains it: "So I live my life in this earthly body by trusting in the Son of God who loved me and gave himself for me" (Galatians 2:20b).

Without question, no man, woman, or child can have a relationship with the Lord without changing their residence to the Kingdom of God. How deceived we are if we think otherwise. Jesus says, "If the world hates you, remember that it hated me first. The world would love you as one of its own if you belonged to it, but you are no longer part of the world. I chose you to come out of the world, so it hates you" (John 15:18–19). Followers of Jesus are hated by the world because the world hates our Lord; therefore, we are no longer welcome in its confines. Because the world hated Jesus, we who follow him can expect that many people will hate us as well. If circumstances are going too well, ask yourself if you are following Christ as you should. For that reason, we must make sure it is not at the cost of following Jesus halfheartedly or not at all. The Apostle John warns us:

Do not love this world nor the things it offers you, for when you love the world, you do not have the love of the Father in you. For the world offers only a craving for physical pleasure, a craving for everything we see, and pride in our achievements and possessions. These are not from the Father, but are from this world. And this world is fading away, along with everything that people crave. But anyone who does what pleases God will live forever. (1 John 2:15–17)

The fact is, we are physical, material people. We often say, "in the world, but not of the world," and yet the greatest problem for most is that we can't make the transition—for we want to hang on to the material.

Some people think that worldliness is limited to external behavior—the people we associate with, the places we go, the activities we can enjoy. Worldliness is also internal because it begins in the heart and is characterized by three attitudes: (1) *craving for physical pleasure*—preoccupation with gratifying physical desires; (2) *craving for everything we see*—coveting and accumulating things, bowing to the God of materialism; and (3) *pride in our achievements and possessions*—obsession with one's status or importance.[1]

Materialism often takes over, at the same rate at which our spirituality declines and decays. "Having" is not the first sin of materialists. The sin that precedes it is the sin of regarding what we have as our own. To those who forget, "having" is not something God makes possible but something they feel they have achieved and thus have a right to. At first, new Christians so love the Lord that they do not see their goods of any consequence, so they are quite willing to give God the glory for giving them what they have. But sooner or later, some forget the source of their material blessings. As they grow older, the sparkle they once had in their eyes begins to die. Sometimes their zeal also dies, and they quit trusting God and start stashing goods.

Jesus encourages us in Matthew 6:33 to treasure the Kingdom of God and his righteousness. When we do, the values of the world at hand will be exposed for what they are. What God wants us to treasure is inward and spiritual. For that reason, Paul offers that to be certain we are daily following Jesus, "Don't copy the behavior and customs of this world, but let God transform you into a new person by changing the way you think" (Romans 12:2a). In reality, the only place reserved for believers in Christ Jesus is the Kingdom of God. For that reason Jesus explicates:

Don't let your hearts be troubled. Trust in God, and trust also in me. There is more than enough room in my Father's home. If this were not so, would I have told you that I am going to prepare a place for you? When everything is ready, I will come and get you, so that you will always be with me where I am. (John 14:1–3)

His words show that the way to eternal life, though unseen, is secure—as secure as your trust in him. There is no old life to go back to. Paul confirms in 2 Corinthians 5:17, "anyone who belongs to Christ has become a new person. The old life is gone; a new life has begun!"

The Scriptures I had read many times before now took on greater meaning. When I read the Bible, words would virtually leap off its pages. My hunger for the Word of God so increased that I could not get enough, and passion for Jesus was now my joy. In the midst of this, I discovered the passage of Scripture that has become the hallmark of my daily life. It is my testimony and my experience: "I have been crucified with Christ. I no longer live, but Christ lives in me. So I live my life in this earthly body by trusting in the Son of God, who loved me and gave himself for me" (Galatians 2:20).

From there, my relationship with God was hard to describe except to say that I wanted more of God and more from God. I wanted intimacy with God through Jesus. I wanted the full rich abundant life promised. I sensed there was more to come, for God knew the desires of my heart. I readily confess that as much as I have read the Scriptures, reflected, studied, and learned from the works of renowned biblical scholars, nothing has brought such profound levels of understanding to me of the inner workings of God than a personal visitation of the Holy Spirit. Never have I felt such intimacy with Jesus than when the Holy Spirit is whispering words of love and forgiveness to my heart. Nothing has brought such excitement to me than the unexpected call of the Spirit. Never has the presence of God been more evident than when the Spirit's words are exciting my passion.

98   A Wonder-Filled Life

In the book *Storytelling: Imagination and Faith*, author William J. Bausch, a retired Catholic priest of the Diocese of Trenton, New Jersey, writes that there are stories that signify self-discovery and the questions that such self-discovery raises:

> In a cassette program, Robert Bela Wilhelm takes the listener on a slow and imaginative trip into the past. The listener is asked to relax and to go back to where he or she came from. There the listener recalls the events and people of his or her story. Although on a journey of self-discovery, the listener stumbles across God. This process is very much akin to the "healing of memories" and secular therapy. The patient in therapy is retelling his or her story, knowing that if the facts cannot be changed, he or she can at least change the interpretation. As a patient sits or lies there with closed eyes, the story pours forth and, often there is a moment of self-discovery. A significant realization dawns and the person is led to exclaim, "So that's why I am what I am! . . . Eureka!" Sometimes too, from the burning bush of their self-discovery, a Voice is heard, calling them by name. Sometimes too, on the Exodus journey, a faint footstep is perceived behind them.[2]

Much like Wilhelm's secular journey to self-discovery, there is a spiritual journey to God's discovery. It is not a stumbling journey to discovery but a deliberate call in the heart and mind. In December of 1976, God granted me a picture of his heart on the wall of my living room and I came to realize that any quest for self-discovery must begin with him, because I had no life without him. In my initial book *Can These Bones Live?* I describe that spiritual moment of vision:

> I was alone when it happened. In my solitude, I became aware of an image projected as a picture upon my living

room wall. It was a startling visitation I later reasoned could only have been God-sent. Muffled voices, garbled, indistinct, seemed to emanate from the picture. Then parts of the spectral portrait became unified as if they were all parts of a mosaic. I rubbed my eyes several times in amazement and incomprehension, not yet sure of what I was seeing. Slowly the vision cleared. Shapes began to form. Then I realized that the activity in the picture was caused by the movement of outstretched hands gesturing in my direction. I perceived them not as a threat, but more as though begging, yearning, beseeching, desiring some response from me. I could not answer at the moment; I was transfixed as if frozen in time. As my perception became more acute, faces emerged from the bleak, grey-red, dimly lit background. Images with eyes that were sad, hopeful, pleading, tears could be seen falling, mouths were opened wide. The people appeared to whisper plaintive words, seeking food, clothing, a place to live, work, a guide to living, sage advice, the Word of God in their lives; hands, faces, voices became incarnate. I was seeing and sensing needs as never before, yet I was unaware of what the vision's portent was for me. In my puzzlement and despair, I began to pray intently for understanding. I wanted to know what I was seeing and why. I waited and listened: nothing; silence. No still small voice, no *gentle whisper*. I began to pray anew, this time with greater concentration and persistence. Again, I waited. I listened more attentively. In my heart, I heard God tell me he had important work for me to do and I needed to yield to him. The assignment meant a complete change of the work I had been successfully engaged in for many years. I would have to leave the business world, abandon my personal goals and the desires I had held since a child. My way of life and my family would be altered irretrievably. No longer was there doubt in my mind and heart of what I had been blessed to witness. This vision became my destiny on earth. I had been called to serve the Lord with all my heart, soul, mind, and strength. At that moment I gave little thought as to how I could run a full-time business, continue to be heavily involved in the community, maintain my loyalty and devotion to Pond Street church and still complete a demanding four-year college program. Relying on my strength it could not be done, so I made a life decision to rely totally on the Lord. I would serve him completely. He would provide these answers and make clear his plans in his own time and schedule. He had captured my heart.[3]

In the succeeding days, God began equipping me for the work ahead in sharing the gospel message, through thirty-two years of pastoral ministry and writing a Christian learning library of books. There the themes, contents, and inner works of my writings were revealed when during nights of intended sleep and rest I was abruptly awakened to experience God's Spirit pouring forth words that have led to the profound discovery of the deep things of God.

That is what the Scriptures mean when they say, "No eye has seen, no ear has heard, and no mind has imagined what God has prepared for those who love him." But it was to us that God revealed these things by his Spirit. For his Spirit searches out everything and shows us God's deep secrets. No one can know a person's thoughts except that person's spirit, and no one can know God's thoughts except God's own Spirit. And we have received God's Spirit (not the world's spirit), so we can know the wonderful things God has freely given us. (1 Corinthians 2:9–12)

After publishing my first book in 2006, God granted me the privilege of writing nine more books through his divine Word, mostly from notes in the wee hours of the morning, including my memoir *The Top of The Stairs*. However, before completing my memoir, my eighth book *Are You Jesus?* was published in August 2017, and then an inexplicable, unsettling thing happened—the divine flow of God's revelation ceased. I was at a loss. My writing was paused. Without the Spirit's illumination, I was an empty vessel at a loss for words. I did not understand why God was silent so I began to pray unceasingly for God to open the door to his heart to me again, fearing that if he remained silent my writing would remain silent also.

I am told that every writer struggles with a condition called "writer's block," where writers lose the ability to produce new work or experience a creative slowdown. I have been advised that writer's block is inevitable and may likely stem from several causes, some originating within the work itself and some created by events outside. The author may run out of inspiration or be distracted by family matters, and for the most part feel as if every creative bone in their body has left and that they are ready to throw in the towel. To this point, my books were all written from notes recorded during early morning visitations of the Holy Spirit; in addition, my experience has taught me that although God does not always use the sound of a human voice, he is faithful to speak clearly and succinctly through his Word. To say the least, I had basked in the luxury of being a recipient.

I desperately wanted to hear God's voice again. Surely the absence of revelation was not a lack on God's part but a failure on the part of the human instrument he used to record and proclaim his message. What soon came to mind was the Scripture passage in 1 Samuel 3:1, "Meanwhile, the boy Samuel served the Lord by assisting Eli. Now in those days, messages from the Lord were very rare, and visions were quite uncommon." Here we learn that God had previously spoken directly and audibly with Moses and Joshua, but now during the three centuries of rule by the judges, his word had become infrequent. Because of sin in Eli's family, God had stopped speaking through Eli the high priest. This caused me to wonder if there was something in my life, family, or work that was displeasing to God. I reflected on my present life and where I might have failed God, and asked him to reveal anything that was standing in the way of hearing him once again.

Of course, a writer can become so content with his heavenly connection that routine, boredom, and repetition may occur, and the author takes for granted the wonderful gift of revelation from the Lord. When this happens, the author often struggles to maintain writing out of determination and training, but no longer hears the thoughts of God revealed by the Holy Spirit. Therefore, to renew or transform the narrative to a deeper understanding, the writer must return to the Source, to hear a fresh word from the Lord. After almost eight months, I feeling very despondent. Then, while attending a weekly Bible study on the book of Hebrews, I heard God's voice again. It came this time during the reading of the Scriptures; however, it was a far different and most unfamiliar way than any previous experience. I heard this:

> Because God's children are human beings—made of flesh and blood—the Son also became flesh and blood. For only as a human being could he die, and only by dying could he break the power of the devil, who had the power of death. (Hebrews 2:14–15)

In illuminating this passage of Scripture, something happened in my spirit that I cannot explain. For the first time, I understood *that the main purpose of Jesus's coming into the world was to participate in death.* The words "participate in death" touched every fiber of my being and I felt an intimacy with Jesus as never before.

I am not sure why I felt those words so deeply; however, it seemed that my sin was intensified and I felt moved to be more than an observer. Maybe it was the time of year just before the Easter season, or maybe it was a feeling that had been lying dormant in my heart. However, what was revealed to me was the fact that the contemporary gospel has left many believers in Jesus Christ emotionally detached from the cross. They readily acknowledge Jesus's death but are content to be mere bystanders, with his death being less personal and more a matter of fact. This left me with a greater desire for intimacy with Jesus than ever before.

In retrospect, the words of Dr. Calvin Miller, poet, pastor, theologian, and professor of preaching at Beeson Divinity School, AL, in his book *Into the Depths of God,* became appropriate at this time: "Deep is not a place we visit in our search of God, it's what happens to us when we find him."[4] It was several days later that I began to understand, as I heard the words of the Spirit. The main purpose of Jesus coming into the world was to "participate in death," for he was the bearer of a new life separate and apart from the old life in the world. This was a life set apart to God, a life to be lived in the presence of the Father. It then became clear that God wanted us to die to live, while Satan wanted us to live his way—to die. This brought me pain to know that Jesus's participation in death was because of my sin and guilt. I recall the Apostle John's declaration in his gospel 1:14: *"So the Word became human and made his home among us. He was full of unfailing love and faithfulness. And we have seen his glory, the glory of the Father's one and only Son."* Though I had taught and preached the message of Incarnation many times, this was different, it was a moment of personal discovery, a moment of God's discovery, a moment that drew me closer to Jesus than ever before. I longed to be there to witness his broken, mutilated body on the cross of which Paul writes Romans 8:3:

> The law of Moses was unable to save us because of the weakness of our sinful nature. So God did what the law could not do. He sent his own Son in a body like the bodies we sinners have. And in that body, God declared an end to sin's control over us by giving his Son as a sacrifice for our sins.

Jesus took our place in a body prepared for him just like ours, he finished the race God had marked out for me and all his created beings. Jesus crossed the finish line without sin, and the prize for his victory was death on the cross. Accordingly, Paul writes:

> I want to know Christ and experience the mighty power that raised him from the dead. I want to suffer with him, sharing in his death, so that one way or another I will experience the resurrection from the dead!" (Philippians 3:10, 11)

When we become one with Christ by trusting in him, we experience the power that raised Jesus from the dead. That same mighty power will help us live morally renewed and regenerated lives. But before we can walk in the newness of life, we must die to sin. Just as the resurrection gives us Christ's power to live for him, his crucifixion marks the death of our old sinful nature.

SIX

FAN OR FOLLOWER

"So I live in this earthly body by trusting in the Son of God, who loved me and gave himself for me."

(Galatians 2:20b)

Have you ever paused for a moment amid the daily pressures of life to ask yourself, "Do I know what is needed to live out this Christian life?" The question might also be asked, "What does it mean to be a Christian?" Or simply, "What is a Christian?"

The query is prompted by the many personages today on TV, radio, magazines, newspapers, and social media who claim to be followers of Jesus Christ. Their exposure often leaves many people confused and left to wonder how believers in Christ Jesus can distinguish the truth when there seems to be little or no similarity in the messages coming forth. How can it be that many who wear the name "Christian" have a scant resemblance to each other. Therefore, the question persists, "What is a Christian?"

The very first chapter of the opening book of the Bible can help lead us to an answer. We are told in Genesis 1:27: "So God created human beings in his image. In the image of God he created them; male and female he created them." The first thing we learn is that Christians bear the identity of Jesus Christ and should seek to model their lives after their Creator. In creation our identity is formed and embedded in the image of God. Though sin distorted it for a time, Jesus Christ came into the world to restore the divine image in us. Paul writes in 2 Corinthians 3:16–18:

> But whenever someone turns to the Lord, the veil is taken away. For the Lord is the Spirit, and wherever the Spirit of the Lord is, there is freedom. So all of us who have had that veil removed can see and reflect the glory of the Lord. And the Lord—who is the Spirit—makes us more and more like him as we are changed into his glorious image.

When Moses came down Mount Sinai with the Ten Commandments, his face glowed from being in God's presence (Exodus 34:29–35). However, the glory that the Holy Spirit imparts to the believer is more excellent and lasts longer than the glory that Moses experienced. The longer our minds are open to see Jesus, the more we can become like him. The truth about Christ's death and resurrection transforms us morally as we understand and apply it to our lives. As our knowledge deepens, the Holy Spirit helps us to change; and the more closely we follow Christ, the more we will be like him.

The fact is, most of us start with good intentions. We believe we have strong reasons to follow Jesus, but somehow along the way our hopes are dashed, we encounter disappointment or discouragement, or expectations are not met, so we quit at the start. We turn off and abandon our goal before we reach the end of the road.

May I be so presumptuous as to ask: Are you following Jesus because of certain expectations? Are you following because of his miracles or his power? Do you follow because of what he has done or is doing in your life, or are following simply because of someone else's testimony? Or do you follow Jesus because he established an intimate relationship with you when you answered his call to "come follow me?"

Following Jesus may mean leaving the crowd. It may mean getting off the broad way and taking the lonely fork onto the road Jesus took: the road of suffering, loneliness, and despair—the road that leads straight to the cross. Is that not what the writer meant when he said, "As the time drew near for him to ascend to heaven, Jesus resolutely set out for Jerusalem" (Luke 9:51)? And from that moment few followed him.

This leads to my second fact of understanding: our identity is confirmed by our integrity. As we live out our lives in the world, the way we live either confirms or denies who we are. One can say from the Scriptures that a Christian is a person who has truly repented of sin, sincerely trusted Jesus Christ for his or her salvation, has acknowledged Christ as Lord, has invited the Holy Spirit to take up residence in their heart, and lives daily in God's presence. Thus, there is no longer a need to guess or hope who you are. You can know with certainty through the Holy Spirit that you are God's child and that you will spend eternity with Christ. Paul uses powerful imagery in 2 Corinthians 3:2b to show that a Christian is recognizable by the way they live when he says: "Your lives are a letter written in our hearts; everyone can read it and recognize our good work among you."

Before we journey further along in pursuit of the question "What is a Christian?" there are two important points I would like to make. The first is that I will be giving a great deal of thought and emphasis to the personal and relational consequences of this self-examination. This is deliberate. It is a counteraction to the undue emphasis placed for so long on the rational and the logical in religion.

I have no desire to set up opposition between reason and revelation—between "knowledge" and "knowing"—for both must be affirmed. However, one's knowledge of Christ is too specific for the inner life. The inner life of Christ is too real, too vibrant. Both are inevitable in religious heritage, both are expressed as knowing Christ, though their different perspectives lead to the possibility of conflict—not merely between different beliefs based on different interpretations of the biblical storyline but also conflicts between those whose faith is scripted and those for whom faith is life. Both are the direct result of experience; however, living faith is an attempt to embody and manifest that experience while reason, far removed from the real encounter, is a result of philosophical alteration and refinement and characterizing of the experience.

The Bible says that good works do not make a person acceptable to God. A person can live to a high moral standard, give money to feed the poor, go to church, and serve his neighbors, and yet not be a Christ-follower or Christian. The truth is, God is the only One who can provide salvation for mankind, through Jesus, and any other attempt to approach God, no matter how sincere, will end in total failure.

Most churchgoing traditional Christians in America can easily accept all of this regarding other religions. However, what many fail to see is that much of what is called Christianity today is nothing but religion. Many are going through the motions, thinking that their observance of Christian virtues will help them obtain salvation, without realizing it is possible to be caught up in the trap of trying to be justified by church attendance and financial receipts just as much as the person who burns incense to idols to appease the gods. What I have learned from experience is that there are great church organizations designed to build up the body of the local church—in contrast to the number of vibrant churches focused on making disciples of Jesus Christ. I confess that before I learned to seek after becoming a follower of Jesus Christ, I gave my all in becoming a valued church member.

Surely this is not true of all Christians. There are followers who walk closely with Christ and hang on his every word. Some hunger for his presence and desire earnestly to obey his every command. Some walk after him, maybe not in perfect step but with a perfect heart, as David did: "I will be careful to live a blameless life" (Psalm 101:2). The idea of perfection does not mean a sinless, flawless existence, as people look for. What it means is completeness, maturity, uprightness, having neither spot nor blemish. It means constant obedience. It means the heart is responsive to God. It means the heart cries out as David's, "Search me, O God, and know my heart; test me and know my anxious thoughts. Point out anything in me that offends you, and lead me along the path of everlasting life" (Psalm 139:23–24). It means that the perfect heart reaches out to allow the Holy Spirit to come and search out our innermost being and remove all that is unlike Christ, so that nothing will be allowed to hinder our becoming more like him. It means others will take notice that we are followers of Jesus.

Look at Matthew 4:19–20: "Jesus called out to them, 'Come, follow me, and I will show you how to fish for people!' And they left their nets at once and followed him." Now, pay particular attention to verse 19, "Come, follow me, and I will show you how to fish for people!" The command to "Come, follow me" (in the Greek, an adverb of place expressing a command) is simple: "your place is following after me." Again, my question is: What does it mean to follow Jesus? Is it an invitation to be rescued from sin or is it is the call of the believer to service? It is no small decision to follow Jesus. It is possible to have heard the Lord's teaching and still not be a disciple, to be an observer without being a player, to be a hanger-on in some great work without pulling one's weight. To be a fan rather than a follower.

Merriam-Webster's dictionary defines a fan as "an ardent admirer or enthusiast," but the word is also a shortened form of the word "fanatic," meaning "marked by excessive enthusiasm and often intense uncritical devotion." Fanatic, in turn, comes from the Latin word *fanaticus*, and the term was once used to describe individuals who had been inspired or captivated by a deity. Still, there's more to being a fan than just the origin of the word. Fans are people who passionately support, admire, and celebrate a particular person, company, product, or brand. Specific "fandoms," or fan communities, even have their own nicknames: "Trekkies" or "Trekkers" are those obsessed with *Star Trek*, and Taylor Swift's fan base consists of "Swifties." These self-assigned labels lend followers a sense of identity and community, and denote a positive, familiar relationship with the object or franchise in question.

A fan may be a devoted admirer, but a follower has accepted a call from his or her master. A fan may be a devotee of one or more celebrities, but a follower will have only one master only. A fan delights in experience, but a follower delights in learning. A fan is following his mentor for pleasure, but a follower is walking in his master's footsteps for uplifting his life. Thus, a follower is excited by the call to follow because they have heard the good news about Jesus. As a result, a fan is an ardent enthusiast without attachment, but a follower is a disciple. A disciple is a follower who has abandoned his or her old life and taken up the life of another. Therefore, in following Christ we set aside our own goals and pleasures to embrace the life God created us for: to know him in a personal way and to make disciples of others by teaching them all of Christ's commands.

When Jesus called Peter and Andrew, their goal was to be successful fishermen. In asking them to forsake their goal for his, Jesus commanded them to follow him and he would make them fishers for people's souls. Jesus did not simply command his disciples to become fishers of people; rather, he promised to make them fishers for people!

One of the most memorable two-day periods in the life of Jesus occurred as he fed five thousand men, which prompted some to want to make him king by force. In the middle of the night, he walked on the sea. The next day, in a synagogue he spoke about himself being the bread of life. But after his message in the synagogue, something horribly sad took place, followed by an inspiring confession. In John's narrative, Jesus says to his disciples:

Anyone who eats my flesh and drinks my blood remains in me, and I in him. I live because of the living Father who sent me; in the same way, anyone who feeds on me will live because of me. I am the true bread that came down from heaven. Anyone who eats this bread will not die as your ancestors did (even though they ate the manna) but will live forever. (John 6:56–58)

After Jesus's pronouncement, "Many of his disciples said, "This is very hard to understand. How can anyone accept it?" (v. 60). And the saddest thing of all occurred: "At this point many of his disciples turned away and deserted him" (v. 66), followed by Peter's dedicated confession:

Jesus turned to the Twelve and asked, "Are you also going to leave?"

Simon Peter replied, "Lord, to whom would we go? You have the words that give eternal life. We believe, and we know you are the Holy One of God." (vv. 67–69)

Ultimately, at this point a large-scale defection from Christ took place. Who were those that turned away? What possible good reason could a person have for deciding that life is better without Jesus than it is with him? Jesus's twelve disciples are distinguished from those in verse 66 who turned away, but others of the multitude of the disciples who followed Christ—who heard him, professed to believe in him, and were baptized in his name—were not true disciples, only nominal ones, superficial ones. It lets us know that many people today are quite happy to call themselves Christians with little or no thought of following Jesus. As Paul Harvey said, "We have drifted away from being fishers of men to being keepers of the aquarium."[1]

What is the problem? Why have we not produced more disciples whose lives emulate Christ? Why is there so little intimacy in our relationship with Jesus? The reason we have so many problems in our churches today is that there are many Christians and so few disciples. S. I. McMillen, in his book *None of These Diseases*, tells a story of a young woman who wanted to go to college, but her heart sank when she read the question on the application blank that asked, "Are you a leader?" Being both honest and conscientious, she wrote, "No," and returned the application, expecting the worst. To her surprise, she received this letter from the college: "Dear Applicant: A study of the application forms reveals that this year our college will have 1,452 new leaders. We are accepting you because we feel they must have at least one follower."[2]

Too many people have yet to get it right. There was only one who had it right and he said, "Follow me"—so if you are not following him you're not right. Jesus said, "I am the way" (John 14:6), the only way, and if you're not walking after me you're lost.

I believe the answer may lie in the fact we are walking too far behind him. There is too much distance between Jesus and us, so we really can't observe his life. We need to close ranks and get closer to him. To that end, we cannot and must not continue for another moment calling ourselves Christians until we can answer the question personally: Do I truly want nothing but Christ? Is he truly everything to me, my purpose for living, my life, my all? Have I counted all things lost for a revelation of him? Have I counted everything worthless that I might win him? Is his call to me to follow him my one life's ambition? Are people drawn to me because I turn them on to Christ, or do I turn them off?

To be a disciple of Jesus Christ there are two words that must stand out: identity and integrity. Our identity is who we are or purport to be. As disciples of Jesus Christ, our integrity is manifest in what we claim to be. Think for a moment: How many people, strangers you come in contact with, want to follow you? Therefore, when we present ourselves to the world, it is his identity that draws people to the Father. Dare we go anywhere or do anything in the name of Jesus until we settle the question first, "Is his life so manifest in me that all men will know that I am His disciple? Will people follow me because they know I have been with Jesus? Will they follow me because 'It is no longer I who live, but Christ lives in me'?"

The only thing we can share with anyone is what Christ has given us. The only words that have real meaning from our mouths are the words lived out in our lives. During a long and fruitful ministry, Paul had these words to say: "you should imitate me, just as I imitate Christ" (1 Corinthians 11:1). We remember Jesus's words, "So you cannot become my disciple without giving up everything you own" (Luke 14:33). The question remains: Are you merely a fan of Jesus or a devoted follower? Because there are varying opinions about who we are and who God calls us to be.

While writing this book, I commissioned a study of believers to respond to the question, "What is a Christian?" or simply, "A Christian is …," with the stipulation that responses should be no more than one paragraph. Responders were told that their answers would be used as material in this book and were given the assurance they would remain anonymous. The query was highly personal and targeted those who claim to believe in Christ and have experienced his life and activities here on earth. Their responses were expected to be derived from intimacy with him, where personal knowledge is paramount. People who answered the questions were from different denominations, multiracial in make-up.

Very few answers were less than a single paragraph, and most were void of the personal pronoun "me." The most common response to the question was, "A Christian is a person who has believed and accepted Jesus Christ as their personal Savior and who practices the teachings of Jesus Christ as they are written in the Bible." Other responses included:

> A Christian is someone who has experienced a second birth and has recognized that Jesus was raised from the dead.

> A Christian is someone whose heart is filled with genuine love and whose daily walk aligns with the will of God.

> A Christian is one who earnestly practices the tenets and precepts of the Divine Scriptures, understanding that Jesus Christ is the way, the truth, and the life.

> One who believes by faith, that Christ is who he says he is and puts into practice and lives following his teaching.

> A Christian is someone whose behavior and heart reflect Jesus Christ.

It must be noted that most of these answers are true and right and grounded in the Scriptures. However, they miss the real point of behind the question, "What is a Christian?" It once again highlights the difference between "knowledge" and "knowing." A person can have a tremendous amount of information about God and yet never get close enough to experience the magnitude of his divine love.

The contemporary church, for the most part, appears oblivious to the fact that intellectual enlightenment has crept in to displace spiritual truth. Human illumination is to "know"; spiritual illumination is a "knowing." The difference in words seems slight; however, the chasm is as vast as eternity. "To know" is of human origin; "knowing" is what is revealed in the heart about God by the Holy Spirit. Knowing fosters spiritual understanding, whereas cognitive knowledge lacks understanding of the things of God, making it difficult to grasp gospel truths and their power and effect.

One can study the Bible and read the Scriptures, even memorize favorite verses, but the Holy Spirit must bring the spiritual revelation that not only must one have knowledge but understand how to live out the Word. How would you recognize a Christian from any other person if you met him or her on the street?

I believe that in responding to this question, we must give some thought to Matthew 4:18–21, where Jesus first called Peter, Andrew, James, and John to follow him, and they all left their present occupations of fisherman at once and followed him. How did these men know what kind of man Jesus was? What did they see in Jesus which compelled them to drop everything and follow him? What did Jesus promise for those who dropped their nets and followed him? Could it be that the Holy Spirit revealed that Jesus was offering them a new radical lifestyle to be lived in the presence of the Father?

Did Jesus not say in John 10:10, "My purpose is to give them a rich and satisfying life"? Does this not give added weight to the question "What is a Christian?" Every day God allows us to live, we are defining ourselves as Christ in the world. Our hunger for the inmost things of God is what defines us, and our light should be relatively indistinguishable from Christ himself. This prompts the queries: Why have we not become the salt of the earth? Why have we not become the light of the world? Why have we not done more to change the world? Why is it so hard for us to break the stranglehold of the world in our lives?

Scripture is clear why Jesus took on a robe of flesh, why Christ came into the world: "This is a trustworthy saying, and everyone should accept it: 'Christ Jesus came into the world to save sinners'" (1 Timothy 1:15). And yet, his coming had a deeper, more encompassing purpose, which is imbedded in John the Baptist's warning to repent and prepare for the coming Messiah: "Turn from your sins and turn to God, because the Kingdom of Heaven is near" (Matthew 3:2). This tells us that Jesus came not only to save us from sin but also to show us how to live as faithful subjects in his kingdom. When John writes in his gospel (1:14), "So the Word became human and lived here on earth among us," he is stating that God in Christ entered human history as a man, and that when he came to earth the Kingdom of God was birthed. And so the Kingdom of God is among us is both a present and future reality. Jesus came into the world to destroy sin and to establish his reign and rule in the hearts of men who had lived under the authority of Satan, "the prince of this world," who is the destroyer of life. In contrast, the life Jesus offers is abundantly rich and full. It is eternal, and yet it begins immediately; it is endless.

With that in mind, I ask myself, "As believers, why do we not understand that we are not called to live better in the world, but to live fully and abundantly in the Kingdom of God?" You ask some believers how they are doing and they will often respond, "I'm doing OK, I'm making it," or "I'll get through it." These responses are based on the world's standards of survival. All the while, we are called to thrive in the Kingdom of God. Is it then any wonder why the world fails to recognize us?

That sounds kind of harsh as I write it, but the responses received from this survey have made me wonder. It brings home the point that while Sunday is nice for fellowship or worship, growth does not usually occur from a twenty-minute sermon. It also speaks volumes to leadership, and maybe to a lesser degree of the hunger of people "to know." Somewhat like the first question Jesus posed to his closest followers, "Who do people say that the Son of Man is?" (Matthew 16:13), setting them up for the more personal question which gets to the heart of the matter, his latter query is direct and highly personal and targets those who claim to believe in Christ and have experienced his life and activities here on earth: "But who do you say I am?" (v. 15). The real question is more personal: "If someone met you on the street, would they know you had been with Jesus?" What is a Christian?

Looking back on my church experience, I regret that my initial worship experiences were more about the church family than about discipleship. I had confessed faith in Jesus Christ. I had my name on the church rolls. I was considered a good church member. I was involved in many church activities. I was faithful in attending worship, volunteered wherever help was needed, prayed, ministered to people, helped with the church dinners, all the while thinking "this is what is needed to please God" but always knowing there was more. I was continually asking, "Lord, what would you have me to do?" All the while, I was ignorant that God simply wanted me to be like His Son Jesus. I had been merely practicing outward religion.

But change came in 1973 when a woman member of the small house church across the street came to me, seeking approval for the use of our sanctuary at Pond Street Baptist Church. They were planning to hold revival services but had not yet acquired a building.

Her request was approved, and the first night I found myself with a desire to attend. While entering the foyer of our church I was met by the woman of the neighboring house church, who looked at me quite strangely then asked, "What are you doing here?"

To say the least, I was quite shocked to be asked why I was present at the church I had been attending for the last thirteen years. No one had ever asked me that question before. However, not yet fully recovered from the assault on my self-importance, I answered, "I came for the revival."

She replied, "I thought Baptists didn't usually attend this kind of service."

At the moment, I realized she was right. However, I also knew why I had come. I had been drawn to this place tonight with the prospect of getting to know the Lord Jesus in a deeper and more abiding way. Revival focuses every bit of energy on God. It begins on one's knees in prayer, pleading and petitioning God for a renewed outpouring of His Spirit. It is usually characterized by a powerful soul, hot preaching about Jesus, and deeper intimacy and power from the Lord. I wanted and needed this in my life.

The defining moment occurred some months later, in the fall of 1974, at another revival at the church. This time an evangelist, the Rev. Frank Simmons, was conducting a revival at Pond Street. After a short, powerful challenging sermon he posed the question, "Do you know for sure where you will spend eternity?" The first time he asked I was content not to deal with the question, all the while knowing I did not have the necessary assurance. The question of the writer of Hebrews 2:3 surfaced in my memory: What makes us think that we can escape if we are indifferent to this great salvation that was announced by the Lord Jesus himself?

I knew I had to do something. I wanted to be sure that I was going to spend eternity with the Lord. I threw all caution to the wind, stood up from my front-row seat, and presented my life before the Lord. At that moment I exchanged my name for his. I would no longer be known by my name but by his—the name of Christ. The name "Christian." That night, "I decided to follow Jesus, no turning back, no turning back."

I recall rising from my seat and surrendering my death to Jesus, tears streaming down my face. My heart was sorrowing, repentant, and palpitating wildly. I felt my whole body, mind, soul, and spirit surrendering, and felt some gentle hands lowering me to the floor where I lay for a time. I felt a joy inexpressible and a peace beyond understanding. I had crowned Jesus as Lord of my life and now dwelt in his divine presence. Paul writes, "The Spirit of God, who raised Jesus from the dead, lives in you. And just as God raised Christ Jesus from the dead, he will give life to your mortal bodies by this same Spirit living within you" (Romans 8:11). I had taken on Christ's life.

My old self had been dead and buried, and my new self had taken up residence in me. My life had been exchanged for Jesus's life. My old self had been exchanged for his new self. Jesus said, "My purpose is to give them a rich and satisfying life."

What is a Christian? A Christian is a life. "So I live in this earthly body by trusting in the Son of God, who loved me and gave himself for me." What it means, in effect, is that the Holy Spirit not only makes us like new, he also keeps us like new. "This means that anyone who belongs to Christ has become a new person. The old life is gone; a new life has begun!"(2 Corinthians 5:17). There can be no argument against a changed life. A Christian is a demonstration of a transformed life and this change should be noticed. Transformation is not like changing a suit for each occasion, as we read in 2 Corinthians 3:16–18:

> But whenever someone turns to the Lord, the veil is taken away. For the Lord is the Spirit, and wherever the Spirit of

the Lord is, there is freedom. So all of us who have had that veil removed can see and reflect the glory of the Lord. And the Lord—who is the Spirit—makes us more and more like him as we are changed into his glorious image.

The more closely we follow Jesus, the more we move into his likeness.

SEVEN

LIFE CENTERING

"The world would love you as one of its own if you belonged to it, but you are no longer part of the world. I chose you to come out of the world, so it hates you."

(John 15:19)

Previously I testified of my growing up in my parents' church and all of the prohibitions and restrictions to keep us from the world's evils. Admittedly I often pushed the bounds of their prohibitions because I wanted to see things for myself, and to my surprise I often found many of their embargoes not harmful at all. But please do not misinterpret what I am saying. In 1 Corinthians 10:23 we read, "You say, 'I am allowed to do anything'—but not everything is good for you. You say, 'I am allowed to do anything'—but not everything is beneficial." Surely Paul is not suggesting that one can do anything they want no matter who is hurt by it. Rather, he is suggesting that what we do should not cause another believer to stumble. We should not project our standards on others.

Our actions must be motivated by God's love, so that all we do will be for his God's glory.

However, with my upbringing in my dad's church, there were certain restrictions to overcome and usually, the only one hurt was me. Much later I discovered that some of the things considered worldly were the very things Jesus used in his parables to make a point. Fr. William J. Bausch, in *Storytelling: Imagination and Faith*, suggests that spirituality is rooted in earthiness:

> For us, spirituality is rooted in platonic otherworldliness, not earthiness. But Judaism will have none of this. It is rather rooted in the sensual, the earthy, the Lord's creation (Isaiah 25:6–8): On the mountain, Yahweh Sabbaoth will prepare for all the peoples a banquet of rich food, a banquet of fine wines, of food rich and juicy, of fine strained wines. On this mountain, he will remove the mourning veil covering all people, and the shroud enwrapping all nations and will destroy Death forever.[1]

Here the prophet notes that God is a refuge for the poor, the disadvantaged, and the oppressed. "All the people of the world"— Gentiles and Jews together—at God's messianic feast, will celebrate the overthrow of evil and the joy of eternity with God. Jewish thinking, which is biblical thinking and which was also "Jesus thinking," takes it for granted that the sensual is a blessing and that there is no (spiritual) life without it. In commenting on the Jewish Christian differences, we're always looking elsewhere for God, in the heavenlies. However, the religious Jew finds him right where he's planted: in the here and now, in earthiness.

Forgoing my parents' exclusions and prohibitions in my life and ministry, I feel vindicated for the many times I have found the earthy rich for sermons and spiritual insights. The fact is, there are many very subtle messages behind many of the advertisements we see or hear in the words or phrases coming forth in the media. When watching television or listening to the radio I am particularly interested in the commercials or ads, because over the many years I have been in ministry some of my most notable sermons have come from the themes or messages rooted in these advertisements.

One of the most memorable stories of spirituality rooted in earthiness occurred several years ago as I was watching a television commercial for Travelers Insurance, featuring a nattily dressed man with a derby carrying an oversized red umbrella, going about providing aid for people in distress. At the end of the advertisement, the caption read, "There when you need it." The story so captured attention that I wrote about it in my earlier book *The Crimson Thread of the Bible*:

> Initially, I thought the advertisement a bit amusing and cleverly done. However, the more times it appeared the greater my sense there was a deeper message embedded within. Finally, I realized this man carrying the red umbrella connected me to something or someone far greater than I could ever imagine. During his travels, the umbrella carrier comes across some children caught in a rainstorm and he walks along with them shielding them from the rain with his umbrella. He later makes his way down to a river and encounters a circus troupe stranded because the ferry stopped running with no way to get across to the other side. The man invites them to get into his inverted umbrella and sails across the river, using the umbrella as a boat. From there, he encounters a young boy and girl who are stranded because their bicycles have broken down. The man promptly mounts them on the

124   A Wonder-Filled Life

handle of his umbrella and flies them back home. The last scene of the story was what greatly caught my attention, as the man with the red umbrella was now sitting on a tall building overlooking the city quite pleased with the many smaller red umbrellas below. The caption reads: "There when you need it." This final scene brings to mind the words of the prophet Isaiah as he depicts God watching over His creations and world: "God sits above the circle of the earth. The people below like grasshoppers to him! He spreads out the heavens like a curtain and makes his tent from them" (Isaiah 40:22).[2]

The picture of God over all creation reveals to me how great God's love is for us. This brings forth the most striking imagery as Jesus prays to the Father:

I have given them your word. And the world hates them because they do not belong to the world, just as I do not belong to the world. I'm not asking you to take them out of the world, but to keep them safe from the evil one. They do not belong to this world any more than I do. Make them holy by your truth; teach them your word, which is truth. (John 17:14–17)

Satan is the avowed enemy of Christians, because they are living accusations against the world's immorality and do not cooperate with joining in their sin. Jesus prays for followers of Christ, that they become pure and holy through believing and obeying the Word of God. God's great purpose of our redemption overarches all of life and is seen in the man in the red umbrella sitting on the heights and watching those below with satisfaction. Daily application of God's Word has a purifying effect on our minds and hearts.

Eric Liddell, a Scottish athlete born in China who later served as a Christian missionary, asserts: "You will know as much about God, and only as much of God, as you are willing to put into practice."[3]

The image of God sitting above the circle of the earth immediately brings to mind Troup Jr. High School, in New Haven, CT, where my Social Studies teacher Mrs. Sterling had a huge globe sitting on the far edge of her desk, which she would often spin to show us the various continents. That's where I learned what the world looked like; I must admit I still don't know why Australia doesn't fall off the bottom of the world. With that image in mind, I could envision a Lite-Brite—the small plastic colored plastic peg that illuminates when inserted into a panel— now implanted into the globe with its head protruding on the outside. Imagine that pin is Jesus, speaking to the people: "I am the light of the world. If you follow me, you won't have to walk in darkness, because you will have the light that leads to life." Because the pin is inserted in the globe and the head of the pin is now lit, can you recall Jesus's words in John 14:6: "I am the way, the truth, and the life. No one can come to the Father except through me." Does the vision of the Father overlooking the red umbrellas then make more relevant the above words, "They do not belong to this world any more than I do. Make them holy by your truth; teach them your word, which is truth"? The Father has given his word to people about Jesus. Therefore if we center on Jesus and follow him closely, he will lead us out of the world into God's heavenly abode.

When Liddell says, "You will know as much about God, and only as much of God, as you are willing to put into practice," it means daily focusing on our relationship with God because we desire to be in his presence. What I am suggesting is the adoption of a principle that will take our walk with Christ to a new level in approaching God where he is to be found—in the center of our souls. Centering is the merger of two selves: ours and his. Centering is union with Christ. It is not a union that eradicates either self but one that heightens both, as each is made greater in this union. The fact is, we are never more ourselves and God is never more God than when we enter into union with Christ.

Consequently, we are reminded by Jesus that Christianity is about living. We still live in the world bodily but we are not of the world, because God reigns and rules in the heart. We take up space in the world because, relationally, the Kingdom of God occupies space in the world. Though physically we live in the world, we have been transformed into the kingdom.

Transformation requires the Word of God firmly planted in our minds. In Colossians 3:2–3 we are told that our real home is where Christ lives. Grasping this fact allows us to have a different perspective on our life here on earth—looking at our everyday lives from God's perspective, seeking what he desires, thinking from God's perspective, reading the Scriptures from his perspective, learning and understanding what his will is for us. Taking action on our renewed learning, we are transformed into realizing that indeed, what we think . . . we are. Thus, once God's Word is breathed in, then the renewal, reeducation, and redirection of our minds take place, and transformation is completed.

To understand this truth, one must be aware that there is tension between our old nature and the new nature created in Christ Jesus. The old nature is lived as a physical man in a physical body; the new nature is a spiritual being in a physical body. Our old nature conflicted with Christ; however, our new nature, or "new reality," is in harmony with Christ. There is between the two natures a door which can be opened only from our old nature. Jesus says: "Look! Here I stand at the door and knock. If you hear me calling and open the door, I will come in, and we will share a meal as friends" (Revelation 3:20). Jesus is trying to get through to us—not breaking in, but knocking. He allows us to decide whether or not to open our lives to him or keep his life-changing presence and power on the other side of the door. The choice is to move from the old to the new, from the old physical reality to the new spiritual reality which is where Christ is. In Colossians 3, Paul uses some words that are telling.

> [S]et your sights on the realities of heaven, where Christ sits at God's right hand [in the place of honor and power]. . . . For you died to this life, and your real life is hidden with Christ in God. And when Christ, who is your real life, is revealed to the whole world, you will share in all his glory. (vv. 1, 3–4)

Note the phrases "realities of heaven" and "real life." Paul wants us to know there are two realities in life: Christ's and ours. His is with the Father in heaven. Ours is with him, yet in the world. As new creations in Christ Jesus, our new life and our real life are the same. It is the fullness of life Jesus came to give. This life he offers is abundantly rich and full. It is eternal, yet it begins immediately. Our real life in Christ is lived on a higher plane because of his overflowing forgiveness, love, and guidance: "So I live my life in this earthly body by trusting in the Son of God, who loved me and gave himself for me" (Galatians 2:20b).

Relationally we have become one with Christ and his experiences are ours. To be in a deeper relationship with him, we must move closer to his reality and center our lives on him. Once the door to the old life is closed behind us, the vastness of the ocean of God's presence opens wide to us. Surely, most of us would be apprehensive to approach God with freedom and confidence, but thanks to Jesus Christ by faith we can enter directly into God's presence. With this in mind, I am inclined to think that only when we venture into the realm of the deep can we begin to plumb the vastness and enormity of God. Jesus would probably have used some present-day activity as a parable of spirituality being rooted in earthiness.

Today, in the age of spaceflight, several companies are hoping to launch people on short suborbital trips into space within the next year or two, with many people already signed up. The establishment of a space-tourism industry depends on the development of vehicles capable of launching people into space and returning them to Earth. Any such vehicle will have to be designed with reliability, safety, and comfort in mind. Jesus might use this as a parable, with the main point being that if we think of our old sinful life as dead and buried it is a one-way trip to the Father, safe and secure in the presence and power of the Holy Spirit: "Since you have been raised to new life with Christ . . ." (Colossians 3:1a). Destination: the Kingdom of God. For docking and a rendezvous to occur, we must be in the same spiritual plane as God.

In space, when two satellites or ships want to rendezvous, the one chasing the other in orbit must slow down to catch up; if you increase the speed, you move into a higher orbit than the craft in front and miss it altogether. The way docking is handled by NASA is for the chase vehicle to start in a higher orbit, and then slow down to a lower orbit to match the target vehicle. It is this way with following God. If he is your target, you must get in the same orbit so you can dock securely, open the hatches, and have close fellowship with him. You cannot experience his presence when you're in a different orbit!

This illustration may help us to understand the importance of practicing our belief and faith in the character of God. That practice, I believe, enables you and me to start in a higher orbit and to slow down when we are seeking to connect with God's presence. It is in that connecting, abiding, and finding refuge that our minds, hearts, bodies, and spirits are truly open to the touch of God's miracles and/or blessings.

It is not simply about trying to learn as much as we can about God, nor is it about trying to "acquire" as much of God as we can. That is an impossibility. God is so vast, so big, so everything, and we are so finite.

The question is often asked, "How do we enter into a deeper, more intimate relationship centered on Christ?" I have found the answer to this problem to be simple but always demanding. First, our focus needs to be on hungering after what God wants rather than merely trying to quit what he doesn't. Paul warns in Romans 12:2, "Don't copy the behavior and customs of this world" that are habitually selfish and often corrupting. But simply refusing to conform to these principles is not enough. There must be a deeper, exigent hunger for Christ himself.

Second, we must purpose to live closer to Christ. Here Paul gives testimony: "Yes, everything else is worthless when compared with the priceless gain of knowing Christ Jesus my Lord. I have discarded everything else, counting it all as garbage, so that I may have Christ and become one with him" (Philippians 3:8–9a). Finally, we must live in abundant inwardness. Jesus says John 10:10 (TLB), "My purpose is to give life in all its fullness." He further explains: "I have given them the glory you gave me, so they may be one as we are one. I am in them and you are in me" (John 17:22–23a).

Jesus's desire for his disciples was that they would become one. He wanted them unified as a powerful witness of the same oneness he shares with the Father. It suggests that we willfully focus all of our energies on our relationship with God because we desire his company—to move deeper into God, closer to the heart of God, to a life-consuming art of approaching God where he is to be found, in the center of our souls.

130   A Wonder-Filled Life

Most people live on the periphery of God's empowering. They need to move into the kind of centering prayer life that furnishes them with a dynamic God view. This kind of prayer is a dialogue of lovers. It is interested in a relationship, not answers. Fr. Bausch, in *Storytelling: Imagination and Faith*, writes:

> The Bible is a storybook relating to us in a lively and accessible idiom. None of us has to be a theologian to appreciate the story of the Good Samaritan and no one, however degreed, has a claim on all its meaning. Stories like the Good Samaritan do not give us facts nor do they give us proofs for anything. Instead, they do what they are meant to do: provide us with images and ways of thinking about life's imponderables with God as a reference point. The biblical stories illumine the areas of human experience and show us possibilities. Indeed, the biblical stories go further and invite us to live out these possibilities. This is the area of grace. This is why the sacred stories reveal to us the face of God.[4]

Every person who claims or purports to be a believer in Jesus Christ should have a vision of God that transcends every earthly thing. Some theologians, in describing God, have used the phrase "wholly other"—meaning that God is not one of us, nor is he like us; he is beyond anything we could even imagine, greater than we can comprehend, more magnificent than we could ever describe, good beyond description, powerful beyond description, holy beyond description. Thus, when Isaiah heard the angels singing of God, he learned what God is like—his complete independence of this world, and his involvement with humanity by choice:

> It was in the year King Uzziah died that I saw the Lord. He was sitting on a lofty throne, and the train of his robe filled

the Temple. Attending him were mighty seraphim, each having six wings. With two wings they covered their faces, with two they covered their feet, and with two they flew. They were calling out to each other, "Holy, holy, holy is the Lord of Heaven's Armies! The whole earth is filled with his glory!" Their voices shook the Temple to its foundations, and the entire building was filled with smoke. Then I said, "It's all over! I am doomed, for I am a sinful man. I have filthy lips, and I live among a people with filthy lips. Yet I have seen the King, the Lord of Heaven's Armies." (Isaiah 6:1–5)

In the English language we have words like "good," "better," "best," or "big," "bigger," "biggest." However, the Hebrew language has no such words to express comparison, so they use repetition: "Holy, holy, holy." Even Jesus practiced this when he said, "Verily, verily I say unto you . . .". He meant: what I am about to say is really, really, true. There is no greater truth. When the Jews wanted to say something was the greatest, they repeated the word three times.

This occurs only twice in the Bible. There is Revelation 8:13, where John sees the judgments of God being poured out upon the earth: "Then I looked, and I heard a single eagle crying loudly as it flew through the air, 'Terror, terror, terror to all who belong to this world because of what will happen when the last three angels blow their trumpets.'" It means there can be no greater time of trouble, no greater woe. The only other time this repetition is used is here in Isaiah 6, when the angels cry: "Holy, holy, holy is the Lord of Heaven's Armies! The whole earth is filled with his glory!" The angels are saying: God is the holiest being in all creation. There is no one else like him—nothing—that even approaches God's holiness. He always has been, always will be. Nothing above him. Nothing below him. You can't dethrone him, and he's not going to resign. All power belongs to him.

But for us, it doesn't stop there. When we are confronted with the holy perfection of our God, our own imperfection stands out like a dark stain on a white shirt. We become painfully aware of our own sin. When the prophet Isaiah stood in the presence of our holy, holy, holy God he exclaimed, "It's all over! I am doomed, for I am a sinful man. I have filthy lips, and I live among a people with filthy lips." There is something about being in the presence of God. When we see him, he opens our eyes and we fall on our faces before him in worship. And through our worship, we come to see things as God sees them.

The fact is, we can only know ourselves according to our vision of God. We can only know ourselves after we have been humbled to the dust before the majesty of God. On the other hand, God does not want us to obey him out of fear or cringe before him, but wants people with whom he can speak and who will stand erect in his presence, ready and willing to do his will. The center of our being lies outside ourselves and in the God who made us and calls us into his fellowship. The question is, how do we reach out for God in love? How can we meet God deep in the center of our existence?

The Apostle John, in his first epistle, says that our certainty is based on God's promise that he has given us eternal life through his son Jesus Christ. This is true whether we feel close to God or far away from him. However, if we align our prayers to his will, he will listen—and we can be certain that if he listens, he will give us a definite answer.

And we can be confident that he will listen to us whenever we ask him for anything in line with his will. And if we know he is listening when we make our requests, we can be sure that he will give us what we ask for. (1 John 5:14–15)

My lingering thought is that our vision of the glory of God must be of such grandeur that human words cannot describe it—a vision of a God of such power that no forces of evil can stand against it, so awe-inspiring that the world is drawn to it, so loving that the hardest heart must melt before it, so high and exalted that every knee must bow before it, so exalted that even the multitude of angels worship and praise his glory. Suddenly, as the songwriter says "the things of earth grow strangely dim in the light of his glory and grace."[5] John records his own vision in Revelation 7:9–12:

> After this I saw a vast crowd, too great to count, from every nation and tribe and people and language, standing in front of the throne and before the Lamb. They were clothed in white robes and held palm branches in their hands. And they were shouting with a great roar, "Salvation comes from our God who sits on the throne and from the Lamb!" And all the angels were standing around the throne and around the elders and the four living beings. And they fell before the throne with their faces to the ground and worshiped God. They sang, "Amen! Blessing and glory and wisdom and thanksgiving and honor and power and strength belong to our God forever and ever! Amen."

The crowd in heaven praises God, saying that salvation comes from him and from the Lamb. Salvation from sin's penalty can come only through Jesus Christ. Is this not a reason to praise and worship God? As Paul writes in Philippians 2:9–11,

Therefore, God elevated him to the place of highest honor and gave him the name above all other names, that at the name of Jesus every knee should bow, in heaven and on earth and under the earth, and every tongue declare that Jesus Christ is Lord, to the glory of God the Father.

EIGHT

THE NAME OF JESUS

"God replied to Moses, 'I am who I am. Say this to the people of Israel: I am has sent me to you.'"

(Exodus 3:14)

As a young man growing up in the 1930s in New Haven during the Depression era, I can still hear the stirring call of my mother (with emphasis): "Remember, you are McClures. You look just as good as those Astorbilts, and are just as special." At the time I had only a vague idea of who "those Astorbilts" might be, and even today I can't even imagine resembling those Astorbilts with our homemade clothes and city (welfare) shoes. But we were always led to believe that we were as special and wealthy in our way as those fictitious Astorbilts.

But what made the comparison to the Astorbilts so compelling and believable was her insistence, "You're not like all the other kids; you're McClures." We all know the expression, "What's in a name?" Essentially, it means what someone or something is called or labeled compared to their or its inherent qualities. Hence, a name is much more than just a name! Hidden within may be a special meaning. For my mother, the name McClure was reinforced by the precepts of the church we attended. The earliest picture I have of my parents together is them standing in front of their church in New York, with their hands resting on a Bible. So the McClure name was integrated with the name Jesus, where Christian character was birthed and maintained.

In the Bible a name—whether of man, angel, or deity—sets forth the character of the bearer. We're told the name of Jesus has incredible great power and authority. There is a story in Acts 3 of Peter and John going up to the temple to participate in a three o'clock prayer service:

> As they approached the Temple, a man lame from birth was being carried in. Each day he was put beside the Temple gate, the one called the Beautiful Gate, so he could beg from the people going into the Temple. When he saw Peter and John about to enter, he asked them for some money. Peter and John looked at him intently, and Peter said, "Look at us!" The lame man looked at them eagerly, expecting some money. But Peter said, "I don't have any silver or gold for you. But I'll give you what I have. In the name of Jesus Christ the Nazarene, get up and walk!" (vv. 2–6).

As one reflects on this text, the question surfaces: If the lame man went to the temple to pray, why was he left at the Beautiful Gate to beg? Does it not make sense that if the man went into the temple to be healed, he would have the capacity to make more money than he could by begging? But looking further, I found that because of the man's condition he was not allowed in the temple; only those who were whole could be members of the congregation. The man needed to make a choice either to embrace what was familiar—his lameness—or reach out for something far better—walking, with which he was not familiar.

Surely, we can relate to this man's predicament. I am aware that many people do not like to be compared to an invalid, so they choose to remain as they are. However, the truth is that each person born since Adam has been lame since the fall. We have been lame since we were born of human parents. We have been lame since God pronounced judgment upon sin. And yet, we remain in the same condition, even though Jesus Christ came into the world to die for our sin. "This is a trustworthy saying, and everyone should accept it: 'Christ Jesus came into the world to save sinners'" (1 Timothy 1:15). The truth is, each of us has an area of lameness in our lives. Even if we refuse to face it, even if we won't admit it, there is sin that still plagues.

While most of us do not have the means to live a life of levity, we have succumbed to the notion that our lifestyle represents the good life. When we look in the mirror and don't see any major flaws, can get through a social event without making any major mistakes, or keep a job without getting fired, we think we are all right—except that, if there is something wrong in only one area of life, that area can affect a person's entire life and keep them from functioning as a whole person.

If you go to God and ask him for what you want, don't be surprised if, instead, he gives you what you need. This is what happened when Peter and John confronted the lame man: "I don't have any money for you, but I'll give you what I have. In the name of Jesus Christ of Nazareth, get up and walk." That was not what the lame man asked for, nor what he wanted. But the Scriptures tell that Jesus was just what he needed. We read in Philippians 2:7–11:

When he [Jesus] appeared in human form, he humbled himself in obedience to God and died a criminal's death on a cross. Therefore, God elevated him to the place of highest honor and gave him the name above all other names, that at the name of Jesus every knee should bow, in heaven and on earth and under the earth, and every tongue declare that Jesus Christ is Lord, to the glory of God the Father.

Because the name of Jesus is above every name, because he loved us enough to die for us, and because he was highly exalted by God and given a name in which everything must bow to him in heaven and on earth and under the earth, lameness is subject to the name Jesus. Thus we are told:

Then Peter took the lame man by the right hand and helped him up. And as he did, the man's feet and anklebones were healed and strengthened. He jumped up, stood on his feet, and began to walk! Then, walking, leaping, and praising God, he went into the Temple with them. (Acts 3:7–8)

What we observe in the text is that the man asked for alms—and instead, he got legs. He reminds us of the fact that sin cripples all it touches. The man couldn't walk, work, or worship, so he sat outside at the door begging for money. Laying at the gate he was marred, disfigured, distorted, and cast out. Every day they walked past the man probably resenting him, and now he was running, leaping, and praising God—they couldn't argue with that! This miracle could not be lightly dismissed. Peter could have given him money, but he still would have been the same man! Peter gave him something much better. In the name of Jesus Christ, this man was healed.

How long will you continue to ask for alms when your real need is legs? How long do we continue to ask for physical healing when our spirit is near death? How long will you continue to ask for a hot patch on the outside of your back and avoid your need for healing for what is going on inside?

Behind the name Jesus lies the marching orders for every person who claims his name. Jesus says, "I have been given complete authority in heaven and on earth. Therefore, go and make disciples of all the nations, baptizing them in the name of the Father and the Son and the Holy Spirit" (Matthew 28:18–19). Suppose today you took these words of Jesus seriously, and went out into your cities, towns, neighborhoods, and apartment buildings. Suppose you took the words of Jesus to your friends and family members. Suppose you approached people in the malls and shopping centers and amusement parks. Suppose you stopped to talk to people outside the church on Sunday morning and said, "I don't have any money for you, but I'll give you what I have. In the name of Jesus, get up and walk." What might they say? Suppose they responded to you by asking, "Who sent you? What authority do you have? What are your credentials?"

John writes in chapter 8 of his gospel that this was exactly what Jesus encountered as opposition to his ministry grew steadily from within the ranks of the Jews. To understand this hostility and the basis for the questions posed in this chapter, it is necessary to examine the sequence of events that had taken place in previous chapters. In John 5, Jesus healed a man at the pool of Bethesda on the Sabbath, and in the process dared to say to the man: "Now you are well; so stop sinning, or something even worse may happen to you" (v. 14). He later defended his action by claiming God as his Father and the one who sent him, which prompts John to add, "So the Jewish leaders tried all the harder to find a way to kill him" (v. 18). Further, in verse 20 Jesus claimed to be equal in ability with the Father in raising the dead and then claimed that the Father would testify to this on his behalf.

140   A Wonder-Filled Life

In chapter 6, Jesus feeds five thousand people with five small loaves of bread and two fishes and follows this with, "I am the bread of life. . . . I am the bread that came down from heaven" (vv. 35, 41). Not only did his assertions anger the religious authorities and many other people, but they so offended his followers to the point John tells us, "Many of his disciples turned away and deserted him" (v. 66). Chapter 7 opens, "After this, Jesus traveled around Galilee. He wanted to stay out of Judea, where the Jewish leaders were plotting his death" (v. 1). We are told, "There was a lot of grumbling about him among the crowds" (v. 12). Some people said about Jesus, "'Surely this man is the Prophet.' . . . Others said, 'He is the Messiah.' Still others said, 'But he can't be! Will the Messiah come from Galilee?'" (vv. 40–41). To add to their confusion and anger, Jesus pardons the sin of a woman caught in the act of adultery, and follows this with a most startling declaration: "I am the light of the world. If you follow me, you won't have to walk in darkness, because you will have the light that leads to life" (8:12).

The Pharisees challenged him, "You are making those claims about yourself! Such testimony is not valid" (v. 13). They argued that he had no other witnesses. Then Jesus replied, "I am not alone. The Father who sent me is with me" (v. 16). Jesus's claim of oneness with the Father bordered on blasphemy. His disregard for the Law intruded on their turf. He offered forgiveness, promised hope, attacked religious institutions—and worst of all, he attracted large crowds. "Who gave you authority to do this? Where is your Father?" they asked. "Do you have a sponsor? Who are you?" It is then that the Pharisees declare their own "credentials"—"we are descendants of Abraham" (v. 33), founder of the Jewish nation—and therefore claimed to be children of God. They were unable to understand because they refused to listen and used their stubbornness, pride, and prejudices to keep them from believing in Jesus. Their actions showed they were not children of God but children of Satan. Thus, in verse 53, the leaders question Jesus, "Are you greater than our father Abraham? He died, and so did the prophets. Who do you think you are?"

Now the stage was set for the most astonishing, far-reaching, life-changing, and deeply significant declaration of all time, one that has both present and future implications both for humanity and divinity. The stage was now set to reveal the one who walks, speaks, and acts while knowing that nature, angels, demons, mysteries of life, and death all pay homage at his feet. The one who commands the winds and the waves and they obey at once; who heals all manner of human sickness and even raises the dead; who routs demons, and forgives sins with the authority of God incarnate. Looking centuries ahead, even to the end of the present age, he turns to his questioners and, speaking through all the ages of history, says, "I tell you the truth, before Abraham was even born, I am!" The Phillips translation puts it, "Before there was an Abraham, I am!"

Here lies the key to what I consider to be two of the most important words in all of Scripture, "I am." To the Pharisees, this astonishing claim seemed like mere wild talk and heady nonsense sprung from colossal vanity. Who was this ignorant upstart to try to oust Abraham, making himself the way by which men should steer themselves through life? Ordinarily, egoism is the self-assumption of self-importance based on self-ignorance. However, in the case of Jesus, what he asserted concerning himself was the very opposite of any presuming upon self-importance. By contrast, he reeked of humility and self-denial and simply spoke out of a supernatural fullness of knowledge, which revealed that his coming made no change in God—and though people did not realize it, he was always God, was always Christlike, was always what his self-revelation in our Lord has showed us that he was. What we see through Christ, God always was. "Before Abraham was I am!"

142   A Wonder-Filled Life

Previously, in several cases, Jesus purposely stressing his mystery left his identity open to a wide range of interpretations. However, this time, when the scribes and Pharisees tried to pin him down, he answered, "I tell you the truth before Abraham was even born, I am!" Some 2,500 years after Abraham, along comes Jesus, saying to the Pharisees, "Before Abraham was, I am" —claiming to be one with God, that his name is the name of God, that his power and authority are equal to God. This made the people so furious that "At that point, they picked up stones to throw at him. But Jesus was hidden from them and left the Temple" (v. 59).

Not until it was revealed to me by the Holy Spirit did I understand the deeper meaning of these words, and only then did I realize that it was indispensable to understanding why the words of Jesus were so demeaning and debilitating to the Pharisees. Jesus was revealing an existence that preceded Abraham, not by time but by eternity. What is at stake here is the question of how to reconcile this with the name God spoke to Moses (Exodus 3:14–15): "I am who I am." . . . This is my eternal name, the name to remember for all generations."

The miraculous, divine revelation at the burning bush (Exodus 3:2–5) is among the most powerful and enduring images in human history. So powerful and clear is the revelation of God's name that Moses and the Israelites are inspired to undertake the legendary acts of courage and faith of leading the people out of Egypt. The Israelites' migration story indicates that their wilderness experience was spiritually challenging and physically difficult—and yet they found that the spiritual journey is not a place of exile and abandonment, for God was with them at every moment. The Lord said to Moses, "I have certainly seen the oppression of my people in Egypt. I have heard their cries of distress because of their harsh slave drivers. Yes, I am aware of their suffering. . . . Look! The cry of the people of Israel has reached me, and I have seen how harshly the Egyptians abuse

The Name of Jesus   143

them. Now go, for I am sending you to Pharaoh. You must lead my people Israel out of Egypt" (vv. 7, 9–10).

At first, Moses protested and made excuses to God about his weakness and inability to speak and reluctance to go and bring the Israelites out of Egypt until God gave assurance of his presence: "I will be with you. And this is your sign that I am the one who has sent you: When you have brought the people out of Egypt, you will worship God at this very mountain" (v. 12). Moses responds in faith, and then proceeds to a practical question: How will he convince the Israelites that God has spoken to him?

> "If I go to the people of Israel and tell them, 'The God of your ancestors has sent me to you,' they will ask me, 'What is his name?' Then what should I tell them?"
>
> God replied to Moses, "I am who I am. Say this to the people of Israel: I am has sent me to you." (vv. 14–15)

In the Bible, a name—whether of man, angel, or deity—sets forth the character of the bearer, In this case, the name was a short one—one that would confound a humanity that would question God or ask him what he was. Indeed, he only *is*. All others have been and will be, but God *is*. Though the name of God is too sacred to be pronounced, nevertheless we can begin to see from the narrative what kind of God this was who revealed himself to Moses. He was a mysterious power in whose presence one must take the sandals from their feet and cover their faces. He had a dwelling place in nature, in the mountain and the tree of fire; he knew all that was happening among men. He hated injustice, helped the oppressed to freedom, and punished the tyrant. He could endow people with seemingly miraculous powers and be omnipotent in directing the course of history through men and nature toward his ends. He was the God who, in stressing his mystery, purposely left his analysis open to a wide range of interpretations: "I am," or better, "I will be."

Thus, it's only through Christ and knowing Christ can anyone understand what God is really like. Before Christ came, some people had shadowings of God, some of them quite glorious, of what they felt to be the truth about God's character and nature. But before Christ, you never heard anyone else in history making such exalted, profoundly awe-inspiring, and startling claims for himself as those found in the Gospels. Should we not pause and take careful note of Jesus's to reply to Philip's request in John 14:8–11: "Lord, show us the Father." To which Jesus replied, "Have I been with you all this time, Philip, and yet you still don't know who I am? Anyone who has seen me has seen the Father! So why are you asking me to show him to you? Don't you believe that I am in the Father and the Father is in me? The words I speak are not my own, but my Father who lives in me does his work through me. Just believe that I am in the Father and the Father is in me. Or at least believe because of the work you have seen me do."

All that Christ said and did was the express image of God's very mind and heart. All the works he does are the works of the Father. The writer of Hebrews 1:3 says, "The Son radiates God's own glory and expresses the very character of God, and he sustains everything by the mighty power of his command."

Not only is Jesus the exact representation of God, he is God himself—the very God spoke who in Old Testament times. He is eternal; he worked with the Father in creating the world (John 1:3; Colossians 1:16). He is the full revelation of God. You have no clearer view of God by looking at Christ. Jesus Christ is the complete expression of God in the human body.[1]

The book of Hebrews links God's saving power with his creative power. In other words, the power that brought the universe into being and keeps it operating is the very power that cleanses our sins. In 1:5, the writer notes the Son is greater than the angels: "For God never said to any angel what he said to Jesus: 'You are my Son. Today I have become your Father.'" The "far greater" name that was given to Jesus is "Son." This name given to him by the Father is greater than the names of the angels. John says in the prologue of his gospel (1:3–4), "God created everything through him, and nothing was created except through him. The Word gave life through everything that was created, and his life brought life to everyone." Therefore Jesus points out, "I am the bread of life" (John 6:35); "I am the light of the world" (8:12); "I am the door for the sheep" (10:7); "I am the good shepherd" (10:11); "I am the resurrection and the life" (11:25); "I am the way, the truth, and the life" (14:6); and "I am the true vine" (15:5).

Some people aware of the immensity of his claims may ask, Did Jesus make these claims seriously? The answer is clear when you simply read the "I am"s of Jesus in their setting. Take the first, "I am the bread of life," to which he added, "He who comes to me will never go hungry, and He who believes in me will never be thirsty." Or the second, "I am the light of the world," to which he added, "Whoever follows me will never walk in darkness, but will have the light of life." To the third, "I am the door for the sheep," he added, "Whoever enters through me will be saved." To the fourth, "I am the Good Shepherd," he added, "The good shepherd lays down his life for the sheep." After the fifth, "I am the resurrection and the life," he added, "He who believes in me will live even though he dies, and whoever lives and believes in me will never die." To the sixth, "I am the way, the truth, and the life," he added, "No one comes to the Father except through Me." And to the seventh, "I am the true vine," he added, "If a man

146   A Wonder-Filled Life

remains in me and I in him, he will bear much fruit; apart from me you can do nothing."

So what does this signify? What about these divine assertions of Jesus? What are we to learn here? It means that, primarily, the message of Jesus is himself. He did not come merely to preach a gospel; he *is* the gospel. He did not come merely to give bread; he said, "I *am* the bread." He did not come merely to shed light; he said, "I *am* the light." He did not come merely to show the door; he said, "I *am* the door." He did not come merely to name a shepherd; he said, "I *am* the good shepherd." He did not come really to discuss the resurrection; he said, "I *am* the resurrection and the life." He did not come merely to point the way; he said, "I *am* the way." He did not come merely to plant a vine; he said "I *am* the true vine." Jesus is the absolute answer, the final goal of our human quest. Listen to the living Savior again, as he says over and over in answer to your fundamental needs as a human being, "Before Abraham was, I am." I am now, I am then, I always was, I always will be. . . .

> pleased that is good for them . . . as if He should say, are they weak?—I am strength . . . are they poor? I am riches . . . are they in trouble?—I am comfortable . . . are they sick? I am healthy . . . are they dying?—I am life . . . Have they nothing? I am all things . . . I am wisdom and power . . . I am justice and mercy . . . I am grace and goodness . . . I am glory, beauty, holiness, eminence, renowned, esteemed, perfection, all-sufficiency, eternity . . . I am Lord of Lords, I am King of Kings . . . I am Jehovah, "I AM" . . . Whatever is amiable in itself, or desirable unto them, that I AM . . . Whatsoever is pure and holy . . . Whatsoever is great or pleasant . . . Whatsoever is good

or needful to make men happy, that "I AM.". . . I AM Who I AM![2]

Therefore, God elevated him to the place of highest honor and gave him the name above all other names, that at the name of Jesus every knee should bow, in heaven and on earth and under the earth, and every tongue declare that Jesus Christ is Lord, to the glory of God the Father. (Philippians 2:9–11)

The name of Jesus is so sweet / I love its music to repeat / It makes my joys full and complete, / The precious name of Jesus / Jesus! oh, how sweet the name / Jesus! every day the same / Jesus! let all saints proclaim /Its worthy praise forever.[3]

NINE

THE NEW LIFE

"Humans can reproduce only human life, but the Holy Spirit gives birth to spiritual life. So don't be surprised when I say, 'You must be born again.'"

(John 3:6–7)

Many people go around with certain unexamined assumptions about the world, God, and themselves. Jesus then comes along with a word—that life without the cross is not worth living—causing us to reconsider these assumptions and turning the table on our expectations. The cross defines our goal as believers in Christ Jesus: to become more Christlike. But the question is, why?

Simply put, that is what humanity is supposed to look like. The first two chapters in Genesis depict God's created order and the relationship of mankind to the Creator. God did not create us exactly like himself because God has no physical body; also, we never will be totally like God because he is our supreme Creator. Instead, we are to be reflections of God's glory. Because Adam disobeyed God's command, Jesus came to show us what we were intended to be in the first place.

Thus, to be Christlike is God's desire for us. Failing to understand God's objective in creation is the reason many people are unsuccessful in accessing and living out God's intention for all humankind: life to the full! If indeed this is the reason Jesus came into the world, it would then appear to be of such great importance that every person should search unceasingly to find this life. In an earlier book, *Made for Glory*, I noted:

> In Jesus's life, we see how God thinks and therefore how we should think. Jesus was also a model of what we look like and what we are to become. The fall damaged the image of God in us, so Jesus's coming provided a visual picture of what we are meant to look like. He gave us a clear picture of the image and likeness of God in creation. Jesus says: "The thief's purpose is to steal and kill and destroy. My purpose is to give them a rich and satisfying life" (John 10:10). In contrast to Satan, who comes to take life from us, Jesus comes to give us life, abundantly rich and full right now. His life is eternal, yet it begins immediately and is lived on a higher plane. Jesus's life shows us how to live as image-bearers and gives us the power to live in that way. Consequently, the truth about Christ in creation is critical to our understanding of incarnation, crucifixion, resurrection, and recreation. If this were not so, we would not know that the good news is *truly* good news.[1]

In particular, writers have special themes they are addressing which brings us to consider: What about Jesus himself? He told stories and was a master of parables, but was there one central theme that encompassed them all? We must remember that the experience of Jesus came before reflections about him, long after God had set his plan of redemption for his people in motion. This is a way of saying that life came before thought and that God's divine plan came before reflection. What did God have in mind? What about Jesus?

What urges Jesus on is answered in his own words in John 4:34—and it is essential, if we are to understand his life, that we keep his answer in mind: "My nourishment comes from doing the will of God, who sent me, and from finishing his work." That's the essential hinge of Jesus's life, his relationship to the Father. We then discover that the gospel stories and events about Jesus have many levels of meaning, and so provide for each person his or her peculiar response. However, many Jesus stories have become familiar with age and repetition, and have lost their force and their ability to transform. We often think we know exactly what they mean. We are sure we understand what God has in mind. However, in this new place of recognition, where God withholds his word until the designated time, we are called to an unfamiliar place and put in a new setting where we are able to see the truth of Jesus from a different angle. I am not alone in this, of course, for the life of Jesus can be seen on many levels where people have a desire to see and hear the Word of God afresh.

This is not a difficult undertaking. If one is open to hear and listen to the Word of God, understanding will come. In Matthew 13:9 Jesus promises, "Anyone with ears to hear should listen and understand." This reminds us that God's revealed truth is universal and can find a residence in a heart seeking more of him; of course, this is not without discipline.

Secondly, there must be a compelling desire to translate old familiar procedures into new and compelling practices. We must look beyond our limits, and our experiences of limitation, and to submit to the wonder itself, expecting a great surprise. There are two parables of Jesus in Matthew 13 that illustrate my point—the value and worth of pursuing this new life that Christ came to bring:

> The Kingdom of Heaven is like a treasure that a man discovered hidden in a field. In his excitement, he hid it again and sold everything he owned to get enough money to buy the field.
>
> Again, the Kingdom of Heaven is like a merchant on the lookout for choice pearls. When he discovered a pearl of great value, he sold everything he owned and bought it! (vv. 44–46)

The first parable speaks about the Kingdom of Heaven as a treasure more valuable than anything we can ever have; therefore, a person must be willing to give up everything to obtain it. The man in the parable who discovered the treasure hidden in the field came upon it by accident; but when he saw it, he immediately knew its value. Although the transaction cost the man everything, he paid nothing for the priceless treasure itself—it came free with the field. Though nothing is more precious than the Kingdom of Heaven, God gives it to us as a gift.

In contrast to this, the succeeding parable displays another aspect of the kingdom. Jesus casts the merchant (human beings) rather than the Kingdom of Heaven as the precious pearl. The contrast becomes more vivid in the transaction where God pays the ultimate price to possess the pearl: the price he was willing to pay to redeem us was his Son.

Here in these parables, an incredible point is made. Though the pictured treasure in the latter parable is different, the objective outcome for each man is the same. Both men had the same response to their discovery: recognizing their find to be of inestimable worth, both sacrificed whatever was necessary to make it his own. Neither of the purchasers haggled over the price. Nor did they bemoan what their acquisitions would cost them. On the contrary, they made their transactions joyfully, because what both men stood to gain was so tremendous that it made any monetary cost, any sacrifice, any leap of faith insignificant in comparison. It might look like a great "sacrifice" (selling everything—giving everything to buy that single pearl), or like madness to people who don't know the value of pearls, but the gain for each was truly far greater than any cost.

All that being true, there still appears to be a large gap between what the kingdom host (God) in the second parable paid for the precious pearl (human beings), as opposed to what the man in parable one paid for the field. Peter writes in his first epistle:

> For you know that God paid a ransom to save you from the empty life you inherited from your ancestors. And it was not paid with mere gold or silver, which lose their value. It was the precious blood of Christ, the sinless, spotless Lamb of God. (1 Peter 1:18–19)

The message of these very brief parables offers encouragement to us. It's not easy to make a radical investment of ourselves in Christ. It requires an act of faith to live single-heartedly for him. We may find ourselves at different stages in our journey—perhaps reluctant to sacrifice certain things in our lives, perhaps giving up something for a time only to take it back. But there is everything to gain in persevering. As Paul echoes, "everything else is worthless when compared with the infinite value of knowing Christ Jesus my Lord. For his sake, I have discarded everything else, counting it all as garbage, so that I could gain Christ" (Philippians 3:8).

As we come to recognize the boundless great joy in knowing Christ, we become more like the man in the parable, who discovered a hidden treasure in the field and found that the Kingdom of Heaven came free with the field. In Ephesians 2:8–9, Paul speaks about salvation as a gift: "God saved you by his grace when you believed. And you can't take credit for this; it is a gift from God. Salvation is not a reward for the good things we have done, so none of us can boast about it." We become Christians through God's unmerited favor—not as the result of any effort, ability, intelligent choice, or acts of service on our part—and yet how often Christians, even after they have received the gift of salvation, feel obligated to try to work their way to God. They fail to understand that grace costs them nothing but cost God everything, and that when one reaches out to receive it, the Kingdom of God is the hidden treasure.

In John 3, there is the story of a man named Nicodemus, who might well be the man in the parable who stumbled on the precious pearl of the kingdom and found it too good to be true. At first, Nicodemus was perplexed by Jesus's words, but after contemplating Jesus's offer of life, Nicodemus found it to be a hidden treasure he could not live without. In the opening narrative we find Jesus is in Jerusalem for the Passover Feast. During his stay, Nicodemus, a Pharisee, a Jewish religious leader and member of the ruling Jewish council, approached him. The text reveals that Nicodemus (probably afraid of being discovered by his peers) made an appointment to see Jesus at night. It was not only highly unusual for Nicodemus to approach Jesus at night but hazardous, for daylight conversations between Jesus and the Pharisees tended to be highly antagonistic.

Nevertheless, Nicodemus's desire to learn about Jesus overshadowed any fear. If he was not already sure of who Jesus was, his words revealed that he had a pretty good idea. Nicodemus addressed Jesus as "Rabbi," signifying he regarded him as a teacher. From his salutation, it is obvious that Nicodemus recognized Jesus; and with humility, Jesus accepted the high accolade paid to him by Nicodemus as his just due. The text does not disclose if there was any prior conversation between Nicodemus and Jesus, but we assume that Nicodemus, a Jewish scholar, would be concerned about matters of the law.

However, unknown to Nicodemus, Jesus had already perceived the questions that were uppermost in Nicodemus's mind: How righteous does a man have to be to enter the kingdom? How can one satisfy the demands of the law? Here Jesus's desire for Nicodemus was far greater than Nicodemus's unanswered questions, so when Nicodemus said, "we all know that God has sent you to teach us. Your miraculous signs are evidence that God is with you," Jesus gave a very pointed reply: "I tell you the truth, unless you are born again, you can never see the Kingdom of God" (v. 3).

Upon hearing Jesus's reply, Nicodemus was overwhelmed. It was far more than he expected. However, he realized he had stumbled upon something—an offer to a new life. But what Jesus said to Nicodemus was not as startling as it was puzzling. By their own merits and hereditary claims as children of Abraham, the Pharisees believed the kingdom already belonged to them. Fully aware of this, Jesus then emphasized his previous assertion: "I assure you, no one can enter the Kingdom of God without being born of water and the Spirit" (v. 5). How seemingly innocent and how intuitive the statement of Jesus, and yet how profound and far its reach.

Not only did Nicodemus not fully understand Jesus's assertion, but his response in verse 4 exposed the fact that his thoughts were on an earthly plane rather than in the heavenly realms: "What do you mean? . . . How can an old man go back into his mother's womb and be born again?" Like Nicodemus, we must examine Jesus's words about the new birth for ourselves if we are to come to the truth—others cannot do it for us.

For many today, the problem is that Jesus's words in this narrative have been vastly misused and misunderstood, and have caused much frustration and disappointment in those who question the efficacy of their faith. The term "born again" has been applied to many things other than to what Scripture ascribes it to: from presidents to sports figures, sporting events, and even whole cities. Years ago, there was a supposedly washed-up athlete who made an amazing comeback. I also read of a movie actress who after many years finally had a hit motion picture on her hands. These occurrences are akin to other events of similar type—rescues from the brink of obscurity, where the resurgence was described by reporters as "born again." This causes some consternation and surprise for many who then encounter the phrase. It is disturbing that these words first spoken by Jesus to Nicodemus, and reported by John, have been bandied about so freely and are so often used in secular terms. Yet in the Christian community, we embrace the term with a great deal of ignorance, suggesting a need for us as members of the household of faith to reexamine what "born again" really means.

After his baptism, wilderness temptation, and the imprisonment of John the Baptist, Jesus makes an incredible announcement: "The time promised by God has come at last! . . . The Kingdom of God is near! Repent of your sins and believe this Good News!" (Mark 1:15). Jesus was announcing that the reign and rule of God was at hand. This is what the gospel is all about. This is the good news for all humankind: God inaugurating his spiritual rule and reign in the people's hearts and the world, seeking to reconcile all things to himself, to reverse the sentence of the first Adam, and to establish a people in the likeness of the second Adam, Jesus Christ. It is a breathtaking story of a fulfilling and fulfilled purpose—and the truly marvelous news is that all men, women, and children are invited to share in this purpose of God in Christ Jesus.

Whatever our calling or work in the world may be, whatever our addiction may be, whatever our sin may be, we are called to repent and believe the gospel and to lose ourselves in Christ. The good news is that it is no longer a dream: "The Kingdom of God is near!" In Jesus's second parable above of a merchant on the lookout for choice pearls, we see the unfolding of God's plan of redemption for his fallen creations, for it concludes: "When he discovered a pearl of great value, he sold everything he owned and bought it!"

Therefore, it is important for us not to reject Jesus's words that the Holy Spirit gives new life from heaven, for the necessity of it is absolute and universally binding. The law of nature found in Genesis 1 is inescapable. We all bring forth "of like kind." Try as we might, we will only have mortal children who are issued birth certificates the instant they are born, along with the death certificate. However, while on the way, a new life from heaven is offered. To be born again of the Spirit, by the same power that raised Jesus from the dead where God is both Father and Mother to us, gives us eternal life just as our natural parents give us mortality. The need for "new birth" is the need to be free of the sin image and experience a new life in Christ—bearing the image of the heavenly, partaking in the divine nature, and knowing that our sins are forgiven.

The dilemma is, many believers today have never completed a "new" birthing experience. They have heard of Jesus, practice religion, may have even joined a church, but have never fostered a relationship with Jesus Christ as Savior and Lord. They are more adept at keeping traditions, rituals, repetitions, procedures, rules, or religious teachings, and live mostly by the guidelines of contemporary society. Sadly, they have never submitted to Jesus as Lord, and tend to think only in material terms—i.e., what can be perceived through the senses is real. Things of the Spirit are foreign to them. The reason for failure is that their core teaching has left them as drones, hovering between the old life which has died and the new life promised by Jesus.

After many years of observation, I believe I now understand why this essential requisite between a new believer and God fails to take place. The detachment is not necessarily caused by any past sin or disobedience on the part of a believer, because through Jesus they have been forgiven. However, they are ignorant of the fact they *are* birthed into a new home—never before seen, never before experienced, and never before lived, with scant knowledge of life in the Kingdom of God.

A child birthed into the world arrives with a societal mandate that the newborn baby must receive instruction, education, modeling in growth, and how to live in their new environment. The first thing the child becomes aware of is complete dependence on their parents. They are virtually helpless at this point and have to rely on their parents for everything. They see their parents walking upright and are convinced that they must grow to emulate them. To achieve this, they are confronted with educational requirements, physical nourishment, and tools for life living in the world. They are taught the rules, regulations, behavior, and responsibility to others and themselves. And at a certain age, society holds them solely responsible for their sin and disobedience or obedience to the law.

Just like a natural birth into the world, those who repent of their sin acknowledge and believe in the death, burial, and resurrection of Jesus Christ, and experience a new birth (spiritual birth) into the Kingdom of God. They immediately become aware of the parent, God the Father, just as in the secular. However, there is no law or dictate, only a manual of instruction (the Bible) handed to them, and their growth can only come by adopting and obeying the Scriptures on how to live in God's presence. They have no previous experience in this spiritual kingdom, no knowledge of what behavior is required for the Kingdom of God. There are no educational requirements for living in their new home. There is no awareness that they have been evicted from their old home and that it is gone forever.

Paul says, "anyone who belongs to Christ has become a new person. The old life is gone; a new life has begun!" (2 Corinthians

5:17). This ends any connection to their old life. Though they are still physically in the world, they cease to be of the world. At this point, without scriptural understanding, these new believers are in limbo if they have not moved into their new home.

The Scripture says we are to "Think about the things of heaven, not the things of earth. For you died to this life, and your real life is hidden with Christ in God" (Colossians 3:2–3). There is only one place believers are now welcome. The world now hates them. The world doesn't want them, for it is no longer their home. They are ignorant of this fact and become disappointed and frustrated in attempting to find peace, abundance, and a fulfilled life as Jesus promised. There is no personal connection with the Father, and a gap exists in the parent-child relationship, which has been missing since birth. To live out the fulfilled abundant life that Jesus gave his life for, the parent-child relationship must be restored.

As previously noted in John 3:3, 5, Jesus said no one can see or enter the Kingdom of God without being born again. Being born again initiates the parent-child relationship. Therefore, paralleling the secular system, at birth, we are obligated to present a basic understanding of scriptural truths, teaching believers how to live in the Kingdom of God under God's lordship. There we learn who we are, *whose* we are, and who God would have us to be.

The new life is the quickening or birthing experience of the Holy Spirit, which propels a person into the heavenly realms. The fact is, at the moment of conversion we do not merely turn over a new leaf; we begin a new life under a new master. Our hunger for the inmost things of God is what now defines us, and our light should be impossible to tell from that of Christ himself.

However, we must honestly confess that our light has not been homogenous with Christ; rather, it has been undifferentiated from the world. This prompts the query: Why have we not become the light of the world? Why have we not done more to change the

160   A Wonder-Filled Life

world? Why is it so hard for us to break the stranglehold of the world in our lives?

Scripture is clear why Jesus took on a robe of flesh and came into the world. The more I read the Scriptures and reflect on Jesus coming into the world "to participate in death," the more I realize how little I understand the effect Jesus's death has on my life. I sense we should be much closer to Jesus, and that there should be an intimacy far beyond anything we have ever known. The writer of Hebrews 2:16–17 says,

> We also know that the Son did not come to help angels; he came to help the descendants of Abraham. Therefore, it was necessary for him to be made in every respect like us, his brothers and sisters, so that he could be our merciful and faithful High Priest before God. Then he could offer a sacrifice that would take away the sins of the people.

The words "brothers and sisters" suggest a close familial relationship, that we are of the same family. That we share as brothers and sisters. Further, the writer says, "So now Jesus and the ones he makes holy have the same Father. That is why Jesus is not ashamed to call them his brothers and sisters" (v. 11). Here, the Scriptures make clear that as believers in Jesus Christ we all have the same Father. What an incredible statement! What a profound thought—to think we are siblings with Jesus and share the same Father!

In Luke's gospel, chapter 3, we are afforded essential hereditary information about Jesus's ancestors. Luke's record begins with Jesus, travels back through forty-two generations, and ends up at the feet of God. A similar genealogy in Matthew 1 goes back to Abraham, showing that Jesus was related to all Jews; however, Luke's genealogy goes back to Adam, showing that Jesus is related to all human beings: "Kenan was the son of Enosh. Enosh was the son of Seth. Seth was the son of Adam. Adam was the son of God" (Luke 3:38). This is consistent with Luke's picture of Jesus as the Savior of the world.

And yet, Jesus's coming had a deeper, more encompassing purpose, which is imbedded in John the Baptist's warning to repent and prepare for the coming Messiah: "Turn from your sins and turn to God, because the Kingdom of Heaven is near" (Matthew 3:2). Jesus came not only to save us from sin, but also to show us how to live as faithful subjects in his kingdom. When John writes in his gospel (1:14), "So the Word became human and lived here on earth among us," he is stating that God in Christ entered human history as a man, and when He came to earth the Kingdom of God was birthed.

If we understand that our real home is where Christ lives, it will give us a different perspective of our life here on earth. We will put heaven's priorities into daily practice, and concentrate on the eternal rather than on the temporal. If a person has been raised to where Christ now sits in the place of honor at God's right hand, then is it not a certainty that our new life must be lived in the same place as Christ—the Kingdom of God, under God's reign and rule? Are we not told that because Jesus is there, our real life is there also?

How sad it is for people who have received new birth to fail to understand that their new life rejects them from the world and ejects them into a new place, a new station, and a change of address. This mandates a change in our way of thinking. Only in the Kingdom of God can we live out Jesus's declaration: "My purpose is to give them a rich and satisfying life."

TEN

KINGDOM LIFE

"Seek the Kingdom of God above all else, and live righteously, and he will give you everything you need."

(Matthew 6:33)

Previously I stated how deeply I was affected by the idea of kingdom living—the most notable outcome being that Christ now makes his home in my present mortal body and that I live daily in his life. The Scriptures assure me that my former life has been crucified with Christ on the cross, now dead and buried, never to rise again. As Paul confirms in 2 Corinthians 5:17, "This means that anyone who belongs to Christ has become a new person. The old life is gone; a new life has begun!" This newness of life is from God, who simply desires our old self and permission to build; the power for daily living is supplied by the Holy Spirit.

Still, some people try to earn their way to God by keeping a set of rules: obeying the Ten Commandments, attending church faithfully, or doing good deeds, but all they earn for their efforts is frustration and disappointment. However, the way to God is already open, and one can become his child simply by putting their faith in Christ—no longer trying to reach God by keeping rules, but becoming more and more like Jesus by living for him day by day. Thus, believers in Christ find that their whole way of looking at the world changes. How analogous are the words of Dr. Bill McDowell in his article "A Motif for Living":

> What I beg to suggest is that we assemble for ourselves a fit motif for living. What do I mean by motif? It is a dominating idea to give purpose and stability to our lives; an arresting concern that so completely absorbs us until we find ourselves discarding the disturbing, disastrous, disintegrating forces, and becoming instead unified, directional persons. By motif, I mean also a guiding principle that will always—in fair weather or foul—be the hallmark of our behavior.[1]

Can there be any more of a guiding principle of our behavior than being a resident in the kingdom, abiding in God's presence? If we understand that our real home is where Christ lives, we will have a different perspective of our life here on earth. Instead of looking at the obstacles and difficulties we daily encounter, we will now look to God's promise of supply. We will look at life from God's perspective, seeking what he desires, and measuring our success or failure by God's standard rather than by the world's. The more we regard the world around us as God does, the more we live in harmony with him.

The gospel writers agree that all during Jesus's ministry his emphasis and focus were on comparing daily life in the Kingdom of God. Most of his hearers were challenged about the importance of the Kingdom of God. Many of Jesus's sermons were to prepare people for living in the Kingdom of God. With that in mind, I ask myself, "As believers, why do we not understand that we are not called to live better in the world, but to live fully and abundantly in the Kingdom of God?" For many Christians today the Kingdom of God is nonexistent, confusing, or shrouded in great mystery; yet the kingdom was the subject of many of Jesus's parables in which he revealed its nature, its order, and its growth.

The simple and most profound definition of the kingdom is "the reign and rule of God in the human heart." What this means is, the kingdom is a spiritual reality embodied in Christ. It is not visible but invisible, not of this world but in this world, not of man but God, not temporal but eternal. Today the kingdom takes on a physical, outward manifestation: the church. Each of us is "the pearl of great price" for which God emptied, bankrupted the Kingdom of Heaven to purchase. We are the blank check of Calvary. We are the objects of divine favor. We are the recipients of unexpected, undeserved, mercy. We are the canceled check of grace.

With that in mind, never has there been a time more important to teach, preach, and emphasize the gospel of the kingdom, for never have we known such evil, hate, and disaster close at hand. Along with this, I have never sensed such confusion in the church—which means, as Christians in general, we are in deep trouble. In this environment, many have found that religion is not enough to meet their deep needs. Religion does not satisfy their hunger, nor does it bring peace. There is much more that is needed for our living in this world today. Having said that, the question is: What is the Kingdom of God? How do we understand the kingdom Jesus preached? Where is this Kingdom of God and how does one access it?

In the simplest nontechnical terms (my own): The Kingdom of God is embodied in Jesus. It is where God reigns and God rules. Therefore, the Kingdom of God is where every believer in Christ

Jesus takes up residence. Every person who desires a personal relationship with the Lord Christ is called to live in his kingdom.

During his time on earth, Jesus spoke of the Kingdom of God on numerous occasions, describing his teaching and preaching as the good news of the kingdom (Luke 4:43; 8:1). Jesus taught his disciples that they were to pray that God's kingdom would come (Luke 11:2). Jesus instructed his disciples to proclaim the Kingdom of God (Luke 9:2), and many of the parables were illustrations used to instruct us regarding his kingdom. The epistles of the New Testament also mention the Kingdom of God often. The apostles wrote about inheriting the Kingdom of God and the establishing of the Kingdom of God. All of this leaves me with a question of great importance: If the focus of Jesus's preaching was the Kingdom of God, and more than two-thirds of the Gospels is about the Kingdom of God, and the Kingdom of God is where God dwells and the place every believer is to live, why is there so little mention of the kingdom in contemporary preaching?

In posing this question I thought of the idiom, "Putting the cart before the horse." This means the thing that should come second is put first, or to reverse the proper order of things or events. Jesus gives us the proper formula:

> So don't worry about these things, saying, "What will we eat? What will we drink? What will we wear?" These things dominate the thoughts of unbelievers, but your heavenly Father already knows all your needs. Seek the Kingdom of God above all else, and live righteously, and he will give you everything you need. (Matthew 6:31–33)

Here then is the recipe for everything else you need, even for God's power. "Seek the Kingdom of God above all else, and live righteously, and he will give you everything you need." Surely, this is what we are to seek. If we look to God he will look to our needs, worries, fears, provisions. Our problem is in not putting him first.

Haddon Robinson, pastor, theologian, Harold Ockenga Distinguished Professor of Preaching, and former interim president of Gordon-Conwell Theological Seminary, points out that one old recipe for rabbit started out with this injunction: "First catch the rabbit." Says Robinson: "The writer knew how to put first things first. That's what we do when we establish priorities—we put the things that should be in place in their proper order."[2] Further, as Richard Foster says in *Celebration of Discipline*, "the person who does not seek the Kingdom of God first, does not seek it at all."[3] If you reverse the order, Scripture says in Haggai 1:6:

> You have planted much but harvest little. You eat but are not satisfied. You drink but are still thirsty. You put on clothes but cannot keep warm. Your wages disappear as though you were putting them in pockets filled with holes!

When we put our needs first, everything in life becomes topsy-turvy. The promises of God seem empty and unfulfilled. The reason we have so much trouble is we let Jesus be king only in certain areas. We obey where we want and rebel where we don't want—and at that moment he ceases to be king. The only way to get our lives in order is to unseat ourselves, to follow his direction, to allow *God* to reign over our kingdoms, to glorify Jesus to reign in our life his way. Why? Because Jesus said, "I have told you all this so that you may have peace in me. Here on earth you will have many trials and sorrows. But take heart, because I have overcome the world" (John 16:33).

This may shock you, but 119 times Jesus mentions the Kingdom of God. The rule of God. The reign of God. The King's will is being done. Lives are changed. People transformed. Victorious

168   A Wonder-Filled Life

living. Learning to love the unlovable. Heaven, now! Even after his resurrection, what does Jesus talk about? "During the forty days after he suffered and died, he appeared to the apostles from time to time, and he proved to them in many ways that he was actually alive. And he talked to them about the Kingdom of God" (Acts 1:3). Jesus came not only to save us from sin but also to show us how to live as faithful subjects in his kingdom. God, in Christ, entered human history as a man, and when he came to earth the Kingdom of God was birthed.

Teaching on the necessity of living in the kingdom of God has been relatively obscured in contemporary society. And yet, the Old Testament revealed it; the New Testament built upon it; and John the Baptist, the last of the Old Testament prophets, announced it as a "voice crying in the wilderness," quoting the prophet Isaiah's announcement seven hundred years before Christ: "Listen! It's the voice of someone shouting, 'Clear the way through the wilderness for the Lord! Make a straight highway through the wasteland for our God!'" (Isaiah 40:3). Isaiah, along with most of the prophets, called the people of Judah to commit themselves first to God and then to the king; but they rejected God's kindness, choosing instead to seek help from other nations. Despite their disobedience, God would make matters right—but the prophecy would not be fulfilled in their lifetime:

> For a child is born to us, a son is given to us. The government will rest on his shoulders. And he will be called: Wonderful Counselor, Mighty God, Everlasting Father, Prince of Peace. His government and its peace will never end. He will rule with fairness and justice from the throne of his ancestor David for all eternity. The passionate commitment of the Lord of Heaven's Armies will make this happen! (Isaiah 9:6–7)

Since the New Testament builds upon the literal meaning of the Old Testament message, a study of both testaments reveals that the Lord's plan for his kingdom dominates history from the first creation to the new creation.

The Old Testament predicts a coming earthly kingdom, a kingdom that will be fulfilled someday through the embodiment of Jesus Christ, the second Adam, the One who fulfills the covenants of Scripture. It is the kingdom which began when Jesus himself entered human history as a man. The exact phrase "Kingdom of God" does not show up in the Old Testament, although "kingdom of the Lord" does appear in 2 Chronicles 13:8: "Do you think you can stand against the kingdom of the Lord that is led by the descendants of David?"

When the northern and southern kingdoms of Israel went into exile, the prophets before, during, and after the exile made it clear that despite Israel's earthly failure God would not abandon His plan to reign over the whole world through his chosen human king. How would this reign manifest itself? What would be necessary for God to reverse the failure of Israel to be a light to the nations and extend the kingdom across the earth?

First, God will bring about a new exodus. This exodus, however, will not be a mere deliverance from Israel's earthly enemies. Instead, God will come in power to deliver his people as he ushers in the new creation itself and renews his reign over his people. Isaiah 35:1–4 says,

> Even the wilderness and desert will be glad in those days. The wasteland will rejoice and blossom with spring crocuses. Yes, flowers and singing and joy will be abundant! The deserts will become as green as the mountains of Lebanon, as lovely as Mount Carmel or the plain of Sharon. There the Lord will display his glory, the splendor of our God.

With this news, strengthen those who have tired hands, and encourage those who have weak knees. Say to those with fearful hearts, "Be strong, and do not fear, for your God is coming to destroy your enemies. He is coming to save you."

There is also talk of God's kingdom in Daniel 6:26: "I decree that everyone throughout my kingdom should tremble with fear before the God of Daniel. For he is the living God, and he will endure forever. His kingdom will never be destroyed, and his rule will never end." Thus, the *concept* of God's kingship is present throughout the Old Testament. However, the problem is that too many scholars and theologians automatically assume that the Kingdom of God refers only to greater spiritual realities concerning salvation, and either ignore or deny outright a literal ultimate destiny of humanity and an earthly kingdom. Nevertheless, if we are going to make sense of Jesus's preaching and teaching about the Kingdom of God we must remember: the most important teaching on the kingdom in the Scriptures, both old and new, is that *God is King*. So we must turn to this idea first.

John the Baptist, in Mark 1:7–8, first announced Jesus's coming as the *embodiment* of this new life to be lived in the kingdom:

Someone is coming soon who is greater than I am—so much greater that I'm not even worthy to stoop down like a slave and untie the straps of his sandals. I baptize you with water, but he will baptize you with the Holy Spirit!

In Matthew 5–7 Jesus, teaching the Sermon on the Mount on a hillside near Capernaum declared the *boundaries* for the kingdom. In 5:3–12 (NIV), in what are called the Beatitudes, Jesus said:

Blessed are the poor in spirit, for theirs is the kingdom of heaven.

Blessed are those who mourn, for they will be comforted.

Blessed are the meek, for they will inherit the earth.

Blessed are those who hunger and thirst for righteousness, for they will be filled.

Blessed are the merciful, for they will be shown mercy.

Blessed are the pure in heart, for they will see God.

Blessed are the peacemakers, for they will be called children of God.

Blessed are those who are persecuted because of righteousness, for theirs is the kingdom of heaven.

Blessed are you when people insult you, persecute you, and falsely say all kinds of evil against you because of me.

Rejoice and be glad, because great is your reward in heaven, for in the same way, they persecuted the prophets who were before you.

In John 14:6 Jesus defines the *entrance* to the kingdom: "I am the way, the truth, and the life. No one can come to the Father except through me." In John 3:3–7 Jesus states the *requirements* for the kingdom:

"I tell you the truth unless you are born again, you cannot see the Kingdom of God." "What do you mean?" exclaimed Nicodemus. "How can an old man go back into his mother's womb and be born again?" Jesus replied, "I assure you, no one can enter the Kingdom of God without being born of water and the Spirit. Humans can reproduce only human life, but the Holy Spirit gives birth to spiritual life. So don't be surprised when I say, 'You must be born again.'"

Paul says in 2 Corinthians 5:17, "anyone who belongs to Christ has become a new person. The old life is gone; a new life has begun!" It means that having died to the old life, a new life is birthed into the Kingdom of God. The Scriptures assure us in Ephesians 1:4 that the Kingdom of God is divine fulfillment of God's eternal plan for humanity, Even before he made the world, God loved us and chose us in Christ to be holy and without fault in his eyes.

> For you know that God paid a ransom to save you from the empty life you inherited from your ancestors. And it was not paid with mere gold or silver, which lose their value. It was the precious blood of Christ, the sinless, spotless Lamb of God. God chose him as your ransom long before the world began, but now in these last days he has been revealed for your sake. (1 Peter 1:18–20)

And in Matthew 6:25–27, 31–33 Jesus says:

> That is why I tell you not to worry about everyday life— whether you have enough food and drink, or enough clothes to wear. Isn't life more than food, and your body more than clothing? Look at the birds. They don't plant or harvest or store food in barns, for your heavenly Father feeds them. And aren't you far more valuable to him than they are? Can all your worries add a single moment to your life? . . .

> So don't worry about these things, saying, "What will we eat? What will we drink? What will we wear?" These things dominate the thoughts of unbelievers, but your heavenly Father already knows all your needs. Seek the Kingdom of God above all else, and live righteously, and he will give you everything you need.

Our education begins with reading Scriptures with the divine instruction to seek the Kingdom of God above all else. We turn to the book of beginnings, Genesis, which commences the story of creation with the words, "In the beginning God . . ." Genesis means "beginning," "start," or, "the origin or mode of formation of something." However, we must remember that Genesis was not the beginning of human history. That took place in eternity, in the mind of God, long before the Genesis story of creation unfolded. As Paul writes in Ephesians 1:5, "God decided in advance to adopt us into his own family by bringing us to himself through Jesus Christ. This is what he wanted to do, and it gave him great pleasure."

During his time on earth, Jesus spoke of the Kingdom of God on numerous occasions, describing his teaching and preaching as the good news of the kingdom. The apostles wrote about inheriting the Kingdom of God and the establishing of the Kingdom of God. All of this leaves me with a question of great importance: If the focus of Jesus's preaching was the Kingdom of God— the kingdom where God dwells and the place every believer is to live—why is there so little mention of the kingdom in contemporary preaching?

Many will admit how much they have struggled to find peace in their life. Maybe you have long been seeking something from God and you are disillusioned and disappointed—or to be blunt and honest, what you want from him just is not happening. Many people cry out, "I want God to do something for me." I want financial help. Help me get my family problems straightened out. I want that job, that promotion. I need God to heal my brokenness. Take away this worry, fear. Help my children. I need guidance, direction in my life. "Do it, God, please!"

Is any of this familiar? Will you admit you wonder why all these problems exist when you thought that after conversion to Jesus Christ you would have a better life, a stress-free life? Are you not frustrated because God's not coming up with the goods? When it doesn't happen, are you disillusioned with the church and with God himself? Maybe you think God doesn't hear you. Maybe you think He doesn't care. And yet you know He does—but He's not doing anything!

Maybe then, the question needs to be asked of *you*: If you want God to do what you require of him, are you doing what he requires of you? *First?* Are you seeking him first in your life before anything else? Do you know that the focus of Jesus's preaching was the Kingdom of God? Are you aware of all God's promises you will find in the Kingdom of God?

On one occasion God promised that the power of the Holy Spirit would be given so that his will would be done on earth as in heaven. This means that the kingdom takes on a physical, outward manifestation, the church. In the world but not of the world. In the kingdom, God sits on the throne of our lives. God reigns and rules over us, and we are under his lordship. We follow his direction and let him take over, to be king in all areas of our lives.

Franz Joseph Haydn (1732–1809), the great composer, was present at the Vienna Music Hall, where his oratorio *The Creation* was being performed. Weakened by age, Haydn was confined to a wheelchair. As the majestic work moved along, the audience was caught up with tremendous emotion. When the passage "And there was light!" was reached, the chorus and orchestra burst forth in such power that the crowd could no longer restrain its enthusiasm. The vast assembly rose in spontaneous applause. Haydn struggled to stand and motioned for silence. With his hand pointed toward heaven, he said, "No, no, not from me, but from thence comes all!" Having given the glory and praise to the Creator, he fell back into his chair exhausted.[3]

With that, I urge you to raise your sights to heaven and bow before the Lord of creation. I urge you to worship Christ on the throne.

John records in Revelation 1:10, "It was the Lord's Day, and I was worshiping in the Spirit. Suddenly, I heard behind me a loud voice like a trumpet blast." John later adds, "Then as I looked, I saw a door standing open in heaven, and the same voice I had heard before spoke to me like a trumpet blast. The voice said, "Come up here, and I will show you what must happen after this" (4:1). . . .

> Then I saw a scroll in the right hand of the one who was sitting on the throne. There was writing on the inside and the outside of the scroll, and it was sealed with seven seals. And I saw a strong angel, who shouted with a loud voice: "Who is worthy to break the seals on this scroll and open it?" But no one in heaven or on earth or under the earth was able to open the scroll and read it. Then I began to weep bitterly because no one was found worthy to open the scroll and read it. But one of the twenty-four elders said to me, "Stop weeping! Look, the Lion of the tribe of Judah, the heir to David's throne, has won the victory. He is worthy to open the scroll and its seven seals."
>
> Then I saw a Lamb that looked as if it had been slaughtered, but it was now standing between the throne and the four living beings and among the twenty-four elders. He had seven horns and seven eyes, which represent the sevenfold Spirit of God that is sent out into every part of the earth. He stepped forward and took the scroll from the right hand of the one sitting on the throne. And when he took the scroll, the four living beings and the twenty-four elders fell down before the Lamb. Each one had a harp, and they held gold bowls filled with incense, which are the prayers of God's people. And they sang in a mighty chorus:

"Worthy is the Lamb who was slaughtered—to receive power and riches and wisdom and strength and honor and glory and blessing." And then I heard every creature in heaven and on earth and under the earth and in the sea. They sang:

"Blessing and honor and glory and power belong to the one sitting on the throne and to the Lamb forever and ever." And the four living beings said, "Amen!" And the twenty-four elders fell down and worshiped the Lamb. (Revelation 5:1–14)

"[A]t the name of Jesus, every knee should bow, in heaven and on earth and under the earth, and every tongue declare that Jesus Christ is Lord, to the glory of God the Father" (Philippians 2:10–11). There can be only one king in the Kingdom of God, and it can be no other way. As John the revelator writes, "On his robe and thigh was written this title: King of all kings and Lord of all lords" (Revelation 19:16).

SECTION II

So I live in this earthly body by trusting in the Son of God, who loved me and gave himself for me.

ELEVEN

LIFE IN THE BODY

"For the Kingdom of God is not a matter of what we eat or drink, but of living a life of goodness and peace and joy in the Holy Spirit."

(Romans 14:17)

In the fall of 2019, midway through the writing of my memoir *The Top of the Stairs*, I ceased all activity on the book for fear that once the book was completed God would call me home. I had the conviction that this would be the last of my books. I was felled by a stroke in August of 2018; and a month later, on September 20, I had a catherization of my heart which confirmed AFIB and congestive heart failure. Aside from that, my wife of sixty-three years had recently been confined to a nursing home in January. So I withdrew from writing. To clarify, it was not that I feared dying but that I would be leaving a ministry with no one in sight to carry on the work. In *The Top of the Stairs* I wrote,

But one morning during my worship time, I was listening to music and heard the song, "I Exalt Thee." God took that moment to remind me that in my eighty-seven years of life on this earth I had experienced moments of sadness and joy, laughing and weeping, spiritual perceptions and insights, a still small voice, waves pounding the beach, brilliant sunsets, and music in rain. I had always thanked him for these experiences. What was different about what I was now going through? I then recalled my answer to a previous question, Have I resolved my view of life after death? Without hesitation, I knew in my heart that nothing had changed in how I felt about dying, because nothing had changed in how I felt about Jesus. I now saw the same things I'd seen when I first met him in the canes and crutches at the top of the stairs.[1]

I was reminded that the apostle Paul's whole purpose in life was to speak out boldly for Christ and to become more like him. Thus Paul could confidently say that dying would be even better than living because in death he would be removed from worldly troubles, and he would see Christ face to face. He testifies in Philippians 1:20–22:

> For I fully expect and hope that I will never be ashamed, but that I will continue to be bold for Christ, as I have been in the past. And I trust that my life will bring honor to Christ, whether I live or die. For me, living means living for Christ, and dying is even better. But if I live, I can do more fruitful work for Christ. So I really don't know which is better.

Those who do not believe in Jesus's death, burial, and resurrection are satisfied that life on earth is all there is. However, they are unaware that heaven is not a bad deal. Therefore, we who do know ought to stop complaining and asking "Why me?" We ought to stop feeding our sickness and saying, "I need more faith." A lot of people will feel better if they would stop concentrating on their sickness and start resting their health on God's promise. Furthermore, if you focus too much on sickness you won't see Jesus, the healer. Paul further writes:

> So to keep me from becoming proud, I was given a thorn in my flesh, a messenger from Satan to torment me and keep me from becoming proud. Three different times I begged the Lord to take it away. Each time he said, "My grace is all you need. My power works best in weakness." So now I am glad to boast about my weaknesses so that the power of Christ can work through me. (2 Corinthians 12:7–9)

Christ is never strong in us until we are weak. As our strength diminishes, the strength of Christ grows in us. When we are entirely emptied of our strength, we are full of Christ's strength. As much as we retain of our own strength, we lack Christ's. Therefore, since we are made strong by our areas of need, we must treasure our wounds and celebrate our hurts. Therefore, through all of our trials and sickness, we can only boast of what Christ has done and continues to do daily in our lives.

With that in mind, let me make something very clear. For many years I thought my worldly accomplishments and successes were my own doing. I merely wanted God to stand by if I needed help. But after reading Isaiah 6, I found that I was bankrupt. I saw in myself what Isaiah saw after seeing the glory of God. It was then I confessed: "It's all over! I am doomed, for I am a sinful man. I have filthy lips, and I live among a people with filthy lips. Yet I have seen the King, the LORD of Heaven's Armies" (v. 5). When I saw the Lord, self died. When self dies, we not only find out who we are but we move deeper into his presence and find out what God has for us to do. Then, the glory of glories! We discover they are one and the same. What God has for us to do is who we are. It is then we testify: "My old self has been crucified with Christ. It is no longer I who live, but Christ lives in me" (Galatians 2:20). The ultimate purpose of Christians is to glorify God, and yet the tiniest of gods are to be found in the "mirror of me" where most of the world's masses worship. Some may occasionally peer past the edges of the mirror to see the vastness of God beyond it, but most continue to adore the little image of themselves, always asking at every turn, "What's in it for me?"

But praise—authentic adoration—smashes such little altars. Those who turn from the mirror and turn to God see the heavens opened and hear the seraphim crying, "Holy, Holy, Holy is the Lord Almighty." There you will see the Lord, high and lifted up. There you will praise him, no longer having confidence in your abilities but now confessing confidence in God's power in your life over every circumstance and be forever free of your ego, echoing, "It is no longer I who live, but Christ lives in me."

When Paul said, "For to me, living means living for Christ, and dying is even better. But if I live, I can do more fruitful work for Christ" (Philippians 1:21–22), he was not suggesting that in his strength he can do more by living. Rather, he was stating that because he had been crucified with Christ, the Holy Spirit who now had taken up residence in his body by faith could work through him unrestrained. It freed him to focus and concentrate on being more like Jesus.

This lesson was learned by King Jehoshaphat of Judah, who found out that when one allows God to take over there is nothing to fear. When the nation of Israel was faced with disaster, Jehoshaphat called on the people to get serious with God, so they could devote extra time to separating themselves from the daily routine, consider their sin, and pray to God for help. In 2 Chronicles 20:1–2 Jehoshaphat was told:

> After this, the armies of the Moabites, Ammonites, and some of the Meunites declared war on Jehoshaphat. Messengers came and told Jehoshaphat, "A vast army from Edom is marching against you from beyond the Dead Sea. They are already at Hazazon-tamar."

Jehoshaphat responded by praying to God for help: "O our God, won't you stop them? We are powerless against this mighty army that is about to attack us. We do not know what to do, but we are looking to you for help" (v. 12). He committed the situation to God because his people were God's people. He professed complete dependence on God, not himself, for deliverance. God answers through the prophet Jahaziel, saying:

> "Listen, all you people of Judah and Jerusalem! Listen, King Jehoshaphat! This is what the Lord says: Do not be afraid! Don't be discouraged by this mighty army, for the battle is not yours, but God's. Tomorrow, march out against them. You will find them coming up through the ascent of Ziz at the end of the valley that opens into the wilderness of Jeruel. But you will not even need to fight. Take your positions; then stand still and watch the Lord's victory. He is with you, O people of Judah and Jerusalem. Do not be afraid or discouraged. Go out against them tomorrow, for the Lord is with you!" Then King Jehoshaphat bowed low with his face to the ground. And all the people of Judah and Jerusalem did the same, worshiping the Lord. (vv. 15–18)

This narrative alerts me to the fact that the battle is not ours but God's. It highlights our human limitations, which are surrendered to God's strength to work through our weaknesses. No longer do we pursue selfish desires. Therefore, we no longer need to fight, for God fights for us—and God always triumphs. The enemy is already defeated. We have assurance, "My old self has been crucified with Christ. It is no longer I who live, but Christ lives in me."

Before my "Kingdom Living" experience with the Holy Spirit in 1977, I did not understand what it meant to stand still and allow God to fight my battles. From my personal experiences growing up with prejudice and being relegated to the second-class citizenry in society, I had to be more assertive and aggressive to survive. Thus I had a difficult time allowing anyone even God to take leadership in my life. As previously mentioned, I hung on my mother's words, "It doesn't matter what anyone says about you; it doesn't make you any better or worse than you really are." I thanked my mother for the wise words that I lived by. If I knew myself and loved myself, I could hold my head up high in any situation. Thus, I often went ahead of God and trusted my instincts.

My first real experience of change happened at the aforementioned conference, when I had just completed a seminar on "The Life in the Spirit" with a group of people from a local church in Rhode Island. I realized there was so much that I was missing. I had a desire to know Jesus in a more personal way. I wanted to know him better and I wanted to be closer to him. I wanted intimacy with God. I desired to know his will for me and to have the courage to follow his divine direction. Amidst my prayers, I sensed God's absolute purity. I was awed by his holiness.

From that moment on, my life began to change. My desire was simply to become more like Jesus. When I read the Bible, it took on new life. My hunger for the Word of God increased so that I could not get enough, and passion for Jesus was now my joy. In retrospect I felt very much like the prophet Isaiah in chapter 6, where the writer says, during the year King Uzziah died, Isaiah who had walked with God and had grown more sensitive to spiritual, eternal values—suddenly became aware, behind all ceremony symbolism and pomp. There was a moment he was standing solitary, alone with God, and saw the Lord seated on a throne, high and exalted. At that moment the divine presence of God flowed like deep waters over his soul, and from that day the vision of holiness and sovereignty of God became the radiance of all his seeing.

This is the essence of religious faith. It is not to believe certain things or possess certain habits, traditions, and relationships, but to believe God and believe *in* God—to trust him because we know he alone is real. The God Isaiah saw was a God of indescribable glory and beauty. It was not possible for him to even verbalize—the Lord he saw was too great for description, too glorious even look upon, an experience so humbling that Isaiah could not lift his eyes to the glorious face. All he could see was the majestic sweep of radiant garments, and hear the winged creatures singing, "Holy, holy, holy is the Lord of Heaven's Armies! The whole earth is filled with his glory" (Isaiah 6:3). This was the vision that steadied Isaiah on the threshold of his career and lodged in his heart the fearless courage to face the obstinacy and opposition of men.

Assuredly, much more depth and detail could be said about the vision, and the temple, and the seraphim who attended the Lord on the throne. However, since time will not allow such an undertaking I will address my thoughts to the fact that a vision of the Lord may be the expressed need of every person today. Accordingly, I find something very clear, practical, and definite in Isaiah's announcement.

Note, the prophet Ezekiel not only sees but knows when and how he saw. "On July 31 of my thirtieth year, while I was with the Judean exiles beside the Kebar River in Babylon, the heavens were opened and I saw visions of God" (Ezekiel 1:1). Likewise, Paul testified, "As I was on the road, approaching Damascus about noon, a very bright light from heaven suddenly shone down around me. I fell to the ground and heard a voice saying to me, 'Saul, Saul, why are you persecuting me?'" (Acts 22:6–7). It was the voice of the Lord whom he was destined to serve. So too Isaiah could point to the map of his life and say, "It was in the year King Uzziah died that I saw the Lord."

Today, all of us must reflect and ask ourselves the question, "When did we encounter the real presence of the Lord?" How many of us can mark the moment we met Jesus and our lives were changed? How many can point to an event in life more important than the day Christ came to live inside of us? Should it not be that we remember the most important event in our lives? If this is not what God is trying to point out for all of us, why would he mark this as the pivot point of this story? Is Uzziah still alive in us or can we say today as Isaiah, "One day my Uzziah died and I saw the Lord"? This is especially significant to me, for I was a member of a church in Providence for twelve years before my Uzziah died and I saw the Lord. Nearly twenty years have passed since that crisis in my life, but I still point to that night in Pond Street Baptist Church, while posing as deacon, when in the midst of a revival an eternal transaction between Christ and my soul took place.

King Uzziah had been a strong ruler and successful soldier and most likely had been Isaiah's patron, so it is probable that to some degree Uzziah had unconsciously become Isaiah's idol. His death not only left an empty throne but left Isaiah wondering what to do next. It is not difficult for me to picture Isaiah's sorrow. However in an instant, darkness turned to light. What the prophet did not realize was this was the opportunity needed by the real occupant of the throne to present himself as "Lord of Heaven's Armies," and to reveal himself as the God who transforms the whole of life.

The more I reflect on this text the more I am convinced that the spirit of King Uzziah is alive and well in many people today and stands over against God, inhibiting the vision of the real presence of the Lord. Are you aware that Uzziahs come in many forms, in many ways, and are probably the greatest hindrance for many people in the contemporary church? Many today focus on denominations, liturgies, music, emotion, or a great preacher, and miss the God of grace and indescribable glory.

Some may wish to dispute my contention; others may wish to ignore their blindness. However, one of the most sobering passages in Scripture is found in Jesus's letters to the seven churches in the book of Revelation. The church in Laodicea had become so lukewarm, distasteful, and repugnant that Jesus issued warnings to repent: "I know all the things you do, that you are neither hot nor cold. I wish that you were one or the other! But since you are like lukewarm water, neither hot nor cold, I will spit you out of my mouth!" (Revelation 3:15–16). The church in Laodicea was complacent, rich, and felt satisfied, but they did not have Christ's presence among them. Christ knocked at the door of their hearts, but they were so busy enjoying worldly pleasures that they didn't notice he was trying to enter.

Too many professing Christians have soundproof partitions erected between the ears, and do not allow the creative action of the Holy Spirit to penetrate the whole of life. In so doing, they fail to realize there is more lurking beneath the comfort, complacency, and dryness they are presently experiencing. However, when their Uzziah is removed, they begin to suspect there is more to this thing called religion and may begin to suspect their temples are yet to be filled by the Lord of Heaven's Armies.

The apostle Paul says, "And so, dear brothers and sisters, I plead with you to give your bodies to God because of all he has done for you. Let them be a living and holy sacrifice—the kind he will find acceptable. This is truly the way to worship him" (Romans 12:1). To see the Lord, some things must be allowed to die. Some habits and traditions must be buried; prejudices and fears must be crucified; idols must be destroyed; thrones must be vacated and torn down; sin must be exposed; pride and self-centeredness must give way to humility and self-denial; and the indescribable vision of the Lord must become sight. Surely, it is no easy matter to convince people who are enjoying the fruits of long material prosperity that there is a veil over their temple. However, if one truly desires to know the real presence of the Lord, one must seek to expand their pilgrimage of the mind and offer themselves up to the Lord.

Allow me to illuminate your minds to the real outcome of Isaiah's, or any other person's, experience in the temple—and the resulting change in life when God opens a person's eyes to the wonderful vision which transfigures religion to worship of a holy God, in which the heart cries out, "I saw the Lord. He was sitting on a lofty throne, and the train of his robe filled the Temple."

After I departed from Pond Street Baptist Church, my experience with Christ was still very much in focus. It seemed almost surreal, as if the person I once was no longer existed. The many experiences in my life seemed distant, and my life now began to merge into God's divine plan. In particular, my heart was changing toward people. I saw them through different eyes. The anger I once felt because of isolation and rejection due to my color was waning, and I began to see people's needs before I saw their color. God was preparing me for what was ahead. I cannot help thinking now that God was fashioning me to be his eyes and heart for a ministry in

Westerly, Rhode Island. Calvin Miller, in his book *The Unchained Soul*, tells the story of how

> Scottish patriarchs looking for walking sticks always passed over the untried wood of the lower slopes. They climbed to the wuthered heights to search for rods made strong by storm and wind. These iron-strong canes were once young trees that fought the icy Northers. With each storm, they bent and twisted and broke a bit inside. But gradually each inner scar became the steely fiber they bought with every storm that endured. Only such woody steel will serve as the rod of God.[2]

Conversely, Miller warns,

> But do not let their majesty delude you. These mighty rods were once just spindling trees. Therefore, never bless the rods; rather, bless the gales that broke their sinews, lacing them with stone, until the storms they so despised had changed them into scepters.[3]

God uses our experiences to fashion us into rods that he can use for his glory. He merges us with him so that we might share in his divine nature. Many times I had been vulnerable and felt beaten up, rejected, and broken, but along with each act of bigotry, each derogatory word, each accusation, God was fashioning a stronger, more confident, more durable, and wiser man to accomplish the task he had set before me. In the process, I learned that those experiences which do not break us make us stronger and wiser. When we see a vision of God we are to share the vision of God's heart with his people, and it is required that we are faithful to believe

190   A Wonder-Filled Life

in its divine outcome. To see the real presence Isaiah saw we must not pray for vision; we must pray for God to prepare our hearts to receive a vision. The initial steps toward seeing the Lord of Heaven's Armies are to:

Approach God with nothing in our hands.

Acknowledge our utter aversion to sin and our need for forgiveness and mercy.

Desire to have the veil removed from our eyes.

Long for God's holiness and purity to be made manifest in you.

Yield your heart to God's love, and thirst for his presence to flood your life.

Be open for his life to be formed in you by the Holy Spirit.

Be expectant for "the evidence of things we cannot yet see."

Behold vision.

Once vision is realized in the heart, the recipient must embrace it, nourish it, and cherish it. It is a gift of God for his people. The receiver of vision must then be isolated from all past experiences, habits, and cognitive knowledge. The visionary's eyes must have a single focus to see what others cannot see. Once we comply, we find that the Uzziahs that blocked our vision are removed. We discover a larger conception of God, a fuller knowing of God, a more intimate presence that fills, thrills, and transforms every aspect of life, body, soul, and spirit. God himself promises to effect this wonderful transformation in us, and only He can do it.

We can change our clothes, our habitation, our outward manners, but not our hearts. We can change our approach, we can feign love for our brothers, we can change churches, but we cannot change not our hearts. The depth of need renders it too much for a person. The heart of stone is too cold to feel its need and too dead to strive after a better condition. This is the dangerous result of sin: the conscience is seared, the guilt of sin and its danger are not felt, the appeals of divine grace are not heeded. Rain and sunshine cannot fertilize a granite rock.

But now God promises to do what no human being can ever accomplish for themselves: he will take away the evil, remove the rebellion, take away the desire to sin, remove the heart of stone. He will give a new nature. He will give a heart of flesh. He will inspire power into this new nature by putting a new spirit in his children. When God's word reaches the heart through the power of his Spirit, a new feeling is awakened and an inward and therefore secret change takes place in the believer. God is now all around us, all over us, all under us, all through us, all behind us, all before us, and all in us. Then the deep cry of the heart can arise from within us: "It is no longer I who live, but Christ lives in me. So I live in this earthly body by trusting in the Son of God, who loved me and gave himself for me."

TWELVE

LIVING ROOTS

"Then Christ will make his home in your hearts as you trust in him. Your roots will grow down into God's love and keep you strong."

(Ephesians 3:17)

At that American Baptist Conference Center in Green Lake, Wisconsin, not only did I learn about kingdom living but I also learned that what I had always taken for granted in living out my faith was the starting point of what God wanted for me. Indeed! I now realized that there was much more flourishing beneath the surface to go. Paul said, "Your roots will grow down into God's love and keep you strong" (Ephesians 3:17–18). I believe that what Paul is suggesting is that the love of God is so complete and of such a degree that we are not able really to comprehend the depth or quality of it, because it lies far deeper than our intellectual understanding. However hard you try, you can never escape from his love. When you feel shut out or isolated, remember that you can never be lost to God's love. Paul also writes,

193

And I am convinced that nothing can ever separate us from God's love. Neither death nor life, neither angels nor demons, neither our fears for today nor our worries about tomorrow—not even the powers of hell can separate us from God's love. No power in the sky above or in the earth below—indeed, nothing in all creation will ever be able to separate us from the love of God that is revealed in Christ Jesus our Lord. (Romans 8:38–39)

This helps me to understand more fully Jesus's declaration in John's gospel, "For God so loved the world that he gave his one and only Son, that whoever believes in him shall not perish but have eternal life" (John 3:16, NIV). For a long time, I failed to comprehend that which is simply stated elsewhere by John: "God is love" (1 John 4:8). What is probably the most familiar, most often quoted, most well-known, and most loved passage of Scripture in the entire Bible, "For God so loved the world that he gave his one and only Son" frequently is misinterpreted by emphasizing the quantity of God's love, and in doing so misses what I believe to be Jesus's intent.

John had lived with Christ, had seen him work, and perceived his ministry to people. John enjoyed fellowship with the Father and the Son all the days of his life; hence, I do not believe the passage is speaking of the capacity or quantity of God's love, but it is speaking of its special quality. Its relational aspect. Its never-ending eternal nature. It means, "In such a way, God loved the world that he gave. . . ."

A certain medieval monk announced he would be preaching next Sunday evening on "The Love of God." As the shadows fell and the light ceased to come in through the cathedral windows, the congregation gathered. In the darkness of the altar, the monk lighted a candle and carried it to the crucifix. First of all, he illumined the crown of thorns; next, the two wounded hands; then the marks of the spear wound. In the hush that fell, he blew out the candle and left the chancel. There was nothing else to say.[1] The great lovers of God are those who love Jesus not because of what he's done for them but because he died for them.

Accordingly, the prescription for understanding the love of God is to allow the Word of God to penetrate the depths of our being and to draw our nourishment from him, which is often expressed by words such as "deep" or "depths." Calvin Miller, in his book *Into the Depths of God*, notes: "Deep is not a place we visit in our search for God, it is what happens to us when we find him."[2] Have you ever wondered what might happen to us when we find ourselves in the depths with God, where far below the noisy, trashy surface of the ocean things are now quiet and serene? The first thing one discovers is there is no longer any fear of the depths, because of God's presence. No sound breaks the awesome silence of the ocean's heart. In the depths, one loses all sense of contact with the surface and is lost in the vastness and endlessness and mystery of its depths. In the depths of real inwardness lies the treasure.

> For his Spirit joins with our spirit to affirm that we are God's children. And since we are his children, we are his heirs. Together with Christ, we are heirs of God's glory. But if we are to share his glory, we must also share his suffering. (Romans 8:16–17)

Contrary to this, many Christians live on the surface, whipped by the tumultuous circumstances of their days. And yet those who plumb the "deep things of God" discover true peace for the first time. It is not simply about trying to learn as much as we can about God, nor is it about trying to get or acquire as much of God as we can. That is an impossibility because God is so vast, so big, so *everything*, and we are so finite. The task is to allow ourselves to move deeper into God, closer to the heart of God—to be centered in God, which is the merger of two selves: ours and his. Centering is union with Christ. It is not a union that eradicates either self but heightens both. The sacred individuality of each is made greater in this union. The fact is, we are never more ourselves and God is never more God than when we enter into union with Christ. It means willfully focusing on our relationship with God because we desire his company. It is a discipline of the heart. It is the life-consuming art of approaching God where he is to be found—in the center of our souls.

Unfortunately, many people live on the periphery of God's empowering. They need to move on into the centering prayer life which furnishes one with a dynamic God view. This kind of prayer is a dialogue of lovers. It is interested in a relationship, not answers. Centering prayer wants God alone—all of God—more of God—only God. It draws us inward, closer to the heart of God, as a beautiful and gentle reminder of our purpose, seeking God and his will first. Then, real change follows effortlessly, without the struggle to change ourselves. His love transforms us as we continue to keep our eyes fixed on him and not on the things of this world.

Jesus's counsel to be in the world means that we must walk through a sinful, fallen culture, giving it hope only because we remain in conversation with God as we walk through it. We are writing our best self-definitions, one centered prayer at a time. Our hunger for the inmost God thrills us and defines us. Such prayers tell us throughout our lives who we are. Such prayers at last leave us indistinguishable from Christ himself. It is so simple yet we miss it, thinking that we must strive to be more Christlike. We become as he is in this world by following his example: dying to self, loving as he loved, giving as he gave. We put our hands in his as he draws us closer to the kingdom within. As Paul affirms,

> Then Christ will make his home in your hearts as you trust in him. Your roots will grow down into God's love and keep you strong. And may you have the power to understand, as all God's people should, how wide, how long, how high, and how deep his love is. (Ephesians 3:17–18).

God's love is so complete it reaches every part of our experience. For a long time, I struggled with going deeper with God, for the word "deep" conjured up thoughts of my first real experience with water while in the United States Navy boot camp. I was pushed off a tower into a pool and left to struggle on my own to the surface. My avoidance of deep water was justified until I realized that a deeper relationship with Christ would require entering the place where he makes his abode. In Colossians 2:7 (TLB), Paul says: "Let your roots grow down into him and draw up nourishment from him." In 1 Corinthians 2:10, we are told that the Holy Spirit shows us even God's deep secrets. Jesus says that unless we join with him and remain in him we will be unfruitful: "Yes, I am the vine; you are the branches. Those who remain in me, and I in them, will produce much fruit. For apart from me you can do nothing" (John 15:5). It raises the question, how deep are we willing to go to meet with God? How much will we allow ourselves to be drawn into the depths of God?

In Ezekiel 47 there is a compelling narrative of the stream of water flowing east from beneath the door of the temple and passing to the right of the altar on its south side. In verses 2–5 the writer said:

> The man brought me outside the wall through the north gateway and led me around to the eastern entrance.

There I could see the water flowing out through the south side of the east gateway.

Measuring as he went, he took me along the stream for 1,750 feet and then led me across. The water was up to my ankles. He measured off another 1,750 feet and led me across again. This time the water was up to my knees. After another 1,750 feet, it was up to my waist. Then he measured another 1,750 feet, and the river was too deep to walk across. It was deep enough to swim in but too deep to walk through.

What is significant in this text is the word "led." You cannot be led unless you have decided to follow. You cannot be led unless you submit. God will not drag you, coerce you, drive you, blackmail you, but he will lead you. Eventually, the water becomes too deep to cross, which means we are simply to be immersed in it. I cannot help think of how God's grace is like a stream that grows and grows. The narrator describes it as ankle-deep water, and then "knee-deep," and then water up to the waist, but soon becomes a river that cannot be crossed. When reflecting on it, I am amazed that from the center of my shallow tidal soul I have immediate access to the vast oceans of God's presence:

Do not be afraid, for I have ransomed you. I have called you by name; you are mine. When you go through deep waters, I will be with you. When you go through rivers of difficulty, you will not drown. When you walk through the fire of oppression you will not be burned up; the flames will not consume you. For I am the Lord, your God, the Holy One of Israel, your Savior. (Isaiah 43:1–3)

Are we not to trust the word of the Lord? Should we not be willing to dive to the depths of the river where we can be alone with God—away from the surface noise, away from the trash, even away from the boats that could carry us across—and go deeper into his presence?

Ezekiel's flood should not threaten us. We need not fear going deeper. Did God not promise, "When you go through rivers of difficulty, you will not drown?" Trying to go through rivers of difficulty in your strength, you are more likely to drown. But if you invite the Lord to go with you, he will not only protect you but his power can transform you, no matter how lifeless or corrupt you may be. Even when we feel messed up and beyond hope, his power can heal us. In verses 6–10 of Ezekiel 47 the man asked,

> "Have you been watching, son of man?" Then he led me back along the riverbank. When I returned, I was surprised by the sight of many trees growing on both sides of the river. Then he said to me, "This river flows east through the desert into the valley of the Dead Sea. The waters of this stream will make the salty waters of the Dead Sea fresh and pure. There will be swarms of living things wherever the water of this river flows. Fish will abound in the Dead Sea, for its waters will become fresh. Life will flourish wherever this water flows. It is here the Holy Spirit regenerates all who would come to him."

Jesus promises,

> "Anyone who is thirsty may come to me! Anyone who believes in me may come and drink! For the Scriptures declare, 'Rivers of living water will flow from his heart.'" (When he said "living water," he was speaking of the Spirit,

who would be given to everyone believing in him.) (John 7:38–39)

Those who have dared to live the deeper life never meant to orient their preferences around the meditative life; it's just that once you've been to the Great Barrier Reef in Northern Queensland, Australia, wading pools hold little interest. At the Great Barrier Reef, one can walk seventy to ninety miles out into the ocean. It is a great place for snorkeling. Snorkelers float face down on top of the water, with a mask and breathing tube that extends above the water. However, there are scuba divers who go to the end and plunge themselves into the water, diving beneath the clear waters and burying themselves in the wonder of the mysterious ocean depths. Scuba diving takes many hours or years of learning to go deep. The problem is, the snorkelers can use the same language as divers. They can both describe the beauty of the reef, the many beautiful fish that swim there, the sea creatures, the reeds, and the coral, for the metaphors pass close. However, they are not the same.

What I believe to be the great problem with us as Christians today is that we continue to talk to each other about our shallow experiences and fail to realize we have simply been snorkeling. We have yet to descend to the depths of the ocean. Instead, we keep filling our lives with the same old appetite for spiritual expression, rarely stretching ourselves or expanding our horizons. But when we reach for God in love, and God reaches back, he meets us deep in the center of our existence, where, "no eye has seen, no ear has heard, and no mind has imagined what God has prepared for those who love him" (1 Corinthians 2:9).

How difficult it is for most of us to grasp the essence of God elucidated by the three simple words, "God is love." How difficult to simulate or express this type of love called for by God: "We love each other because he loved us first" (1 John 4:19). It is one thing to say you love Jesus, but the real test is your willingness to serve him. Not just because you reasoned with your head it's the thing to do, not because you walked the road together and saw the miracles, not because he protected you from the stormy seas of life, not because he blessed you when you least expected it, but more than that—because he died for you. It is so far beyond human ability to define or understand God's everlasting love; however, we must try if we are to draw closer to Christ.

To help our understanding, Paul says "Let your roots grow down into him and draw up nourishment from him." We are to become like the roots of plants anchored in the soil. The plant receives water and nutrients as the roots absorb, and the plant matures. The deeper the roots go, the more benefits they provide to the soil. While alive and active, roots redistribute carbon and nutrients throughout the soil. Likewise, a tree can withstand incredibly strong storms like tornadoes and hurricanes, because of their remarkable root systems. The taproot is surpassed by an extensive root system spreading horizontally, and this lateral mass of roots will bring the tree moisture and nutrients for its lifetime.

The giant sequoia redwood trees have a unique root system that is a marvel, compared to their mammoth size. Their roots are relatively shallow. There is no tap root to anchor them deep into the earth. The roots only go down six to twelve feet, and yet these trees rarely fall over. They withstand strong winds, earthquakes, fires, storms, and prolonged flooding. One might ask, how can something up to five hundred tons, reaching more than 350 feet in height, and living for many centuries remain standing with roots only going down about ten feet? Their root system is intertwined with the other redwood trees, literally holding each other up. The trees grow very close together and are dependent on each other for nutrients. Only redwoods have the strength and ability to support other redwoods. So, beneath the surface of these humongous, tall, statuesque trees are roots like an army of men who have their arms interlocked, standing, and supporting each other. They prevent the adversities of life from knocking each other down.

The lesson learned from plants and trees is that we cannot remain in limbo without the life-giving nourishment of the Holy Spirit. We must choose to live and grow, or die. Our roots must go down into the soil of God's marvelous love to gain nutrients for life. As Paul cautions,

> And now, just as you accepted Christ Jesus as your Lord, you must continue to follow him. Let your roots grow down into him, and let your lives be built on him. Then your faith will grow strong in the truth you were taught, and you will overflow with thankfulness. (Colossians 2:6–7)

If there is one most important thing I have learned in life, it has been to not forget my roots. I have learned a lot from the trees in my backyard. After being called to pastor Pleasant Street Baptist Church in Westerly, I bought a home in a neighborhood with few trees but many houses. Soon I planted more than thirty trees around my property, most of them given to me by one of my parishioners. Among these trees were two red maple seedlings, which I bought to provide some diversity and color among the other trees. Knowing nothing about gardening I pruned the lower branches of one of the maples, and soon realized my ignorance. I noticed this particular tree was growing straight up to the sky tall and stately, while the other red maple remained full, spreading its branches outward. What I became aware of is that the two trees resulted in different shapes, but both were beautiful because of the nourishment they received from the soil.

Is that not like what God does in us? If we remain in him, he fashions each of us into a beautiful image unlike any other. Note Jesus's words in John 15:5, "Yes, I am the vine; you are the branches. Those who remain in me, and I in them, will produce much fruit. For apart from me you can do nothing." Here, Jesus describes the essence of the fruitful life he came to bring us, as he said in John 10:10, "My purpose is to give them a rich and satisfying life." The King James Version of the Bible puts it, "that they may have life, and that they may have it more abundantly." Jesus says, "Yes, I am the vine; you are the branches." The image of a branch gaining all its sustenance and strength from the parent vine is a beautiful description of our total dependence upon God, without whom we can do nothing.

I have always been fascinated by genealogy; it has led to some significant discoveries and many surprises about my roots. At present, my family genealogy contains 787 people, and my paternal DNA suggests links to Nigeria, Cameroon, Mali, Ireland, and Scotland. This research created in me a desire to search further, which led me to the realization that the Word of God contained all the answers to the information I was seeking. There is a genealogy in Luke 3:23–38. At first, I did not discover the information I was looking for—probably because like many other Bible readers, I thought genealogies are not very exciting. However, on further searching I came across a most amazing fact: my roots are birthed in eternity. In the very last verse (38) I read these words: "Kenan was the son of Enosh. Enosh was the son of Seth. Seth was the son of Adam. Adam was the son of God." Hallelujah! I was so joyful in knowing that indeed our roots go back to eternity. Even though Adam disobeyed God, we are still connected to him by the sacrifice of Jesus Christ on the cross.

Satan tries to tell us that we are hopelessly lost because of sin, but that is a lie. Satan tries to deceive us that we have no worth and should simply give up. He tries to tell us that because of Adam, our roots are forever severed from God. However, the Word of God declares otherwise: "No power in the sky above or in the earth below—indeed, nothing in all creation will ever be able to separate us from the love of God that is revealed in Christ Jesus our Lord" (Romans 8:39). By faith, we must stay connected to God every second of every day, to live the most God-honoring and abundant life of peace and fruitfulness in Christ Jesus.

Receiving Christ as Lord of your life is the beginning of your life with Christ. You must continue to follow his leadership by being rooted, built up, and strengthened in the faith. You can live for Christ by committing your life and submitting your will to him. The key is centering on Christ and grounding yourself in his Word. God seeks those who love him and who hunger for things: "'No eye has seen, no ear has heard, and no mind has imagined what God has prepared for those who love him.' But it was to us that God revealed these things by his Spirit. For his Spirit searches out everything and shows us God's deep secrets" (1 Corinthians 2:9–10).

The ultimate redeeming hunger is to be changed to the glory of his image—to be conformed to his image. Paul expressed this desire for conformity in many ways, but my favorite appears in 2 Corinthians 3:18: "So all of us who have had that veil removed can see and reflect the glory of the Lord. And the Lord—who is the Spirit—makes us more and more like him as we are changed into his glorious image." We look into the glass and see Jesus, and are given life by our desire to become Christ in the mirror. When we reach for God in love, and God reaches back, he meets us deep in the center of our existence where our roots were first fashioned in eternity. As Paul writes:

Even before he made the world, God loved us and chose us in Christ to be holy and without fault in his eyes. God decided in advance to adopt us into his own family by bringing us to himself through Jesus Christ. This is what he wanted to do, and it gave him great pleasure. Amen. (Ephesians 1:4–5)

THIRTEEN

SPIRIT LIFE

"He is the Holy Spirit, who leads into all truth. The world cannot receive him, because it isn't looking for him and doesn't recognize him. But you know him, because he lives with you now and later will be in you."

(John 14:17)

The eternal significance of what the Christian life is really like necessitates a pause at the doorway of discovery, to examine an important consideration. In the introduction of this book, we began a conversation about the experience of living a transformed life. The supposition is that each time a person expresses a desire to be closer to Jesus, he or she is speaking of a hunger for a deeper, more intimate relationship with the Lord.

Have you ever halted your activities for a moment to ask yourself, do I know what is needed to live out this Christian life? Or the question might be, what does it mean to be a Christian? I have become more aware that many who wear the name "Christian" are not sure what it means, and there are few who live in such a way that their lives preclude any questions at all.

208 A Wonder-Filled Life

The first thing that helps in our understanding is that a Christian bears Christ's identity, and models his or her life after their Creator. We are told:

> Then God said, "Let us make human beings in our image, to be like us. They will reign over the fish in the sea, the birds in the sky, the livestock, all the wild animals on the earth, and the small animals that scurry along the ground." So God created human beings in his image. In the image of God he created them; male and female he created them. (Genesis 1:26–27)

Further, in chapter 2, verse 7, we learn, "the Lord God formed the man from the dust of the ground. He breathed the breath of life into the man's nostrils, and the man became a living person."

It is critical to our understanding that in creation, God is already revealed as a trinity of persons. Why is this so important? The fact is, one cannot understand the Christian life without a clear sense of the role of the triune God. Within his mysterious being, God is Father, Son, and Holy Spirit. The designations are just ways in which God is God. Within the Godhead, there are three persons who are neither three Gods nor three parts of God, but coequally and coeternally God. At the outset, please know that I am aware that the doctrine of the Holy Trinity has found consensus in Christendom and that the term "Trinity" is widely used in every area of Christianity: in preaching, in writing, in music. And yet, because the term "Trinity" is found nowhere in Scripture, some think that it does not exist. Are the phrases "three-in-one," "triune God," or any similar term for God to be discarded, then? Must we be resigned to understanding the Trinity simply by faith? I think not.

Notice the plural pronouns "us" and "our" in Genesis 1:26: "Then God said, 'Let us make human beings in our image, to be like us.'" Though not a complete list, the following are a few references in Scripture that support the fact that God is one, in trinity:

- The Father and I are one (John 10:30).

- After his baptism, as Jesus came up out of the water, the heavens were opened and he saw the Spirit of God descending like a dove and settling on him. And a voice from heaven said, "This is my dearly loved Son, who brings me great joy" (Matthew 3:16–17).

- Therefore, go and make disciples of all the nations, baptizing them in the name of the Father and the Son, and the Holy Spirit (Matthew 28:19).

- Anyone who has seen me has seen the Father! (John 14:9).

These biblical references raise some important questions. Did Jesus's coming not reveal the Father? Did Jesus not promise to send the Holy Spirit after his return to heaven? Was it not the Holy Spirit's role to reveal Jesus? This being true, should there not be clear teaching in Scripture on the relationship between the Father and Son and Holy Spirit?

In Genesis 1:1 we are told: "In the beginning, God created the heavens and the earth." In the beginning, before time was, God chose to create the world as an expression of his love. He created the world and people—he made something from nothing. "And the Spirit of God was hovering over the surface of the waters" (v. 2)—God's Spirit was actively involved in creation. "Then God said, 'Let there be light, and there was light'" (v. 3)—God spoke into the darkness, and his Spirit empowered his words. "And God saw that the light was good" (v. 4)—now light had overcome the darkness. The Bible further supports the fact that along with God his Spirit was present in creation: "For the Spirit of God has made me, and the breath of the Almighty gives me life" (Job 33:4); "Then you send your Spirit, and new life is born to replenish all the living of the earth" (Psalm 104:30, TLB).

In many ways, the contemporary church has shied away from conversations about the Holy Spirit as a living presence in our lives. Too often the Spirit is spoken of only because of its unique relationship within the Trinity: God the Father, God the Son, and God the Spirit. The clearest teaching on the Holy Spirit in the life of a believer is found in John 14:15–17, where Jesus promises the Holy Spirit:

> If you love me, obey my commandments. And I will ask the Father, and he will give you another Advocate, who will never leave you. He is the Holy Spirit, who leads into all truth. The world cannot receive him, because it isn't looking for him and doesn't recognize him. But you know him because he lives with you now and later will be in you.

Jesus was soon going to leave the disciples, but at the same time he would remain with them. How could this be? How could Jesus be in two places at the same time? The Advocate offers support, strength, and counsel and intercedes when necessary. The Spirit of God himself would come after Jesus was gone, to care for and guide the disciples. Did not the regenerated power of the Holy Spirit come upon the disciples just before Jesus's ascension: "Again he said, 'Peace be with you. As the Father has sent me, so I am sending you.' Then he breathed on them and said, 'Receive the Holy Spirit'" (John 20:21–22)? Was not the Spirit poured out on all the believers at Pentecost? Luke describes it:

> On the day of Pentecost all the believers were meeting together in one place. Suddenly, there was a sound from

heaven like the roaring of a mighty windstorm, and it filled the house where they were sitting. Then, what looked like flames or tongues of fire appeared and settled on each of them. And everyone present was filled with the Holy Spirit and began speaking in other languages, as the Holy Spirit gave them this ability. (Acts 2:1–4)

That sound from heaven was not gradual but rather sudden, "like the roaring of a mighty windstorm." A real attention-getter. It filled the whole house, God's presence was among them in a more personal and powerful way than they had ever experienced before. Everyone was included. And as Jesus promised, the infilling of the Holy Spirit would give them the power to be "witnesses . . . in Jerusalem, throughout Judea, in Samaria, and to the ends of the earth" (Acts 1:8). Thus, it is clear from the Scriptures that at Pentecost the Holy Spirit came to live within us and among us and to make his power available to us for daily living. God is spiritually present everywhere. The Holy Spirit is God living his life out in us, "It is no longer I who live, but Christ lives in me. So I live in this earthly body by trusting in the Son of God, who loved me and gave himself for me" (Galatians 2:20).

Further, the Spirit marks the beginning of the Christian experience. We cannot be joined to Christ without his Spirit (1 Corinthians 6:17); we cannot be adopted as his children without his Spirit (Romans 8:14–17; Galatians 4:6–7); we cannot be in the body of Christ except by baptism of the one Holy Spirit (1 Corinthians 12:13). The Holy Spirit is the power of our new lives, and he begins a lifelong process of change as we become more like Christ (Galatians 3:3; Philippians 1:6). In the good news we see the truth about Christ, and we are transformed as we understand and apply it. As our knowledge of Christ increases, the Holy Spirit draws us to a deeper experience where we become visible reflections of God's glory in our everyday lives.

It is said that many today are unaware of the Holy Spirit's activities, for shying away from the Spirit leaves us empty, powerless, and inadequate to cope with everyday living. But to those who hear Christ's words and understand the Spirit's power, the Spirit gives a whole new way of living. This life-giving Spirit is the same Holy Spirit who was present at the creation of the world, he is the power behind the rebirth of every believer, and he gives us the power we need to live the Christian life. Thus, we dare not cut off a conversation about the Spirit of God who has taken up residence in us. If you are waiting for a certain feeling you may not realize it, but be assured the Spirit has come upon you and in you because God promised he would. In Acts 2:38–39, Peter says this to the people in Jerusalem who were deeply moved by his powerful message about Christ:

> Each of you must repent of your sins and turn to God, and be baptized in the name of Jesus Christ for the forgiveness of your sins. Then you will receive the gift of the Holy Spirit. This promise is to you, to your children, and to those far away—all who have been called by the Lord our God.

There is no need to guess or hope who you are, for you can know with certainty through the Holy Spirit you are God's child and you will spend eternity with Christ. Previously we mentioned the fourteenth chapter of the gospel of John, where Jesus, at the close of his ministry, sets the stage for the continuing presence and power of God in the lives of his people. The reason for concern is that his time on earth was at hand; he knew his disciples would not make it in this world without divine help. He had always been with them, walked with them, talked, taught, and slept with them. In their need he sustained them. But now he has to break the disturbing news to his inner circle of twelve that change is at hand.

He begins, "Dear children, I will be with you only a little longer. And as I told the Jewish leaders, you will search for me, but you can't come where I am going" (John 13:33). Disturbing news indeed! What were they to do now? Their Master, their friend, the one who worked miracles, the one who has sway over nature, the one who speaks peace to the wind and the waves, the one who mends broken bodies and drives out evil spirits, the one who has power over life and death, is going away—and they have no idea where he is going. How can they make it in the world without the one who fashioned the world in the palm of his hands? What would life be like without the presence and power of the Master?

Consequently, Jesus reassures them: "Don't let your hearts be troubled. Trust in God, and trust also in me" (John 14:1). In the dictionary, trust is defined as the belief that someone or something is reliable, good, honest, effective. So for the disciples, trust in God, though unseen, means security. And yet at the same time it is unsettling, because it is only as secure as their trust in Jesus. So here we learn that trusting God is the key to help in time of need. Trust is the key to peace amid the storm. Trust is the antidote for the troubled heart, and in the case of the disciples there was much to consider. They were about to part with their beloved friend. They were about to be left alone to face persecutions and trials. They were without wealth, friends, honor, and it is not improbable to think they felt Jesus's death would be the end of all their dreams.

Surely, for many of us today there are times in our lives when we too are confronted with equally disturbing news as these disciples, such as the impending departure of a loved one either by death or physically moving far away. It could be when we lose a valued possession like a home or a business. It could be when we are in despair, feeling deep sorrow and hopelessness. And yet, even then, Jesus's words ring out: "Trust in God, and trust also in me."

The disciples were eyewitnesses of Jesus's life and teachings, and the Holy Spirit helped them remember without taking away their perspectives. Even today the Holy Spirit can help us in the same way. As we study the Bible, we can trust the Holy Spirit to plant truth in our minds, convince us of God's will, and remind us when we stray from it. But most of all, the Holy Spirit convinces us of life's greatest news: "Christ died for our sins, just as the Scriptures said. He was buried, and he was raised from the dead on the third day, just as the Scriptures said" (1 Corinthians 15:3–4).

So the Spirit tells us that God came in the flesh to a little town in Bethlehem. He tells us Jesus came to die to secure our pardon and that Jesus was crucified and buried in a borrowed tomb, and that early one morning he rose from the dead and was seen by Peter, and then by the twelve disciples, and then by more than five hundred of his followers at the same time (vv. 5–6). But the reality is, it doesn't matter how true all of this is unless one is open and willing and ready to hear the truth of God.

The problem is that many people spend their lives debating the technical aspects of Jesus only to fail, for the simple basic truth lies not in reasoning but rests on the Word of God. The Holy Spirit reveals Jesus as the God of hope in despair, the God of comfort in sorrow, and the God of peace during the storm. The Spirit reveals that Jesus is the God who says "Here on earth you will have many trials and sorrows. But take heart, because I have overcome the world" (John 16:33). Jesus is the God who says to the sick and afflicted, "Pick up your mat and walk" (John 5:11). He is the one who spoke through the prophet:

> When you go through deep waters, I will be with you.
> When you go through rivers of difficulty, you will not

drown. When you walk through the fire of oppression, you will not be burned up; the flames will not consume you. (Isaiah 43:2)

To be sure, the Holy Spirit makes the Word of God real, living, and powerful in people's lives. His witness gave birth to the church; and today, he is still witnessing to the hearts of men and women that Jesus is Savior and Lord. But the part that he reveals to me, that makes me want to give all to him, is when he assures me I that have access to the Father and will never again be an orphan. Paul writes,

For all who are led by the Spirit of God are children of God. So you have not received a spirit that makes you fearful slaves. Instead, you received God's Spirit when he adopted you as his own children. Now we call him, "Abba, Father." For his Spirit joins with our spirit to affirm that we are God's children. (Romans 8:14–16)

Here Paul uses adoption to illustrate our new relationship with God. In Roman culture, the adopted person has lost all rights in his old family and gained all the rights of a legitimate child in his new family, becoming a full heir to his new father's estate. Likewise, when a person becomes a Christian, he or she gains all the privileges and responsibilities of a child in God's family. One of these outstanding privileges is being led by the Spirit, who becomes our witness that we now live in the supernatural realm of the Spirit. We are in the natural world but not of the world for our physical existence in the world is being filled, led, controlled, and guided by the Spirit. We read,

Those who are dominated by the sinful nature think about sinful things, but those who are controlled by the Holy Spirit think about things that please the Spirit. So letting your sinful nature control your mind leads to death. But letting the Spirit control your mind leads to life and peace. (Romans 8:5–6)

It's about ordinary men and women and children like you and I, taking orders from Jesus to heal the sick, raise the dead, cleanse those with disease, drive out demons, experience supernatural power, do the miraculous, live in the supernatural realm of the Spirit. I am not aware of anyone today who doesn't need the Holy Spirit's direction for every part of their lives. We need the Spirit's power in our daily living, and we need the Holy Spirit's guidance for every decision we make. Remember, Satan knows who we are; he knows those who are his and he knows who is gone from him. That is why God sent the Holy Spirit to reveal the truth to you and me. All that is required is for us to be open to hear his voice.

Paul affirms, "no one can say Jesus is Lord, except by the Holy Spirit" (1 Corinthians 12:3). In Acts 2:17 Peter declared, "'In the last days,' God says, 'I will pour out my Spirit upon all people.'" Be assured, "all people" includes you and me. The promise is ours. We've got to stop sitting on the sidelines, watching others. We've got to stop trying to get power, prestige, and position in the world. Rather, we need to start walking and living in the supernatural realm. Claiming church membership is a pitiful substitute for an intimate relationship with the living Lord. One needs a true, life-changing conversion to Jesus Christ; true godly sorrow; true repentance for sins; submission of the will; the giving up of your anger, stubbornness, pride, insecurity; and taking on the attitude that Christ Jesus had.

How does this change of mind and attitude come about? How does one come to know this new kind of life? God promises, "'In those days when you pray, I will listen. . . . If you look for me wholeheartedly, you will find me. I will be found by you,' says the Lord"

(Jeremiah 29:12–14a). When you truly seek God, something happens. If you don't believe it, come with me. Let's follow his sandalprints in the sand. Let's sit on the cold, hard floor of the cattle stall in which he was born. Let's smell the sawdust of the carpentry shop. Let's walk with him along the hard, dusty trails of Galilee, and feel the gratitude of the leper as his sores are healed. Let's smile as we see Jesus's compassion with the woman at the well. Let's try to stay awake as we enter the garden and witness his agonizing prayer as "He prayed more fervently, and he was in such agony of spirit that his sweat fell to the ground like great drops of blood" (Luke 22:44). Let's feel the shame as we hear the words of the prophet: "We turned our backs on him and looked the other way. He was despised, and we did not care" (Isaiah 53:3). Let's cringe as we hear the hissing of Satan's hell. Let's flinch and agonize as we feel the pounding of the nails driven into his flesh. Let's weep as we see his blood-stained body slump in death and hear his cry to his Father, "It is finished."

But now, let's raise our voices in praise with the women as we arrive at the empty tomb. We came to see him, but the angels say: "Don't be afraid! . . . I know you are looking for Jesus, who was crucified. He isn't here! He is risen from the dead, just as he said would happen. Come, see where his body was lying" (Matthew 28:5–6). And then, at that moment something happens: a word is placed in a deep crevice of your heart that causes you, ever so briefly, to see his face. It is then you recall his words: "He will be killed, but three days later he will rise from the dead" (Mark 9:31). Suddenly it's as if you are hearing it for the first time, and one more piece of the puzzle falls into place. Someone touches your painful spirit as only one sent from God could do. Suddenly you hear a whisper in your ear, "Greetings"—and there he is: Jesus. The man. The God-man. The bronzed Galilean who spoke with thunderous authority and loved with such childlike humility.

Gone is the pomp of religion. Dissipated is the fog of theology. Released are the claims of goodness and morality. Momentarily lifted is the haziness of self-centeredness—and there he stands, Jesus, Jesus the Christ. The glory of God. God himself. The Lord of lords. The King of kings. The God who claimed to be older than time and greater than death. The God of blood-stained royalty, the God of silent tears, the God who wrote his eulogy before the world was made. The God with a heart of compassion and love. The Lion of Judah, the Lamb sitting on the throne, the perfect sacrifice. He is alive. There he stands: Jesus. Did you see him? Do you see him now? Those who first saw him were never the same. Remember Thomas: "My Lord and my God" (John 20:28). Remember Mary: "I have seen the Lord" (John 20:18). But Peter was overwhelmed: "We have seen his majestic splendor with our own eyes" (1 Peter 1:16). We were eyewitnesses of his Majesty. We have seen Jesus.

So as we approach him today with our five senses, we may be thinking that we can't perceive God's presence. Maybe we can't see what Peter saw, maybe we can't touch him, maybe we can't feel him—but we can know him. His glory is here. His wisdom and power are here. His Spirit permeates this place. God stays invisible, but walks next to you in his Word. Instead of God speaking to you face to face, God speaks to you through his Spirit. This is how you connect to the invisible God and all of his glory. This is how you can witness the living Lord today. This is how a change of mind and attitude come about. This is how one comes to know this new kind of life—Spirit life.

Accordingly, I have discovered something interesting. In Psalm 51, when David confessed, "Against you, and you alone, have I sinned; I have done what is evil in your sight," God gave David covering for his confession. He said, "My grace is sufficient for you. My grace is greater than all your sins." Today I believe many people fail to confess because they're afraid the news will be spread all over town. We must learn to stop pointing fingers. We must learn to forgive and forget, and restore God's covering of grace. We must learn how to love each other once again.

David sinned. He committed adultery and murder. God forgave him and God used him. Peter denied Christ three times, turned his back on him. And yet God said to Peter after Pentecost, "You go and preach." Peter preached, and three thousand were saved. After that, Peter and John healed a lame man at the gate called Beautiful, and found themselves confronted and questioned by the religious authorities. But Peter and John, now living in the supernatural realm of the Spirit, were unafraid. The Scriptures reveal,

> The members of the council were amazed when they saw the boldness of Peter and John, for they could see that they were ordinary men with no special training in the Scriptures. They also recognized them as men who had been with Jesus. (Acts 4:13)

That is it—that is the answer to the question, "What does it mean to be a Christian?" Peter and John, ordinary men with no special training, were now filled with the Holy Spirit and living in the awesome power of God. That same promise of power is available to you and me today, if we are open to receive it. The Kingdom of God is at hand. Kingdom living is present and available now. It's here where you and I live. It is where God lives. It is where God *is*.

Many who wear the name "Christian" will testify that they can't see God with their physical eyes, nor touch God with their hands, but one thing is certain: they know God in their spirit. Let your mind be changed and believe the gospel. Let your heart repent and receive forgiveness. Let your spirit be open and submissive, and be merged with his Spirit. Jesus came to establish God's kingdom in this world now. You can live in the supernatural realm in victory now and forever. This is why one can say: I don't know what it is, I don't know how it comes, I don't know when it comes, I don't know where it comes from, but I know him. I know Jesus.

FOURTEEN

RIVER OF LIFE

"Anyone who is thirsty may come to me! Anyone who believes in me may come and drink! For the Scriptures declare, 'Rivers of living water will flow from his heart.'"

(John 7:37–38).

For many years I have loved the narrative of Ezekiel 47:1–9, of the divine river flowing down from the temple of God. As a preacher I had, for many years, a burning desire to preach from this text. However, somehow I was prevented from doing so until many years later, when the Holy Spirit pointed out that there was much in the narrative I could not understand. God's desire was to have a deeper relationship with me, to receive the richness of his word embedded within its depths.

In 1 Corinthians 2:7 and twenty other times in the New Testament, Paul speaks of "the mystery of God," of God's secret wisdom "that was previously hidden"—his offer of salvation to all people. Originally unknown to humanity, this plan became crystal clear when Jesus rose from the dead. His resurrection proved that he had power over sin and death and could offer us this power as well. His plan, however, is still hidden to unbelievers because they either refuse to accept it, choose to ignore it, or simply haven't heard about it. I am convinced today that lodged in the deep waters of our text is much God wants to reveal to us of his unfathomable nature and his wonderful plan. As Paul writes, "it was to us that God revealed these things by his Spirit. For his Spirit searches out everything and shows us God's deep secrets" (v. 10).

At the outset let me be clear: we do not go deep to study God; we go deep to taste his reality. In such an experience, we cannot define God, for he is not definable. But we do, ultimately, define ourselves. In the depths, we meet our smallness, our powerlessness, our helplessness, and our need. We see God's significance by turning from our insignificance. There in the depths, our ears are shamed by rich silence. Our eyes discover what can't be humanly seen. Our minds are challenged by the inscrutable wall of the mystery of godliness. Thus, our smallness becomes his glory, and hungering for conformity to Christ is the treasure.

However, to desire only what Christ gives and not to desire Christ himself is to never own the greater treasure of his indwelling presence. What stops us short of a deeper relationship with God is the fact that we are content to play in the shallow suburbs of the deep things of God. Our superficial spirituality holds nothing exciting and nothing profound, but it is safe. And yet, this state of reality in which we can truly know ourselves lies so near to us. It is utterly accessible. Yet only a few ever know or pass its gates with any regularity. As Dr. Calvin Miller states in his book *Into the Depths of God*, "Deep is not a place we visit in our search for God, it is what happens to us when we find him."[1]

As a young boy growing up in the city, we were a distance from water. Consequently, I never had the opportunity nor desire nor inclination to go to a beach or learn to swim. But many years later I found myself in the US Navy boot camp, where one of the requirements was to jump off a tall platform into the water down below. To say the least I was scared to death. Looking down at that pool, I wondered how I came to be standing on that platform in the first place—until it came to me this was the price of joining the Navy Reserve to make some extra money.

From that moment on, my memory is vague. All I remember is being in the water and struggling to get to the top because I was too young to die. A few moments later (which seemed like an eternity), I found myself outside of the pool gasping for air. I must confess that since that moment I have had a fear of swimming pools and deep water. It causes me to wonder if that was not the reason I was prohibited from preaching on the water flowing down from the throne of God.

Since then I have learned much about God, about life, about being in over my head. About a God who promises no matter how deep the water is, we are safe in him. It's about leaving the shore of stagnant, disappointing superficial Christian living and wading out into the deep spiritual waters of the kingdom life. It's about the God who promises, "When you go through deep waters, I will be with you. When you go through rivers of difficulty, you will not drown" (Isaiah 43:2a).

In John's gospel, chapter 4, we find the narrative of a conversation between Jesus and a Samaritan woman who had come to draw water from a well. First of all, this woman was a Samaritan, a member of the hated mixed race; she was known to be living in sin and was in a public place. No respectable Jewish man would talk to a woman under such circumstances. But Jesus did. During their conversation, Jesus gave the woman an extraordinary message. In verse 10 he tells her of God's gift of "living water," and then follows in verses 13–14 by saying, "Anyone who drinks this water [of the well] will soon become thirsty

224   A Wonder-Filled Life

again. But those who drink the water I give will never be thirsty again. It becomes a fresh, bubbling spring within them, giving them eternal life." The woman could only wonder what Jesus meant by "living water." John explains later in his gospel:

> On the last day, the climax of the festival, Jesus stood and shouted to the crowds, "Anyone who is thirsty may come to me! Anyone who believes in me may come and drink! For the Scriptures declare, 'Rivers of living water will flow from his heart.'" (When he said "living water," he was speaking of the Spirit, who would be given to everyone believing in him. But the Spirit had not yet been given, because Jesus had not yet entered into his glory.) (John 7:37–39)

In speaking to the woman at the well, Jesus used the term "living water" to indicate eternal life; but here in John 7 he uses it to refer to the Holy Spirit. The two go together. The Holy Spirit regenerates all who would come to him and gives them new life. Since Jesus already knew everything about this woman and offered her eternal life, no one needs to hide ever again. No one needs to feel condemned. No one needs to feel all is hopelessly lost. God's power can transform even the vilest of us, God's power can change even the most sinful among us. Even when we feel messed up and beyond hope, his power can heal us. And what is best of all, he accepts our true self. The songwriter is right in saying, "Just as I am, Thou wilt receive / Wilt welcome, pardon, cleanse, relieve / because thy promise I believe / O Lamb of God, I come, I come!"[2]

Many Old Testament passages also speak of thirsting after God as one thirsts for water. Psalm 42:1 says, "As the deer longs for streams of water, so I long for you, O God." Isaiah 55:1 asks, "Is anyone thirsty? Come and drink—even if you have no money! Come, take your choice of wine or milk—it's all free!" Zechariah

13:1 directs, "On that day a fountain will be opened for the dynasty of David and for the people of Jerusalem, a fountain to cleanse them from all their sins and impurity." In Psalm 36:9 God is called the fountain of life, and in Jeremiah 17:13 the fountain of living water.

These scriptural references draw us irresistibly to Ezekiel's vision of the river from the temple, where he saw water flowing from the throne of God. Here the water illustrates God's grace like a stream that grows and grows and grows until it transforms everything, no matter how lifeless or corrupt it may be. What is so amazing about this vision is that when I reflect on it, I am amazed that from the center of my shallow tidal soul I stand on the banks of a deeper, more intimate, more intense experience with God. I have immediate access to the vast oceans of God's presence challenging me to grow in him.

But sadly, many see the river flowing by but fear getting too close. They fear getting into the stream, for they are afraid that God may require more of them than they are willing to give. Much like Elijah's contemporaries (1 Kings 18:21), they stand "wavering between two opinions." They also may be described as like the scribe in Mark 12:34 who was, "not far from the Kingdom of God." These are people who stand at a distance from God and do not enter into the more intimate life of the Spirit. They hear the Word but do not ask; they feel the emptiness but do not seek; they see the door but do not knock. They remain on the outer fringes because they will not yield themselves to Christ in heart and life. They, in essence, are afraid of getting in over their heads.

The temple narrative begins in Ezekiel 47:1:

In my vision, the man brought me back to the entrance of the Temple. There I saw a stream flowing east from beneath the door of the Temple and passing to the right of the altar on its south side. The man brought me outside the wall through the north gateway and led me around to the eastern entrance. There I could see the water flowing out through the south side of the east gateway.

Measuring as he went, he took me along the stream for 1,750 feet and then led me across. The water was up to my ankles. He measured off another 1,750 feet and led me across again. This time the water was up to my knees. After another 1,750 feet, it was up to my waist. Then he measured another 1,750 feet, and the river was too deep to walk across. It was deep enough to swim in, but too deep to walk through. (Ezekiel 47:1–5)

The writer first describes the water as being ankle-deep, and then knee-deep, then up to the waist, which soon became a river that could not be crossed. I believe this signifies stages of growth and change in a believer's life. When ankle-deep, God calls for commitment. Knee-deep is a call for surrender. Waist-deep is a call for emptying of self. And when the water is deep enough to swim in but too deep to walk through, I think of the many times we feel we can't make it in life. We are overwhelmed and can't see our way out of our troubles. It feels like we are in over our heads. It is at this point that God is calling us to yield to his filling.

How many of you have stood on the banks and thought, "I just can't make it": sickness, job, lack of money, children out of control, problems with a spouse? The reason it causes us to worry is it's the biggest pond we've seen and we can't swim across it. However, it may be that we are not to cross it, but rather to be immersed in it. God wants us to follow him into the deep, to dive into the depths of the river where we can be alone with him—away from the surface noise, away from the trash, or the boats that might carry us across, but deeper into his presence.

We need not fear going deeper, because God promises, "When you go through deep waters, I will be with you" (Isaiah 43:2a). In Exodus 12:37, after 430 years of captivity, Moses along with "the people of Israel left [Egypt] and started for Succoth. There were about 600,000 men, plus all the women and children." Following God's instructions, they traveled toward the sea, with Pharaoh and his armies in hot pursuit. The Israelites soon find themselves between a rock and a hard place—the Red Sea in front and Pharaoh's men, horses, and chariots coming up behind. The Israelites grumbled and complained, as there seemed to be no apparent way of escape. However, God, true to his word, opened up a dry path through the sea and each one arrived safely.

When you find yourself caught in a problem and see no way out, don't panic: God is there and he will open up a way out of "no way." Forty years later, Joshua and the Israelites "arrived at the banks of the Jordan River where they camped before crossing" (Joshua 3:1). There the writer tells us:

It was the harvest season, and the Jordan was overflowing its banks. But as soon as the feet of the priests who were carrying the Ark touched the water at the river's edge, the water above that point began backing up a great distance away at a town called Adam, which is near Zarethan. And the water below that point flowed into the Dead Sea until the riverbed was dry. Then all the people crossed over near the town of Jericho. (vv. 15–16)

God had parted the waters of the Red Sea to let the people out of Egypt, and here he parted the waters of the Jordan River to let

228   A Wonder-Filled Life

them out of Canaan. These miracles showed that God is faithful. God keeps his promises.

For Ezekiel, God's promise was realized as the people of Israel had turned from God and the Lord departed the temple. But now, in fulfillment of his promise of restoration, God's return to the throne signals the prophecy of that redeeming power which Jesus Christ would introduce to the world. In chapter 43 the writer describes the Lord's return to take his rightful place on the throne in his temple:

> After this, the man brought me back around to the east gateway. Suddenly, the glory of the God of Israel appeared from the east. The sound of his coming was like the roar of rushing waters, and the whole landscape shone with his glory. (vv. 1–2)

Here the writer gives us insight into God's promise for the future. His return to the temple portends the blessings reserved for the restored remnant, the time when God's name will be glorified and he will live among his people forever. Now that he has resumed his rightful place on the throne, a fountain stream issues from under the temple altar. Its waters rise from the temple rock and deepen as it flows, becoming a river that would irrigate and revitalize whatever is barren in the land.

In pausing for a moment to comprehend this vision, we find a most significant discovery: Jesus Christ is the divine source of the river. We recall he said to the Samaritan woman, "If you only knew the gift God has for you and who I am, you would ask me, and I would give you living water" (John 4:10). With that in mind, allow me to make three important points concerning this wonderful river.

1. *The river's source is from the throne of God.* The Holy Spirit, like this river, came directly from the Father's throne. The

writer says, "There I saw a stream flowing eastward from beneath the Temple threshold." The stream emanated from the very dwelling place of God. The river of life has its source in the divine, in God himself, in his Fatherly yearning, in his boundless pity, in his redeeming purpose, in his infinite mercy, from his unyielding love, from his bounteous grace. The heavens pour down the rains which feed the springs, which grow the food which sustains life and make the rivers of the earth. But from the clouds, from one whom "the heaven of heavens cannot contain," comes that River of Life which a sinful, despairing, hopeless world is waiting to receive.

2. *The next thing to note about this river is its course—it came from the altar, the place where the sacrifice was made.* The Water of Life, the precious Holy Spirit John talked about, comes directly from the altar of Christ's sacrifice, the cross. In Matthew 20:28 Jesus says: "For even the Son of Man came here not to be served but to serve others, and to give his life as a ransom for many." The Holy Spirit came only after the death of Jesus on the cross, "But in fact, it is best for you that I go away, because if I don't, the Advocate won't come. If I do go away, then I will send him to you" (John 16:7). Thus, the truth of God in the gospel of Jesus Christ includes the truth we most want to know concerning ourselves—our nature, our character, our position before God. It also includes the truth we most want to know concerning God—his character and disposition, his purpose of mercy, his supreme act of self-denying love, his overtures of grace and his summons to eternal life.

3. *The third truth of this wonderful river is its sovereign virtues: healing and cleansing.*

230   A Wonder-Filled Life

> There will be swarms of living things wherever the water of this river flows. Fish will abound in the Dead Sea, for its waters will become fresh. Life will flourish wherever this water flows. Fishermen will stand along the shores of the Dead Sea. All the way from En-gedi to En-eglaim, the shores will be covered with nets drying in the sun. Fish of every kind will fill the Dead Sea, just as they fill the Mediterranean. But the marshes and swamps will not be purified; they will still be salty. Fruit trees of all kinds will grow along both sides of the river. The leaves of these trees will never turn brown and fall, and there will always be fruit on their branches. There will be a new crop every month, for they are watered by the river flowing from the Temple. The fruit will be for food and the leaves for healing. (Ezekiel 47:9–12)

The stream that bursts from the temple is to flow through the dry ravines of the eastern wilderness until it reaches the Dead Sea, water so salty that nothing can live in it. And yet these desolate waters will be miraculously healed by the coming of the divine waters. The Dead Sea here represents the world in its sin, or that portion of mankind—men, women, and children—who feel themselves so sunken, worthless, despairing, unwanted, and unloved. These waters have the power to transform us no matter how lifeless or corrupt we may be, even when we feel messed up and beyond hope.

Please take note that these temple waters were not confined to the bracing heights of Jerusalem. They could not contain themselves in those upland regions; they could not remain shut up in the sacred enclosure. They were not just for the rich, the strong, the mighty, the powerful, but were destined to flow out for the good of all the people.

Jesus Christ did not intend to reserve his rich gifts for a few saintly souls already safely gathered into a church. He had no satisfaction in giving his life just to save a few. His grace was chiefly given for those who hunger and thirst and long for his presence. His gifts are for the world mired in sin and desolation. Thus his gathering flood cannot rest until it finds the level of the Dead Sea. The living water Jesus offers is the source of new life. It revives and sustains. It finds men, and women, and children in spiritual death, and imparts a new life of hope and peace and joy. Peoples who seemed wholly lost to self-righteousness are regained. Homes that appeared hopelessly darkened with sin and shame are made light with beams of truth and grace. Hearts that were desolate and deathful are filled with indescribable joy and immortal hope. Lives that were hardened, and rebellious, and living for self are renewed by a sovereign grace. Everything lives where this blessed river flows, for it is the one great cleansing power of all mankind. Once a small stream, it is now a broad deep river that nothing or no one can alter, waters of which are inexhaustibly full with kindness nothing can measure. It has come down these many centuries, it has girdled the whole earth, and it will flow on and on until all people from all nations have been renewed. Did God not promise restoration centuries ago through his prophet Joel?

> Then, after doing all those things, I will pour out my Spirit upon all people. Your sons and daughters will prophesy. Your old men will dream dreams, and your young men will see visions. In those days I will pour out my Spirit even on servants—men and women alike. And I will cause wonders in the heavens and on the earth—blood and fire and columns of smoke. The sun will become dark, and the moon will turn blood red before that great and terrible day of the Lord arrives. But everyone who calls on the name of the

Lord will be saved, for some on Mount Zion in Jerusalem will escape, just as the Lord has said. (Joel 2:28–32)

We are talking about a life-giving Spirit that has the power to heal us today. We are talking about the power of the Holy Spirit in your life and mine. God the Holy Spirit can heal broken hearts. He can heal broken lives. He can heal broken dreams. He is a Spirit who flows with healing power right now. He is the living water who can even heal and bring to life anything dead in you.

I challenge you to bring that which is broken to the Lord Jesus, and watch him heal it by his power! I challenge you to bring that life mired in sin and allow the Holy Spirit to bring healing to your soul and glory to your heart. I challenge you to come for cleansing beneath the flood. I challenge you to step out into the healing stream of living water. Do you not recall Jesus's words, spoken even before his time on earth in Isaiah 43:1–3?

But now, O Jacob, listen to the Lord who created you. O Israel, the one who formed you says, "Do not be afraid, for I have ransomed you. I have called you by name; you are mine. When you go through deep waters, I will be with you. When you go through rivers of difficulty, you will not drown. When you walk through the fire of oppression, you will not be burned up; the flames will not consume you. For I am the Lord, your God, the Holy One of Israel, your Savior."

The Scriptures reveal that God is faithful, that I can trust God. I am told that God does not lie and that what he promises comes to pass. It tells me that everything this river touched was transformed with its life-giving power. Notice that Ezekiel 47:9 repeats twice that everything the river touches will live! When the Spirit of God moves into your life, there will be a renewal. When God moves in, he will change things! He can take that which was dead and make it live. When you throw yourself on the mercy of the river and allow the Spirit of God to have the absolute right of way in your life, you will experience a new beginning.

In the concluding book of the Bible, John the Revelator gives the final invitation, "The Spirit and the bride say, 'Come.' Let anyone who hears this say, 'Come.' Let anyone who is thirsty come. Let anyone who desires drink freely from the water of life" (Revelation 22:17). And, finally the benediction: "Amen! Come, Lord Jesus! May the grace of the Lord Jesus be with God's holy people" (v. 20–21).

FIFTEEN

WONDER-FILLED LIFE

"For the Kingdom of God is not a matter of what we eat or drink, but of living a life of goodness and peace and joy in the Holy Spirit."

(Romans 14:17)

Recently a friend asked me, "What is your favorite Christmas movie?" At first, I was taken aback, for I had to confess that I had been to very few movie theaters before adulthood. This was not a boast, simply a resurfacing of painful childhood memories.

As previously mentioned, growing up in a Pentecostal Holiness Church, there was a pecking order of attaining righteousness by rejecting anything considered worldly. The church had a set of rules and restrictions that maintained that most worldly activities were sinful or just off-limits. At the top were smoking and drinking; however, movies ranked just below these vices, with many church members refusing to attend even something similar to *The Sound of Music*. Any music other than church music was considered an abomination, quite possibly demonic in origin. So when I was asked about my favorite movie, deep feelings of inner loss surfaced. And yet, I do have vivid memories of two movies I saw when I was a child. Rules or not, I did on occasion sever the bonds of parental control, although not without retribution.

Looking back on that particular time of my youth, I now realize that I lived my life vicariously through my sister Debbie, who was two years older than me. Debbie was the rebellious side of my emerging personality that I devoutly wished I could unleash but was too fearful of the predictable consequences. For Debbie, the expression of her will was of tantamount importance. She shrugged off the punishment she was dealt as the cost of having the experience. I admired her enormously for doing what I wanted to do. I wanted to fit in and be accepted by her because her life seemed more exciting than mine.

Admittedly, I had not bought into the church doctrine as much as I bought into my parents' discipline, but I now realize there was little difference between the two when it came to restrictions. I could not understand why we weren't allowed to do what many of my friends did. I often wanted to test my parents' rules. For me, a restriction was like a tantalizing "wet paint" sign, and I was inclined to touch it and see if it was wet. If so, I might find out what wet paint was like. Among other things, my wet paint was going to the movies, which was on our forbidden list. Nevertheless, Debbie's influence still won out over the punishment. Whenever I had the opportunity, I went along with her.

I recall the time I went to my first movie and how excited I was. One day, Debbie told me she wanted to see *Call of The Wild* with Clark Gable and Loretta Young. It was about a man who travels across Alaska during the Klondike Gold Rush and finds another Yukon-bound man, who treats his sled dogs cruelly. The man purchased a dog named Buck, who leads the way toward the gold. He finds a woman recently abandoned by her husband in the Alaskan wilderness, and the couple develops a romance. What I remember most about this picture is the beautiful huskies pulling the sleds.

I also remember vividly the night the Dixwell Avenue Community House basketball team, the Rangers, was scheduled to play a team from Bridgeport. "The CUE House," as they called it, was just down the street from our home. Debbie wanted to go to a movie with her girlfriend across the street, so they let me tag along. They only had to ask me once to see *The Adventures of Robin Hood* featuring Cornell Wilde and Olivia DeHavilland. It was a great picture about Robin Hood, who stole from the rich to give to the poor. I do not know how much I learned about benevolence that night, but I certainly learned that my sin was hard to hide. As luck would have it, when we returned home from our night on the town we never noticed that the lights were out at the CUE House. We were greeted at the door by my mother, who seemed unusually interested in the outcome of the basketball game. She asked, "How did you enjoy the game?"

Feeling quite bold, I answered, "It was very good."

Her next question was, "What was the score?" Before I could conjure up an answer she said, "Don't keep lying. The Rangers game was postponed this evening." In recalling the movie I also remember the punishment. Wet paint was all over my hands.

Paul reminds us in 1 Corinthians 6:12, "You say, 'I am allowed to do anything'—but not everything is good for you. And even though 'I am allowed to do anything,' I must not become a slave to anything." While all things may be permitted, some things aren't good for us. Since then I have learned that God does not waste a lot of time telling you, "don't smoke, don't chew, or go with girls who do." Rather, he is saying: only Christ, all of Christ, Christ alone.

I have asked God many times how to stop sinning, how to resist temptation, how to put off unholy desires. His reply was and still is: more of Christ, only Christ, Christ alone. When Christ becomes your life, what is there left to deny? If self-denial does not lead to the fullness of Christ, then it is merely an exercise.

The one serious mistake many make is emphasizing "quitting," rather than "starting"—always trying to quit this or quit that. I must confess that for much of my Christian life I too have been trying to quit those things I felt were a barrier in my devotion to Christ. As noted, this erroneous view came because of my upbringing in the church my parents attended. Later it seriously occurred to me that we do not become vibrant believers in Christ Jesus because of the things we quit, nor do we endear ourselves to God because of all we lay aside at conversion. Rather, it is what we *take up* that catches heaven's esteem. As Dr. Billy Graham said,

> Christianity is not a long list of restrictions. It flings open the windows to the real joy of living. The cosmos would have us believe that following Christ is nothing but "thou shalt not." The cosmos would have us believe that Christianity is a killjoy, a stolid kind of life, unnatural and abnormal. . . . But the evidence in the Bible is to the contrary. Christ said, "I have come that they may have life and that they may have it more abundantly" (John 10:10). And those who have been truly converted to Jesus Christ know the meaning of abundant living.[1]

This is a paradox trip for Christians. The term "paradox" is from the Greek word *paradoxon*, which means "contrary to expectations, existing beliefs, or perceived opinion." It is a statement that appears to be self-contradictory or silly but which may include a latent truth. To be sure, it is often easier to explain what a paradox is by giving examples. A paradox is often used to challenge the mind and make you think about the statement in a new way, to introduce intrigue and question common thoughts. Take the statement "Less is more." This statement uses two opposite words that contradict one another. How can less be more? The concept behind this statement is that what is less complicated is often more appreciated. Other examples of paradoxical statements are "You can save money by spending it"; "I know one thing; that I know nothing"; "This is the beginning of the end"; and, of course, "jumbo shrimp." Paradoxes play an important part in furthering our understanding of literature and everyday life.

A careful look at the Bible will reveal how much of our faith is paradoxical, and how Jesus emerges as the chief architect of this paradoxical faith. Years ago I would have been embarrassed or in fear of rejection if had I told someone I that had not been to movies because my parents thought movies were corrupting and to be shunned as other things of the world, and that therefore I had to obey my parents' restrictions. After almost sixty years of ministry, I have learned that movies and other forms of entertainment, TV, advertising, commercials, and media may be corrupting in how they are used; however, Jesus used parables and stories to introduce the spiritual blessing of the kingdom.

Unfortunately, we're often looking elsewhere for God. And yet, the fact that Jesus was God in the flesh indicates God was literally among us, with us—as he still is today.

Once there was a man who had grown weary of life. Tired to death. So one day he decided to leave his town, his ancestral village, to search for the perfect Magical City where all would be different, new, full, and rewarding. So he left. On his journey, he found himself in a forest. So he settled down for the night, took out his sack, and had a bite to eat. Before he turned in for sleep he was careful to take off his shoes and point them in the new direction toward which he was going.

However, unknown to him, while he slept a jokester came during the night and turned his shoes around. When the man awoke the next morning he carefully stepped into his shoes and continued to the Magical City. After a few days, he came to the Magical City. Not quite as large as he imagined it, however. It looked somewhat familiar. He found a familiar street, knocked at a familiar door, met a familiar family he found there and lived happily ever after.[2]

This is as good a story as any to comment on the differences between Jew and Christian. We're always looking elsewhere for God, in the Magical City in the sky. Secular spirituality is made up of the search for meaning outside of a religious institution; it considers one's relationship with the self, others, nature, and whatever else one considers to be the ultimate. Often, the goal of secular spirituality is living happily and/or helping others.

It brings to mind my favorite movie of all time, *It's A Wonderful Life*. There are countless movies that fans return to again and again at Christmastime, but *It's a Wonderful Life* is a strong contender for the most beloved holiday movie of all time. It certainly is a great movie for that time of year, but its heartwarming story provides some beautiful lessons that can be enjoyed no matter what the calendar says.

George Bailey is a salt-of-the-earth kind of guy who constantly has his dreams thwarted because he's always looking out for his friends and family. Ever since George was knee-high to a grasshopper, he's wanted to travel to exotic locales and build big things like skyscrapers and airstrips, but just when it seems he's about to get started on making his dreams come true, some crisis happens that causes him to put them on the back burner so he can take care of other people.

Things come to a head one Christmas Eve when George's absentminded uncle misplaces $8,000 of the building and loan's cash funds. Losing the money would mean bankruptcy for the Bailey Building and Loan, and criminal charges for George. At the end of his rope, George decides to commit suicide so his family can cash his $15,000 life insurance policy and pay off the $8,000 debt. Just before George leaps from a bridge to his icy, watery death, his guardian angel, Clarence Odbody, jumps into the river and pretends he's drowning. George, being the big-hearted guy that he is, saves Clarence.

While they're drying off, Clarence tries to talk George out of killing himself. When George bitterly wishes that he'd never been born, Clarence sees a way to convince him not to commit suicide. Through angelic powers, Clarence shows George what his family and Bedford Falls would have been like if George Bailey had never existed. First George finds his younger brother died because George wasn't there to save him; then he envisions the quaint Bedford Falls turned into sleazy Pottersville. His mother is a bitter widow who doesn't recognize him, and people are living in slum apartments instead of the nice homes George's building and loan funded. Worst of all, George's wife is an old maid and none of their beautiful kids exist.

As you can guess, George sees the light and begs to live again. His wish granted, he runs joyously through the streets yelling "Merry Christmas!" to everybody. He arrives home to find the authorities with a warrant in hand for his arrest, but George doesn't care; he's just happy to hold and kiss his kids. His wife comes in shortly after, followed by what seems like the entire town. The townsfolk all donate enough money to save George and the building and loan; George's old childhood friend lends George $25,000; and George's war-hero brother arrives to declare George "the richest man in Bedford Falls."

George realizes what a wonderful life he has, by seeing what the world would be like without him. He never lived the adventure he thought he wanted, but he finally sees that what he has is the true meaning of life. He has a community of love, hope, and wisdom gained through life experience. He learns that despair and darkness do not have the last word, for he receives the rare grace to know the light and goodness his life has brought to other people. What I also find most interesting is among the giant pile of cash, George finds the copy of *Tom Sawyer* that Clarence carried around, with this inscription: "Dear George: Remember no man is a failure who has friends." George could not even begin to know how true and personal this was in the embodiment of Tom Sawyer's life.

In an earlier book, *Are You Jesus?*, I stated that when we seek out God in present circumstances, we more often than not find within a hidden meaning for present-day situations. The images and actions of Mark Twain's characters in his books are compelling evidence of this fact, as there is familiarity enough to our own lives for us to see ourselves, yet they are different enough for us to see new possibilities, inviting us to places beyond where we are now. Through Tom Sawyer and Huckleberry Finn, we are presented with visual images that capture the reality of a life that is compelling—a life hardly seen in the daily activity of today's world, but one promised by Jesus in the Kingdom of God. We are reminded of Jesus's words, "Let me teach you, because I am humble and gentle at heart, and you will find rest for your souls" (Matthew 11:29):

> There are many pictures of Huckleberry Finn and Tom Sawyer doing what they seem to be best at. Simply living. On the cover of his book, Huck is seen from behind standing before the stream with a large straw hat covering his head, a fishing pole in one hand slung over his shoulder, and in his other hand holding a fish he has just caught. In another portrayal he is seen lying on his right side with his right leg

bent and left leg extended, holding a fishing line in his right hand and puffing on the corn cob pipe held in his mouth, shielded from the sun by a large straw hat. Another picture finds Tom sitting down, relaxing, with his back against a very large tree holding the familiar pipe in his mouth, his straw with frayed edges lying on the ground. Still, of the many images of Huck, the one that seems to particularly capture the essence of meaning finds him lying down in a canoe floating lazily down the river, gazing peacefully up at the sky, while exhaling a puff of smoke from the pipe he is holding in his hand, and the caption reads, "Taking a rest." Once again, Mark Twain's characters open the door of recognition and illumination that often they embody unknowing similarity to understanding God's desire for us.[3]

If ever there was a visible depiction of what life would be like for one in light of God's presence the psalmist's words capture it (4:7–8): "You have given me greater joy than those who have abundant harvests of grain and new wine. In peace I will lie down and sleep, for you alone, O Lord, will keep me safe." Two kinds of joy are contrasted here—inward joy that comes from knowing and trusting God, and happiness that comes as a result of pleasant circumstances.

The actions of Huck remind me of George Gershwin's lyrics for "Summertime," from the 1935 opera *Porgy and Bess*. The lyrics are indicative of the phrase "just living" as viewed in the lives of Mark Twain's characters.

Summertime, and the livin' is easy
Fish are jumpin, and the cotton is high
Your daddy's rich, and your mamma's good lookin'
So hush little baby, don't you cry

244   A Wonder-Filled Life

One of these mornings, you're going to rise up singin'
Then you'll spread your wings And you'll take to the sky
But till that morning, there's nothing can harm you
With daddy and mamma standing by.[4]

Please do not misunderstand. I am not suggesting that because "the livin' is easy," all one does in Christ is just hang around and do nothing. On the contrary, the images manifested are to suggest that life is much different in the Kingdom of God only because one has the security of God's presence. Because the life one lives is lived by faith in Jesus, you find yourself doing the things of God naturally. As I also said in *Are You Jesus?*,

In all of Jesus's teachings, he stressed the fact that there is a standard of conduct for believers. He contrasted kingdom values (which are eternal) with worldly values (which are temporary). By contrast, the Kingdom of God is where the rejected are received, the blind see, the lame walk, the lepers are cured, the deaf hear. None were more shunned by their culture than the blind, the lame, the lepers, and the deaf. They had no place, no name, no value; they were a blight on the culture, embarrassments to society, excess baggage on the side of the road. I daresay we all know people like that. They don't have fancy clothes, aren't always clean-shaven, and don't always smell right or look right. They don't live in the big house; some do not have houses at all. And yet, when you think about it, we could be one of them, asking, "Are you Jesus?"

Some folks look down on this sort of person, shun them, reject them, and sometimes even church people walk on the other side of the street. But let me assure you, the

Kingdom of God is made up of folk like you and me, and those whom others call trash. But we are all equally treasures. In a society that has little room for second fiddles, that's good news: Jesus told John that a new kingdom was coming—a kingdom where people have value not because of what they do but because of "whose" they are. Therefore, the question is not how I feel about my neighbor, nor how I feel about my brothers and sisters; the question is how I feel about Jesus who said: "When you did it to one of the least of these my brothers and sisters, you were doing it to me."[5]

SIXTEEN

LIFE PROMISE

"So I live in this earthly body by trusting in the Son of God, who loved me and gave himself for me."

(Galatians 2:20b)

Today I am convinced that if we were to read the Bible devoid of our intellectual knowledge of God, without much of our accumulated personal baggage, we would find the Word of God more compelling, appealing, and understandable. In Jesus's prayer to his Father in Matthew 11:25, he said, "O Father, Lord of heaven and earth, thank you for hiding these things from those who think themselves wise and clever, and for revealing them to the childlike." Does Jesus not suggest that the way to a more intimate relationship with him is to be open and relate as a child and parent?

Jesus gives only two options for understanding the Word of God: "the wise and the clever," or the "childlike." Most people would exclude themselves from the former; however, if one does not approach the Scriptures as a child before a loving parent it leaves no middle ground. Understanding will not take place. I note this because the words of the Bible reflect the life of Jesus, and that when mind and spirit merge transformation takes place. Paul says: "Don't copy the behavior and customs of this world but let God transform you into a new person by changing the way you think. Then you will learn to know God's will for you, which is good and pleasing and perfect" (Romans 12:2).

Therefore, the question arises: Are we close enough to Jesus to sense his very presence? Are we close enough to Jesus that we desire to live in abundant fullness with him? Are we close enough to Jesus to feel the same attraction as the men who dropped their nets when he said, "Come follow me?" Are we close enough to Jesus to acknowledge that our life and our worth comes only from him? Are we close enough to Jesus to know his very thoughts? We are told in Philippians 2:5, "You must have the same attitude that Christ Jesus had." Jesus likewise encourages us in Matthew 6:33, "Seek the Kingdom of God above all else, and live righteously, and he will give you everything you need."

Through the Holy Spirit, we can begin to know God's thoughts, talk with him, and expect his answers to our prayers. An intimate relationship with Christ comes only from spending time consistently in his presence and his Word, and humility is the fastest way to it. However, it calls for our self-abandonment, self-surrender, and willingness to follow no matter where he leads. What God wants us to treasure is inward and spiritual. The promise of new life is the incentive for many people to follow after Jesus, which is a noble aspiration, a good thing. However, there is a higher motivation and greater compulsion that should propel the cadence of one's steps, keeping Jesus in close sight.

We follow after Jesus because we love him, but what is the most compelling reason of all is the fact that he first loved us. Jesus's death on the cross is the greatest expression of the love of God known to mankind. Consequently, God's love, the source of all human love, is the highest purpose of all. It spreads like fire when kindled in our hearts by the Holy Spirit. But be forewarned, you won't understand love, you won't know how to love, you can't fully receive love, until you surrender to the fact that God loves you (unconditionally), warts and all. When you surrender to God's love, you realize all your worth and that everything now comes from God. You are no longer your own. Paul confirms this in 1 Corinthians 6:19–20: "Don't you realize that your body is the temple of the Holy Spirit, who lives in you and was given to you by God? You do not belong to yourself, for God bought you with a high price. So you must honor God with your body."

One would likely question, what do the Scriptures mean when they say that our body belongs to God? Many people are heard to say that they have the right to do whatever they want with their bodies. Although they think that this is freedom, they are saying, "I am enslaved to my desires. My sinful nature is still in control of my body." However, when we become Christians, the Holy Spirit comes to live in us; therefore, we no longer own our bodies. That God bought us "with a high price" refers at that time to slaves purchased at auction.

Although Christ's death freed us from sin, it also obligates us to his service. If you live in a building owned by someone else, you must not violate building rules. Hence, because your body belongs to God, you must not violate his standards for living. The one sure way to adhere to God's building rules, Paul testifies, is to "live in this earthly body by trusting in the Son of God, who loved me and gave himself for me" (Galatians 2:20b). Every day we ask God in prayer, "Your will be done," and often when it comes to the doing we have so much difficulty. What we must still do, as we first did, is say "Lord, I am yours; hope is in my heart." This is what we said to become Christians, and what we must still say to demonstrate our faith.

Be assured that God has good, pleasing, and perfect plans for his children. He wants us to live fulfilled lives as transformed people with renewed minds, desiring to honor and obey him. Because of what Christ has done for us, we are urged to give ourselves as living sacrifices to him. When I meet someone today and they ask, "How are you doing?," I simply reply, "I am living!" My response to the question is not to avoid it, nor is it to suggest that I am hiding a physical or mental disability, nor that I am not sure how to answer it. What I mean to say is that I am living a full rich and satisfying life in Christ in the Kingdom of God.

The very thought of living by faith in Jesus Christ in our frail mortal bodies is hard for many people to process or envision. When I say "I am living," sometimes I get a blank stare or complete silence, or they quickly move on to another subject. At times someone may ask, "What does that mean?" I know it is difficult to understand in this dead and dying world how a person today could be so focused on Christ that every thought, every motivation, and every decision is done in faith. The answer is to let our ordinary senses bring us to the discovery that we no longer have confidence in our abilities to handle difficulties and problems under stress, but have trust in God's power in our lives over every circumstance.

My most recent incident of living by faith in Jesus came suddenly on the morning of Saturday, August 11, 2018, when I sat at my computer screen and just stared, without knowing how to command a simple operation. Mouse in hand, my mind was blank. I realized something was wrong and I did not know how to shut the computer down. I went into my bedroom and lay down on my bed for a few moments, but soon got up because I knew something sinister was happening to me and I had to do something. I grabbed the phone to call my daughter, who lived the next street over, and mumbled some words about how I was feeling. She later told me that the only thing she heard was "hospital," so she came right over while my granddaughter called 911. She found me sitting on the front steps near the door waiting for help, slurring incoherent and unintelligible words. It seemed like an interminable amount of time for the ambulance to arrive, and when the EMTs asked me my name I could only respond with faltering words. It was then I realized I was in the midst of a stroke.

The ambulance headed for Westerly Hospital, but en route was informed that Westerly Hospital did not handle strokes. They gave me the choice of South County Hospital in Rhode Island or L&M Hospital in New London, Connecticut. I chose South County, which was nearer, and when I arrived I lay in the emergency room for a while until a doctor came up and asked me a few questions. A nurse tried to see if I could swallow water, which I failed to do; and the doctor decided to send me to RI Hospital in Providence, where they handled stroke patients.

I arrived at the RI Hospital emergency room about 5:30 in the afternoon, and finally got a bed in the stroke unit about 10:30 at night. The first thing I noticed was that the room was large and had a picture window overlooking Interstate 95. The room was clean and well lit. The nurses were waiting and attended to me, and everything about my admittance went very smoothly. The doctors had already ruled out that it was too late for any intervention for early prevention of the stroke, so the next morning they sent a nurse in with some water and applesauce to see if I could swallow; this time it was successful.

By the grace of God, a day later I started to write words on a pad, and the next day my writing on the pad became understandable. From there, I graduated to verbally making intelligible words and phrases. Since I had been exercising for years, the doctors found that my physical body was not otherwise harmed; they ruled out rehab and decided to release me four days later.

At 6:00 the night before my release, the nurse came in and told me I was being transferred because they needed my room. To say the least, I was very disappointed to leave the room, especially with the hope of leaving the next morning. As I was transported through the long corridors, to an elevator that took me to the ninth floor of another building, worry started to build up as to where I would end up. I had a feeling that I would not like the room they were taking me to, which caused me great anxiety.

When I arrived at the room on the ninth floor of the older building, my heart sank. The room was so different. It was like a shock to my senses and immediately caused depression. I almost felt like it was punishment for my leaving the hospital so soon. There were two beds in the room, and I was stationed at the door which was very large and heavy. The room was poorly lit, with most light coming from the corridor.

I now understand that there was nothing wrong with the room—it was clean, well-attended, and the nurses and attendants were very nice—but at that moment my perception would allow only negative thoughts. I just wanted to be out of there, so I lay awake most of the night. When daybreak came, my thought was that I made it through the night. Just as the doctors had planned, they came to my room about 7:00 a.m. and told me I would be discharged that day, but the specter of that lone night in that room still lingers with me.

On February 20, 2020, I went to the Westerly Hospital emergency room complaining of constant coughing, shortness of breath, and general weakness. In my mind, I was sure that dehydration was the problem, as I had I struggled with it many times in frequent visits to the ER since being first diagnosed with congestive heart failure in 2018, and in early 2019 it was confirmed that I had a leaky valve in the heart. This time I was admitted to the hospital for observation, and various tests showed that my condition was serious. At this point, my cardiologist recommended I be sent to

Beth Israel Deaconess Medical Center (BIDMC) in Boston for a complete workup with the thought that a surgical procedure could be done to repair the leaky heart valve.

To say the least, I balked at the idea. Admittedly I was tired of hospitals and doctors, but my real concern was that this time I would not return from Boston. I thought of all the unfinished work I had: my radio program; my 165 subscribers to my monthly newsletter; and the fact I had just started working on my tenth book, about the life I now live in the body. I must confess that as all of these thoughts came to mind, I shed tears and told my daughter I was not going to Boston. And then to make matters worse, the scene of the ninth-floor room at RI Hospital kept coming to my mind. And yet, I was convinced I had to go because of my cardiologist's insistence that it was a necessary step in my recovery.

Thus, at 7:00 I left Westerly Hospital by ambulance in driving rain, with my anxiety growing by the mile until we arrived at BIDMC around 9:30 in the evening. My fear and trepidation only increased when I arrived at my room and found it was a two-bed room, similar to my room on the ninth floor, and again I was in the bed near the door. I cannot describe the next moments as the EMTs delivered me to my room at BIDMC. My fear and anxiety were growing and I wanted to escape that hospital, all the while knowing there was no escape. I felt as if I was in prison. Once again I started weeping.

At the moment I was prepared to lie awake until the light of day, but amidst my fear and apprehension, I heard the soft voice of the Holy Spirit, reminding me of a promise from God I received in 2001 when I decided to quit the ministry because of surgery for lumbar stenosis, which left me with great pain and barely able to walk. I quote from my earlier book, *Can These Bones Live?*:

> Confirmation came on the morning of Sunday, February 25, 2001. That morning I had scheduled a child

dedication for my granddaughter Charity, who was then four months old. My son Wesley and his wife Vanessa had selected a young Christian couple from Riverside, Rhode Island to be the godparents. I met Jerry and Jan Bradley that morning for the first time when they arrived at church for the dedication. During the ceremony, Charity's face was angelic. She was quietly serene in her beautiful white dress with ruffled bottom, and a bit of lace adorning. It was almost as if we were a bother to her. She hardly whimpered when I held her and offered a prayer of dedication to God on her behalf. My movements were carefully measured during the ceremony that morning, for just ten weeks prior on December 13, 2000, I had undergone back surgery for Lumbar Spinal Stenosis. The nerve alongside my spine was being strangled by the lime buildup of arthritis, causing back pain and severe leg cramping and making it difficult for me to walk. Because of my tenuous physical condition and the fact I was beyond retirement age, I had resigned myself to the fact I would soon have to relinquish the pastorate of Pleasant Street Baptist Church.

When I began to preach that morning I noticed Jan, Charity's godmother, was not focusing on my message but she seemed to be riveted on writing something. This caused me no real concern for we have a page in the church bulletin encouraging people to write notes on the sermon. After the worship service had concluded and the benediction was pronounced, I left the pulpit and proceeded toward my office. It was then Jan stopped me. "I have something for you," she said. My first thought was that in her feverish writing she had penned a critique of my sermon and couldn't wait for me to hear it. In her hand was a note written on a small sheet of pastel paper. She held it out to me and said, "God gave me something to give to you."

When my eyes fell upon the words, tears began to flow making it difficult for me to see well enough to read the rest of what she had written: The note read, "*I have heard your cries. I woke you up many times in the middle of the night. Many times you have tried to quit but I have stopped you. You're not too old. I will strengthen you. I have given you eyes to see beyond what others can see. Take care of the children. You will finish the course.*" For three years I carried this note in my Bible. I wanted it to always be close to me. However, early this year I discovered it was gone. I sat and cried, feeling a great loss because I often looked at it when I was feeling low or uncertain as to my future ministry at Pleasant Street. Though it is gone, most of it I still carry in my heart. It was God's promise to me. How often I am reminded of the words of Martin Luther in that great hymn, "A Mighty Fortress Is Our God": "Did we in our own strength confide, our striving would be losing. Were not the right man on our side. The man of God's own choosing. Dost ask who that may be? Christ Jesus, it is He." Pleasant Street Baptist Church today has a glory all its own. After all, what greater glory could there possibly be than to hear Jesus say, "*Well done, my good and faithful servant*" (Matthew 25:21, 23).[1]

Lying in that hospital bed amidst my fear and apprehension, I heard the words, "You will finish the course." I did not know what the course was that God had prepared for me, and I did not need to know any more. If God said it, I believed his word, and a peace settled over me as the Scriptures say: "Then you will experience God's peace, which exceeds anything we can understand. His peace will guard your hearts and minds as you live in Christ Jesus" (Philippians 4:7).

Nevertheless, it leaves one to wonder how a man that has taught and preached about Jesus's birth, death, and resurrection for more than fifty years would go through such pain and trial in the hospital. Why did he not look to God in his moment of need? Was it the fear of death? Surely it wasn't the fear of death, for that had been settled in the epilogue of my memoir. Was it the fact he left so much unfinished work behind, or was it simply he had forgotten to acknowledge God's presence with him in the past? Did Jesus not say in John 14:1, "Don't let your hearts be troubled. Trust in God, and trust also in me"?

What I now realize is that in the past, when I prayed to God or when he simply showed up because there was a need, it was on behalf of someone else. This time was deeply personal. It was about me, and I needed to hear from God on my behalf. However, I relied on my strength and failed to trust God for the answer.

In 1981 I was called to Pleasant Street Baptist Church as associate pastor, and when pastor Rev. Harold Lambe was called to another church in 1986 the pulpit committee asked me to consider becoming their pastor. I knew that God would not allow me to do otherwise, so on September 28, 1986, I was installed as pastor of Pleasant Street Baptist Church. Shortly after my installation, I heard a voice confirming this was the place God would have me. At that point, I thought my journey as pastor and people would be pretty smooth. I had been in the church the past five years and people had plenty of time to observe me. How wrong I was. My shift in leadership now put me in conflict because people now saw me as one who was hired to do a job for them. They challenged my leadership and confronted me as to who indeed was the head of the church. Was it me as their pastor, the trustees, or heads of long-established boards or committees?

However, we were both wrong, God is the head of the church. In my role as pastor, I needed the people of Pleasant Street to take me seriously. My first address to the congregation was to inform them they could no longer be satisfied with the status quo. I came to establish ministries, to grow the church, and the church would be vastly different both physically and spiritually. I spoke clearly and decisively. "God gave me a vision for this church ten years ago, in December of 1976, and I am here to see it fulfilled."

It was not long after that God spoke. He said to me: "I gave you a vision for your people. It is not your vision, it is mine. I did not tell you to make it happen. I did not tell you to push people around, or manipulate them, or embarrass them beat them or make them feel guilty. I did not give the vision to you or ask you to fulfill it. It is my vision and I will bring it to fruition in my time. All I asked you to do is get people to hear my voice. I will put my vision in their hearts. I will draw them to me." I fell to my knees and began to pray. I asked God for his forgiveness and for those I had wounded. I saw a picture of myself and I was convicted. God had disciplined me.

Another time in February of 1990 I attended a Bible conference at the Dallas-Fort Worth Convention Center with two specific prayers I had jotted down and brought with me from Westerly. Lately I had been feeling a greater need for prayer, more so than ever before. I wanted to understand how to lead my people to greater intimacy with the Lord. I wanted to know how to help them grow stronger, so I asked God to provide me with a prayer partner during my time at the conference. My other request was for direction and insight into the vision for the people at Pleasant Street.

After arriving at my hotel and unpacking, I decided to go down-stairs to have dinner. I was feeling a bit lonely and apprehensive about the proceedings the next morning. I didn't know anyone at the hotel, so I sat over near the low rail, which afforded me a view of people who were checking into the hotel. I was soon roused from my reverie by the sight of two men who entered the dining area and seated themselves at a table far across the room. They had barely sat down when they looked my way. They sat for what seemed like only a moment, then both men got up from the table carrying their trays, and before I realized it they were standing in front of me with trays in hand. One of the men asked, "Are you alone?"

"Yes," I answered with some reluctance.

"May we sit down?" he asked. After preliminary greetings, the next words spoken by one of the men caused my eyes to well up with tears and my heart to leap with joy, for I knew God had heard my prayers. The man said, "We have been praying since we left home that God would provide us with a prayer partner when we arrived here. Would you like to pray with us?" After our meeting, we met each morning from 5:30 a.m. until 6:30 a.m. My two new Christian friends and I spent much time on our knees in the pres-ence of the Lord, seeking his will for our lives. My first request had been answered, and it was a harbinger of more. How like God! And he was not finished yet.

Friday night marked the end of the conference, and all of the conferees had been warned to be in their seats before 7 p.m. or they would have difficulty finding places. That night the Dallas Convention Center was filled to near capacity, so I was pleased to find a vacant seat in the third row, far to the right of the stage. After sitting and waiting for about twenty minutes, I was feeling quite alone because I had missed my two prayer partners. I happened to glance down in front, and I noticed a bit of commotion as a woman in the first row was holding a folded piece of white paper in her hand. She turned and motioned to the woman behind her and leaned back, whispering something to her. Then she placed the paper in the woman's hand. I turned away for a moment, trying to appear disinterested, until I heard the words, "This is for him." I was unaware of who "him" was until the woman now holding the paper reached behind and held the paper out for me to take it. I heard myself ask, "For me? Are you sure?"

I was mystified, for I didn't see who gave the note to the woman in the first row. I took the paper from the woman, still believing a mistake had been made. However, the moment my eyes fell upon the few words contained within, I knew it was for me. Once again it was an answer from God, simple and to the point: "I have heard your prayers for your people, and you will have an answer." Once more, I experienced God's presence in my life, promising he would supply the necessary direction in his time.

Consequently, I can recall many other times that God had been faithful in my life and ministry, but when it came to my trusting him for myself in that hospital I had failed. But now, given another chance, I have learned to trust in God's promise. On May 9, 2021, Mother's Day, I was back in the Westerly Hospital emergency room for severe weakness and shortness of breath, which had been progressing for the last three days. To say the least, I wanted to ride it out, but my two daughters threatened to carry me bodily to the hospital so I went reluctantly. Tests and examination found that my heart rate was in the range of about 33. The doctors thought a newly prescribed medicine was the culprit, or that I needed a pacemaker. They insisted I be taken to the hospital in New London, which specialized in inserting the pacemaker if needed. But first I was in CCU for twenty-four hours to monitor my heart rate, as the suspected medicine got out of my system. This time, since again I had little choice in the decision, I simply said, "I'll go, because God told me I will finish the course."

Admittedly, I do not know what God has in mind. I do not know the course he has set out for me. I do not know when or how I will finish the race, but I do know I will finish the course, for I know who holds me in his hands. I will cross the finish line, for he who is faithful has promised. That is all I need to know because "It is no longer I who live, but Christ lives in me. So I live in this earthly body by trusting in the Son of God, who loved me and gave himself for me" (Galatians 2:20b).

SEVENTEEN

LIVING FAITH

"You love him even though you have never seen him. Though you do not see him now, you trust him; and you rejoice with glorious, inexpressible joy. The reward for trusting him will be the salvation of your souls."

(1 Peter 1:8–9)

"But when the Son of Man returns, how many will he find on the earth who have faith?" That is the question Jesus poses in Luke 18:8, and the question still holds relevance for us today. What will be the true account of our faith when Jesus returns to the earth? What is the true account of our faith today? I would suppose that Jesus asked the question because there is always a danger of our faith diminishing during trial and anxiety and uncertainty.

Hardly anyone today would deny the fact that our faith is being challenged as severely today as ever, amidst the advent of COVID-19. The question that we now ask ourselves is, do we face the future with hearts filled with fear, or do we face the future with a heart full of faith in the goodness of God, and trust that God will enable us by his presence to meet life victoriously?

Often I have been approached by people who are genuinely concerned, and conversely others who have determined that there is a lack in their faith because God has failed to act on their behalf. What kind of answers must I give to those struggling in their faith? First, it may be necessary to determine what Jesus meant when he asked, "how many will he find on the earth who have faith?" I believe it is clear what he is not asking: When the Son of Man comes will he find what faith produces—how many cars, how big a house, how many people prayed, how many healings? No! He is asking whether, when he returns, will he find someone still believing no matter the circumstance?

When President Franklin D. Roosevelt gave his first inaugural address on March 4, 1933, with the nation reeling amid a great worldwide depression, he said, "Let me assert my firm belief that the only thing we have to fear is fear itself." When people forget God, they either tremble in fear as they face the future or they are strongly tempted to make a flight from danger, which takes them away from the place of duty, responsibility, and opportunity.

Time will not allow us to explore the many aspects of faith, so I will proceed on the premise that we are exploring faith in a personal God, maker, and owner of the universe—who in the far distant past, in the mystery of his infinite power and wisdom, determined to send his Son, the Lord Jesus Christ, into this world to die for our sin. This is the starting point for all faith. It begins with Jesus Christ. However, what is of utmost importance to us is how to exercise faith so that God's work is not frustrating. When faith works it is always supernatural, for when you have faith God works. Faith, above all spiritual graces, causes God to intervene in

Living Faith   263

a situation and produce, so faith comes directly out of the heart of God.

The writer of Hebrews 11:1 asserts that "Faith shows the reality of what we hope for; it is the evidence of things we cannot see." Therefore he adds in verse 6, "it is impossible to please God without faith. Anyone who wants to come to him must believe that God exists and that he rewards those who sincerely seek him." Faith means that we no longer have confidence in our abilities but now confess confidence in God's power in our lives over every circumstance. But we must ask: How do we keep vitality in our faith and calling? How do we keep love alive when the crying times and the celebrations of our lives often come together? Staying alive in a living faith is a matter of keeping our focus on Christ at the center.

Many words have been spoken, and much has been written about faith. And yet many fail to understand the what and how of faith. See if any of these questions sound familiar: Is faith really important? If I have faith, can I get what I want? What about the healings and miracles in the Bible that are connected with faith? How did they work? Do some people have more faith than others? What does it mean to live by faith? How can I believe in something I cannot see?

For people who might be pondering the same questions, let us look at the words of Jesus found in John 20. After his resurrection, Jesus made an appearance to his disciples; however, one of the disciples, Thomas, was not present. When told of Jesus's appearance Thomas spoke out in unbelief: "I won't believe it unless I see the nail wounds in his hands, put my fingers into them, and place my hand into the wound in his side" (v. 25). Jesus's resurrection was hard to believe. Indeed, it was a supernatural event outside the realm of human experience, and like many people today, Thomas had trouble believing what he could not see.

Then he said to Thomas, "Put your finger here, and look at my hands. Put your hand into the wound on my side. Don't be faithless any longer. Believe!"

"My Lord and my God!" Thomas exclaimed.

Then Jesus told him: "You believe because you have seen me. Blessed are those who believe without seeing me." (vv. 27–29)

Jesus's statement could be understood to mean, "faith is opening our eyes to God"—or simply put, "faith is seeing God."

In his book *The Knowledge of the Holy*, A. W. Tozer writes, "That our idea of God corresponds as nearly as possible to the true being of God is of immense importance to us." He goes on to say,

The low view of God entertained almost universally among Christians is a cause of a hundred lesser evils everywhere among us. A whole new philosophy of the Christian life has resulted from this one basic error in our religious thinking. For this reason, the gravest question before the church is always God himself, and the most portentous fact about any man is not what he at a given time may say or do but what deep in his heart he conceives God to be like. Left to ourselves we tend immediately to reduce God to manageable terms. We want to get him where we can use him, or at least know where he is when we need him. We want a God we can in some measure control.[1]

If Tozer is right, and I believe he is, then much of our modern theology has robbed our concept of God of the infinite, taken away his sovereignty, and reduced him to a mere replica of ourselves. If what we conceive God to be he is not, how can we rightly

Living Faith   265

think of him? If he indeed is incomprehensible and unapproachable, as Paul says he is, how can we as Christians satisfy a longing after him? And how shall we be held accountable to know what cannot be known?

The answer of the Bible is simply, "through Jesus Christ our Lord." In Christ and by Christ God effects complete self-disclosure, as he shows himself not to reason or intellect but to faith and love. Through the incarnation and the atonement, he reconciles us to himself, and by faith and love we enter in and lay hold on him. So many people are trying to find healing under the guise of everything else that they've missed the healer. So many are trying to get well that they can't find how to lay hold on Jesus. So many are demanding answers rather than being open to the only answer. Though we don't understand, we need to trust the Lord like little children.

Did you ever think some folk are going to die not because of sin but because they want to hold onto this life at any cost? There is a story of one of the great saints of Scotland, Billy Brae, who had hardly known a sick day in his life. Billy spent his entire life preaching and making many converts to the faith. One day Billy got sick and was near death, and as he lay on his deathbed someone asked, "Billy how sick are you?" Billy, in his weakened condition looked up at the man and said, "Oh glory, praise the Lord, I feel like I'm gone to heaven today, and don't you know God said, 'Billy, I ain't ready for you yet.'"[2]

I don't know why some get healed and some don't, but I do know God's got a purpose. I'm going to preach the truth and the whole truth so you can be set free: Don't let anyone condemn you. Don't let anyone lay a guilt trip on you. And don't let anyone tell you that you lack faith. It's right to testify of God's goodness when there's healing and it's right to testify of God's goodness when we can see no healing. Therefore, I know better what Paul means in 1 Thessalonians 5:18, "Be thankful in all circumstances, for this is God's will for you who belong to Christ Jesus." Beloved, this is the key phrase "God's will for you who belong to Christ Jesus." God is sovereign.

I have been often asked by one who is grieving for a loved one, "Why did God let them die?"; or if one is sick or suffering, "Why did this happen to me?" For some, a feeling of guilt is raised when one is prayed for and there is no immediate evidence of a cure. The assumption underlying these and similar cases is that either we failed God, he failed to answer because of some sin, or we needed more faith on our part, otherwise the results would have been quite different. How many would admit to this?

I have a great concern for some of the theology which is being expounded today, as rather than helping those in need it tends to heap condemnation and guilt upon them, heightening their despair rather than lessening it. What is so deceptive about it is there is always a measure of truth in the teaching, and most people who recognize this truth will also accept that which clings to it. For example, prosperity teaching suggests that any person who has enough faith can be certain of good health and riches, and if one is sick and has not received healing or achieved substantial riches then the simple answer is that faith is lacking. Is this true? Is the answer that we are, for the most part, people of inadequate faith? Do our efforts to faith control our healing?

I believe it is time we deal with the whole truth—to get the guilt and condemnation off ourselves and place it where it belongs, that is with Satan. Those comfortable in their belief may not like what I'm about to say. On the other hand, some of you will be happy, for the truth will set you free. As I look at the prospect of faith in sickness and disease, the basis of my contention is that the answer for all of life is found in the sovereignty of God through the

Living Faith   267

Lord Jesus Christ. It's not your faith that determines your healing; it's not how spiritual you are. It's determined by God's will and purpose for you.

Earlier I mentioned the Scripture passage in Hebrews 11:6, from what is called "the faith chapter." From the very first verse, it gives a roll call of heroes and great deliverances of faith. We read it and get happy about it, and why not? Let me share just a few verses:

> It was by faith that Abel brought a more acceptable offering to God than Cain did. Abel's offering gave evidence that he was a righteous man, and God showed his approval of his gifts. Although Abel is long dead, he still speaks to us by his example of faith.

> It was by faith that Enoch was taken up to heaven without dying—"he disappeared because God took him." For before he was taken up, he was known as a person who pleased God. And it is impossible to please God without faith. Anyone who wants to come to him must believe that God exists and that he rewards those who sincerely seek him.

> It was by faith that Noah built a large boat to save his family from the flood. He obeyed God, who warned him about things that had never happened before. By his faith, Noah condemned the rest of the world, and he received the righteousness that comes by faith.

> It was by faith that Abraham obeyed when God called him to leave home and go to another land that God would give him as his inheritance. He went without knowing where he was going. And even when he reached the land God promised him, he lived there by faith—for he was like a

foreigner, living in tents. And so did Isaac and Jacob, who inherited the same promise. Abraham was confidently looking forward to a city with eternal foundations, a city designed and built by God. (vv. 4–10)

Surely, verses 4 through 12 make you want to shout. They make you want to praise the Lord—that's faith, great faith. But don't stop there; read on. Read the whole truth about great faith. In verses 36–39 not all the heroes of faith experienced immediate or even earthly triumph over their circumstances. Why didn't they receive it? The text says "All these people earned a good reputation because of their faith, yet none of them received all that God had promised" (v. 40). The fulfillment of their faith was to come in Christ Jesus. Paul says in 2 Corinthians 12:7–9,

I was given a thorn in my flesh, a messenger from Satan to torment me and keep me from becoming proud. Three different times I begged the Lord to take it away. Each time he said, "My grace is all you need. My power works best in weakness."

Paul had a thorn in the flesh. He asked God to remove it, and God said no. Angels opened the prison doors for Peter (Acts 12:5–11); but at the end of his life, they did not open the prison doors for Paul. The only reason Paul didn't die in prison was that they took him outside and cut off his head. Why? Because he didn't have enough faith? I hardly think so. God didn't heal all in Hebrews 11. They all pleased God through faith, yet all did not receive all that was promised. God planned to perfect us in Christ Jesus.

You ought not to be asking "Why me?" You ought not to be asking, "Why did God let my loved one die?" You're not to be deceived into thinking, "I've done something wrong," and you ought not to question God's will to heal you. You need to know Revelation 12:11: "they did not love their lives so much that they were afraid to die." There is no victory apart from that won at Calvary, by the blood of the Lamb.

A lot of folk are focused on self. When you hear an adverse diagnosis, the first thing that comes up is fear. Do you ask, "Why me?" You begin to fret, you begin to worry, you don't know what to do. I believe Paul supplies the answer: he had released his life to Christ saying, "My old self has been crucified with Christ. It is no longer I who live, but Christ lives in me. So I live in this earthly body by trusting in the Son of God, who loved me and gave himself for me" (Galatians 2:20). Since I am already crucified with Christ, no matter what happens to me I live, yet not I but Christ lives in me.

You want to know what to do about healing, you want to know how to endure suffering, you want to know how to handle sickness. Hebrews 12:2 gives us the answer: "Fix your eyes on Jesus, the author, and perfecter of our faith." He is the divine healer. He heals by the sovereign will of God, and if you don't receive it now he has something better. All healing is under the blood of Jesus. When you are dying and lying in bed, and the devil says, "You ought not to be sick; you must've done something wrong; you shouldn't be suffering; you don't have enough faith, or God would have healed you," don't say, "Woe is me." Don't ask why, don't feel sorry for yourself. Kick those covers off, fight the sickness, fight the sin, fight the deception. Say, "Oh glory, oh glory, hallelujah. Devil, get out of my way; I'm going to heaven. I see Jesus; I'm rejoicing with him. I don't feel ill anymore. I see the healer. I'm purchased by his blood; he paid the price for my life. I trust him because he wants the best for me. You couldn't hold him; you can't hold me. You couldn't deceive him; you can't

270   A Wonder-Filled Life

deceive me. You couldn't kill him; you can't kill me. Even you must one day bow before him. He is sovereign, he is Lord, and I trust my life in his hands." The prophet Habakkuk exults:

> Even though the fig trees have no blossoms, and there are no grapes on the vines; even though the olive crop fails, and the fields lie empty and barren; even though the flocks die in the fields, and the cattle barns are empty, yet I will rejoice in the Lord! I will be joyful in the God of my salvation! (Habakkuk 3:17–18).

If the suffering does not cease, if the pain does not go away, if this old body lies down for the last time, if the shades of death are drawn about me, "yet I will rejoice in the Lord! I will be joyful in the God of my salvation!"

One of the greatest illustrations of faith in the Bible is the story of the three Hebrew boys in Daniel 3. The story, simply stated, is this: It was reported to King Nebuchadnezzar that three young Jewish boys, Shadrach, Meshach, and Abednego, had ignored a decree demanding that at any given time all men should fall down and worship a golden image that the king had set up. Nebuchadnezzar confronted the three boys with the report, along with the threat of a fiery furnace for their disobedience. The men did not deny the report, even though they knew the consequences, nor did they yield to the king's decree; and the threat was carried out. The fact that they were later miraculously delivered may not be the most important part of the story, for the climax it seems to me comes at the point where these men say,

> If we are thrown into the blazing furnace, the God whom we serve is able to save us. He will rescue us from your power, Your Majesty. But even if he doesn't, we want to make it

clear to you, Your Majesty, that we will never serve your gods or worship the gold statue you have set up. (vv. 17–18)

Let us look at this scene to learn the motivation and working of faith. The narrative reveals to us a faith that commands positive action. James tells us in his epistle (2:26), "Just as the body is dead without breath, so also faith is dead without good works." Faith that is not acted upon is not faith. There comes a time in most of our lives when our most splendid declaration of faith is made not with the lips at all but with our life. When the time came for those three young men to declare themselves, they were not asked, "What do you believe?" They were being asked, in a most concretely realistic though inaudible way, "Does your faith command your loyalty? Does your faith elicit your absolute devotion? Does your faith have any real conviction behind it?"

The three young men did not know precisely what God's will was regarding the king's threat, but they did know God's will regarding their action. Listen again to their words: "the God whom we serve is able to save us. He will rescue us from your power, Your Majesty." Our fate might be death; it might be deliverance—we'll leave that with God. But we will not alter our stand. At the center of their faith stood these words: "But even if he doesn't." It tells us that there are times when we must act under a great inner conviction—not because we are courageously unafraid of facing the consequences but because we cannot bear the thought of what our insincerity will do to that one person before whom we stand. So, "even if he doesn't, we want to make it clear to you, Your Majesty, that we will never serve your gods nor worship the gold statue you have set up."

This raises another point: if the three Hebrew boys had escaped only in mind they could have reasoned among themselves that bowing before the golden image could easily be done without mental

272   A Wonder-Filled Life

reservations, i.e., "We can do that and still believe in God. Anything to satisfy the king's whims; it doesn't matter too much." But they could not and would not compromise their faith, for they knew and understood who their God was. Like Abraham; they saw him who was invisible.

This is precisely where we stand today, precisely God's question that must be answered: "But when the Son of Man returns, how many will he find on the earth who have faith?" I believe we can answer today with certainty, for faith is a response inside of you to God's promise, and faith in Jesus Christ is what moves the heart of God to action. The faith that works is more than believing in God—it's believing God. It's more than believing in the Word of God—it is believing that the Word *was* God. It is more than knowledge of God—it is knowing God. It is taking God at his word that all has been accomplished, that you have moved from seeing life with human eyes to looking through God's eyes and seeing what God sees. When that transformation takes place, the invisible becomes visible and you see that "Faith shows the reality of what we hope for; it is the evidence of things we cannot see."

When you are seeing through the eyes of faith, you no longer tell God about your mountains; you now tell your mountains about your God. You no longer send prayers of "Lord, if it is your will," but now you boldly pray, "Lord, let it be so according to your word." When you face life, you now know that if you've got a hassle, God's got a provision and that provision is Jesus. The secret the apostle Paul lived by is that Jesus Christ is alive, and after he saw him risen in his Shekinah glory he said, "I rest my faith totally in him. I rest in his faith, I live in his faith. My hope is in his faith, my peace is in his faith, my joy is in his faith, my faith is his faith; and because of that, faith is my rest and my response to God's initiative in Jesus."

God did it; he took the initiative; he came down to where we are to take us where he is. Faith is not something you work at; the work has already been completed at Calvary, and because it is already done all you can do is merely live in it. Faith that is not says "you do," but faith that is real says, "He did it. God has already done it all in Jesus and I cannot be added to." He says, why can't you trust me? Why do you insist on trying to work on your faith? Real faith is not me making promises and hoping they come true; it is God making promises and me saying, "Thank you; you made the promise, you keep it." When I face the fire it doesn't matter how hot it is; God has promised that it won't burn me. And when I must cross the swollen river of life, no matter how deep, it will not overflow me, for he promised he would keep me above the waves (Isaiah 43:1–3).

So the question never ceases: "But when the Son of Man returns, how many will he find on the earth who have faith?" And how does one have faith that pleases God? Do what makes God happy—accept the finished work of his son Jesus Christ. Believe in the finished work of Jesus on the cross, for what makes God happiest is Jesus. The more Jesus gets famous in your life the happier God will be, the happier you will be, the more of God your life will produce, and the deeper the conviction that "the God we serve is able to save us. But if he chooses not to, we will not waver."

Faith is merely a response to what God has already done. Show me a people who walk closely with God, who actively hate sin, have become detached from this world, and are coming to know his voice, and I will show you people of great faith. Luke tells us in Acts 13, during a period of persecution of the church, that Peter was arrested and thrown in jail to await trial and execution. Herod had boasted, "I'm going to kill you after the Passover," but when the "Angel of God" came to rescue Peter, instead of finding a man in despair, biting his nails, and complaining about his plight, Peter was sound asleep and the angel had to strike him on the side to wake him up. Peter remembered that he had heard Jesus say,

> I tell you the truth, when you were young, you were able to do as you liked; you dressed yourself and went wherever you wanted to go. But when you are old, you will stretch out your hands, and others will dress you and take you where you don't want to go. (John 21:18)

When Peter recalled the words "when you are old," he knew it wasn't his time to die, so he disregarded Herod's threat and went to sleep. God said, "When you are old"—and if God said it, it must be so.

Faith works by hearing the voice of God. But you must first know God to recognize his voice. There is no use telling a man of God what you are going to do with him. There is no use theorizing about what God can and cannot do with someone for whom God has already done great things. You may argue about limitations, debate the impossible, and a believer will still cry out, "God can do anything but fail." If you say to a soul who has experienced God's deliverance that this or that cannot be done, that soul will answer, "God is able." You may not be sufficient for this or that, but God is able. He can bring peace out of confusion, victory out of defeat, triumph out of tragedy, health out of sickness, wholeness out of brokenness, laughing out of weeping, holiness out of sin, and life out of death. God is able. "Faith comes from hearing the message, and the message is heard through the word of Christ."

I spent several years in the church before I heard the voice of God. I was struggling with life, like many today. I thought I could keep it together by myself, but I could not. I tried not to sin, but I couldn't. I tried to plan my life, but I failed. I sought advice from others, but I found many of them were just as bad or worse off than me. And then I found Jesus, when the Spirit of God came to live in me. Just as God raised Christ Jesus from the dead, he raised me and gave me life in my body and my faith became real. That was when I heard the voice of God say to me, "'Count yourself dead to sin but alive to God in Christ Jesus.' Sin has been rendered powerless. You are a dead man." Then I knew my faith was firmly planted in the Word of Christ and I heard these words for the first time: "My old self has been crucified with Christ. It is no longer I who live, but Christ lives in me."

Not long after this, I heard about a city with streets paved with gold. I haven't seen it yet, but I know by faith that one day I will see it, for I will see God face to face. I also know the journey won't be easy, but I've got my eyes fixed on Jesus and I am wearing the shield of faith to ward off the fiery darts of Satan. Faith says to Satan:

"Go ahead and throw everything you have at me. I don't care; give me your best shot. I may stumble once in a while; I may be scarred; I may be knocked down; I may have to smile through the pain. But when you are through, I will still be standing, yet unmoved, for I read in the Scriptures:

"We are pressed on every side by troubles, but we are not crushed. We are perplexed, but not driven to despair. We are hunted down but never abandoned by God. We get knocked down, but we are not destroyed. Through suffering, our bodies continue to share in the death of Jesus so that the life of Jesus may also be seen in our bodies. (2 Corinthians 4:8–10)

"Therefore I am already hearing the sound of many waters rising. I am standing with Jesus, and I know when it's all over I'll still be standing for he who promised is faithful."

EIGHTEEN

THE LOVE LIFE

"Live a life filled with love, following the example of Christ. He loved us and offered himself as a sacrifice for us, a pleasing aroma to God."

(Ephesians 5:2)

In the gospel of Mark, there is a narrative of a Pharisee who questioned Jesus on which was the greatest commandment. By Jesus's time, the Jews had accumulated hundreds of laws. From Genesis through Deuteronomy, there are a total of 613 commandments, as counted by medieval sages, and these commandments include "positive commandments" to perform an act, and "negative commandments" to abstain from certain acts. Some rabbis taught that all laws were equally binding and that it was dangerous to make any distinctions, so this man's question could have provoked controversy among various groups. But Jesus's answer summarized all of God's laws.

The most important commandment is this: "Listen, O Israel! The Lord our God is the one and only Lord. And you must love the Lord your God with all your heart, all your soul, all your mind, and all your strength." The second is equally important: "Love your neighbor as yourself." No other commandment is greater than these. (Mark 12:29–31)

This Pharisee had grasped the intent of God's law—that true obedience comes from the heart. Because all the Old Testament commands lead to Christ, his next step was faith in Jesus himself. This, however, was the most difficult step to take. We do not know if this Pharisee ever became a true believer.

The question that confronts us today is how one understands Jesus's command to "Love your neighbor as yourself." John says in his first epistle:

And this is his commandment: We must believe in the name of his Son, Jesus Christ, and love one another, just as he commanded us. Those who obey God's commandments remain in fellowship with him, and he with them. And we know he lives in us because the Spirit he gave us lives in us. (1 John 3:23–24)

We are to believe not only in Jesus's words but also in his very person as the Son of God. Moreover, to believe in Jesus's name is to pattern your life after his, to become more like him. And if we are living daily in relationship to Christ, we grow to be more like him, which means we grow in love. As we grow in the love of Jesus, we will love one another. John magnificently sums up the essence of God with three simple profound words: "God is love"—adding "and all who live in love live in God, and God lives in them" (1 John 4:16). These three words are so important to understanding love. God does not *do* love, God *is* love. In my book *Almost Persuaded, Now to Believe*, I noted:

In his gospel (3:16) John states what is probably the most familiar, most often quoted, most well-known, and most loved passage of scripture in the entire Bible (John 3:16): *"For God so loved the world that he gave his only Son, so that everyone who believes in him will not perish but have eternal life."* Frequently we misinterpret this text by emphasizing the *quantity* of God's love and in doing so miss what I believe to be John's intent. John had lived with Christ and had seen him work. And John enjoyed fellowship with the Father and the Son all the days of his life, hence, I do not believe the passage is speaking of the magnitude or quantity of God's love, but it is speaking of its special quality. Its relational aspect. If the emphasis was on other than the quality of God's love I would have some deep concern for those who find it difficult to approach God because of their sin. It would suggest that the depth of one's sin would have some bearing on receiving God's forgiveness as more love would be necessary to forgive greater sin. But the fact is we are speaking of "quality" of love rather than quantity which allows even the greatest sin to be treated by God just as any other transgression. It says, *"In such a way, God loved the world that he gave."*[1]

One of the great tragedies of the church in this age, and the source of God's greatest heartache, is that so many believers fail to love. They say the words, "I love you," and for the most part they mean it. However, their grossly inadequate understanding of love is exposed at the first sign of disappointment, or failure, or difference in the other person. When something adverse occurs their love is exposed as highly conditional. The sad truth is that few in the Church of Jesus Christ comprehend what it means to love. I have had many conversations with people over the years, both believers and nonbelievers, and one of the most frequent topics is about love, and in particular God's love for his created beings. And what has been the most difficult thing for many to understand is "How can God love us knowing all the things we have done wrong." How can one grasp the fact that nothing we have done, can do, or will do can make God love us any more or any less. We learn from the Scriptures that in the timeless mind of God before the world was made before we even existed before we were formed in his image and likeness before there was anything to influence his decision, God loved us and chose us in Christ according to his divine plan. Paul writes (Ephesians 1:4):

"Even before he made the world, God loved us and chose us in Christ to be holy and without fault in his eyes. God decided in advance to adopt us into his own family by bringing us to himself through Jesus Christ. This is what he wanted to do, and it gave him great pleasure."

It is hard for many today to understand how God could accept us despite how we have lived or what we have done, but the fact is, he does. Because of Christ God looks at us as if we had never sinned. God had a plan to redeem his fallen creatures which originated in eternity, which means his love for us is not based on what we have or have not done, but solely on his character and being.

The Apostle John the elder statesman of the church, the man who had seen, heard, and touched God in the flesh, walked with him, talked with him, saw him heal, heard him teach, watched him die, met him arisen, and saw him ascend says in his first epistle (4:10): "*This is real love—not that we loved God, but that he loved us and sent his Son as a sacrifice to take away our sins.*" This is a profound statement expressing God's love. Here John tells us (1) Why God creates—Because he loves, he creates people to love; (2) He tells us why God cares—Because he loves them, he cares for sinful people; (3) His love for us caused him to offer a solution to the problem of sin: the death of his Son. (4) We learn why we receive eternal life—God's love expresses itself to us forever. Ever since creation, God's fallen creatures have been the object of his love. John says it most distinctly (4:9): "*God showed how much he loved us by sending his one and only Son into the world so that we might have eternal life through him.*" These words penned by John many years ago are still the motivation for us today. Every moment of inspiration, every thought, every word, every idea considered, every emotion, every tear, and every hope for eternity expressed, is simply a recounting of this wondrous truth of God's Love." John shows that God is the source of our love: that his kind of love is utterly unselfish as God demonstrated in sacrificing his Son for us. Jesus is our example of what it means to love; everything he did in life and death was supremely loving. But what must be understood is this kind of love goes against our natural inclinations. It is impossible to have this love unless the Holy Spirit gives us the power to set aside our natural desires and make us more and more like Christ. I am reminded of Paul's "Prayer for Spiritual Empowering" in (Ephesians 3) in particular (verses 18, 19a):

And may you have the power to understand, as all God's people should, how wide, how long, how high, and how deep his love is. May you experience the love of Christ, though it is too great to understand fully. Then you will be made complete with all the fullness of life and power that comes from God.

Here Paul says, God's love is total. It reaches every corner of our experience. It is wide—it covers the breadth of our experience and reaches out to the whole world. God's love is long—it continues the length of our lives. It is high—it rises to the heights of our celebration and elation. His love is deep—it reaches into the depths of discouragement, despair, and even death. When you feel shut out or isolated, he reminds us that you can never be lost to his love.

> And I am convinced that nothing can ever separate us from God's love. Neither death nor life, neither angels nor demons, neither our fears for today nor our worries about tomorrow—not even the powers of hell can separate us from God's love. No power in the sky above or in the earth below—indeed, nothing in all creation will ever be able to separate us from the love of God that is revealed in Christ Jesus our Lord. (Romans 8:38–40)

Notwithstanding, I must confess that this is beyond my understanding, beyond the grasp of my finite mind. God gave Jesus for the likes of you and me. He gave Jesus for us who are so unworthy and unable to do anything about our plight. He gave Jesus because he so loved the world that he purposed in his heart before the foundation of the world that you and I would be restored to full citizenship in his kingdom. He then put a robe of flesh on his Son that he would become like us to save us from eternal death and hell. He allowed his only Son to die a horrible death, stretched between two thieves with nails in his hands and feet, and with a crown of thorns on his head, only to hear him say, "Father forgive them."

At the height of sin God turned from his Son in his suffering and left him alone, that we might be healed forever. Jesus forgives our sin, washes us in his blood, cleanses us from all unrighteousness, and seats us on his right hand in the heavenly realms. He sent the Holy Spirit to be a deposit, our guarantee that we might be his children in his eternal kingdom. He then assures us that "indeed, nothing in all creation will ever be able to separate us from the love of God that is revealed in Christ Jesus our Lord."

If anyone needed to hear that "nothing in all creation will ever be able to separate us from the love of God" it was Jesus's disciple Peter. The one who was always making a big splash about his commitment to the Lord—"I'll follow you anywhere; I'll never forsake you; I'll never deny you; I'll even die for you." But let me remind you of Peter's failures: He was rebuked by Jesus as a tool of Satan. God spoke from heaven and admonished him to be quiet and start listening. Peter tried to cast out demons like Jesus did and failed. He tried to walk on water, and went under instead. He fell asleep when he should have been praying and watching. But worst of all, he openly denied his Lord three times while Jesus was going through his humiliating mock trial and persecution.

Peter blew it time and time again, and yet this big-mouth braggart teaches us a great lesson: you can't mess up so badly that God can't salvage you. Many people today may be thinking that it's too late or that you've made one mistake too many or that God is just fed up with you and has put you on the shelf. Not so! If you don't believe me, let's look more closely at Peter.

Near the end of the gospel of John, there is a wonderful passage in which Jesus appears once again to his disciples after his resurrection. The apostles, however, are uneasy and unsure about Jesus's unexpected appearances, because he seems to be forever showing up at unusual places and catching them off guard. Here in this text, after some days of no-show, they are back on board their boat fishing. After being out all night and catching nothing, presto! Jesus shows up on the fog-bound shores of the Sea of Galilee, silhouetted against the early gray of the morning.

284   A Wonder-Filled Life

He called out, "Fellows, have you caught any fish?"

"No," they replied.

Then he said, "Throw out your net on the right-hand side of the boat, and you'll get some!" So they did, and they couldn't haul in the net because there were so many fish in it. (John 21:4–6)

Peter, sensing "it's the Lord," put on his tunic (for he had stripped for work), jumped into the water, and headed to shore. Once ashore, Jesus already had, "breakfast waiting for them—fish cooking over a charcoal fire, and some bread" (v. 9). After the others brought the boat in,

"Bring some of the fish you've just caught," Jesus said. So Simon Peter went aboard and dragged the net to the shore. There were 153 large fish, and yet the net hadn't torn.

Now come and have some breakfast!" Jesus said. None of the disciples dared to ask him, "Who are you?" They knew it was the Lord. Then Jesus served them the bread and the fish. This was the third time Jesus had appeared to his disciples since he had been raised from the dead.

After breakfast, Jesus asked Simon Peter, "Simon son of John, do you love me more than these?"

"Yes, Lord," Peter replied, "you know I love you."

"Then feed my lambs," Jesus told him. (vv. 10–15)

Many learned commentators have made attempts to interpret this text, and after two thousand years much is still open to discussion. What is in question here is: Was this experience to remove the cloud of Peter's three-time denial of Jesus at his trial? Was this to restore Peter into the fold of the disciples? Was it because Peter needed special encouragement after his denial? Was it to find out if Peter understood the significance of Jesus's words about death and resurrection? Why would Jesus ask Peter three times if he loved him? What was Jesus referring to when he used the words, "more than these?"

I believe there is much more for us to learn here than even these answers would afford. What I do not believe is that Jesus was testing Peter after his threefold denial so he could restore him, for his death and resurrection had already accomplished that. Admittedly many theologians and scholars and interpreters are much more learned and wiser than me. However, what I contend is that Jesus was simply asking Peter the same questions he places before each one of us today. He was seeking to know if Peter loved him deeply enough to serve him. He wanted to know whether Peter would love him more than any earthly thing. He was asking Peter if he had a real understanding of his death and resurrection and would be willing to sacrifice his life for him.

Before attempting to answer Jesus's query for our own lives, it may be time to pause and try to understand some of the common reasons for our struggles to draw closer to Christ. With that in mind, we may first consider if we have ever decided how much we love Jesus. And if not, why not? One of the first reasons we remain unfulfilled and unhappy in our lives is that we have never decided how much we love Jesus. In our text Simon Peter counts fish—it was, after all, his career, his business, his occupation! Jesus had called him to be a disciple-maker, a fisher of men, but now he's back in the other kind of fishing business again. Jesus challenges him with the supreme question: "Have you ever made a decision, Simon, about how much you love me? Do you love me more than these?" Do you love me more than your daily occupation? Do you love me enough to put me first in your life?

It is one thing to say you love Jesus; the real test is the willingness to serve him. Not just because you reasoned with your head that it's the thing to do. Not because you observed his miracles. Not because he protects you from the stormy seas of life. Not because he blesses you when you least expect it, but more than that—because he died for you. Peter had repented, but here Jesus is asking him to commit his life. Peter's life changed when he finally realized who Jesus was. His occupation changed from fisherman to evangelist; his identity changed from impetuous to "rock"; his character changed from fearful to fearless; and his relationship to Jesus changed—to the point that the religious leaders of the council, after arresting Peter and John,

> were amazed when they saw the boldness of Peter and John, for they could see that they were ordinary men with no special training in the Scriptures. They also recognized them as men who had been with Jesus. (Acts 4:13)

Another reason for a believer's unhappiness and discontent with life is that one has been seeking a relationship without responsibility. Jesus didn't save us to monkey around and dawdle in his love for the rest of our lives. He has a lost world out there that needs saving and he wants us to understand our responsibility. If we love him, there's significant work to be done. If we are unhappy in Jesus, it could be because we have forgotten that God didn't call us merely to enjoy him but to serve him. Jesus calls us, "go and make disciples of all the nations, baptizing them in the name of the Father and the Son and the Holy Spirit. Teach these new disciples to obey all the commands I have given you. And be sure of this: I am with you always, even to the end of the age" (Matthew 28:19–20). The question is, have we even made a single disciple for Jesus?

A further source of unhappiness is: we have failed to commit ourselves. In the John 21 passage we referred to earlier, Jesus is using all the big words: "Simon son of John, do you love me?" Here the Greek word for "love" is *"agape"* (volitional, self-sacrificial love), Peter answers using little words: "Yes, Lord, you know I love you." The Greek word Peter uses is *phileo* (signifying affection, affinity, or brotherly love). "Then take care of my sheep," Jesus said.

Again Jesus repeats the question: "Simon, son of John, do you love me?" *Agape*. And again Peter replies, "Yes, Lord, you know I love you." *Phileo*. A third time Jesus asks Peter the question, changing the word from *agape* to Peter's word *phileo*, as if to ask, "Aren't you even my friend?" Anything less than *agape* is the recipe for failed commitment. Jesus doesn't settle for quick, superficial answers. He has a way of getting to the heart of the matter. Peter had to face his true feelings and motives when Jesus confronted him, but his big failure was to say "Lord" so fast that he didn't really mean it.

How would you respond today if Jesus asked you, "Do you love me?" The question to ask ourselves today is, "Do we really love Jesus? Are we even his friend? Are we willing to love and feed his people?" The truth of the matter is, if our love for Jesus is not *agape* love, it is not love at all.

A fourth reason for our being unhappy and unfulfilled is: we have refused to live by the will of Christ. For many, our blatant confession is, "I just don't want to live by somebody else's will." We rarely ever say this out loud, but it's what we mean. The will of God can lead us into the kinds of commitment we may not want to make. And it's hard to abandon what we want in favor of what God wants! Many people, in reading Paul's declaration in Philippians 4:13, "For I can do everything through Christ, who gives me strength," interpret it to simply mean; "I can do everything through Christ," but they leave out this: only when he is allowed to work his will through our lives.

The prophet Isaiah, in his great chapter on Jesus the suffering servant, said: "We turned our backs on him and looked the other way. He was despised, and we did not care" (Isaiah 53:3). Further in verse 6, he says: "All of us, like sheep, have strayed away. We have left God's paths to follow our own. Yet the Lord laid on him the sins of us all." Further, the Scriptures say, "No one is righteous— not even one. No one is truly wise; no one is seeking God. All have turned away; all have become useless. No one does good, not a single one" (Romans 3:10–12).

Can you even begin to comprehend the depth of our disobedience and sin? Do you not understand that we turned our backs on God and followed our way? We were on the brink of disaster, as a person on a sinking ship in the middle of the ocean. But in our midst of peril, God's Word in eternity before the world was made echoed forth. He spoke it for the descendants of Adam and Eve, and it brought God great joy. It was a word that gathered up all the love, forgiveness, and creativity God had been storing in his heart for his created beings. The word he spoke was "Jesus!" This is the good news.

Note that the prophet said, "Yet the Lord laid on him the sins of us all." Is it not unfair to ask a man born without sin to give his life for another's sins and to overlook their offenses? The answer is: Yes! However, though God hates sin, he loves the sinner. Love is not about fairness. Love is not about desire, lust, or passion. Love has a uniqueness all of its own. God's love was given not in return but simply because those he gave it to could only know him by it. Accordingly, love is not about punishing the guilty offender; love is about the grace of God that is unwarranted, undeserved, unmerited, but extended to the sinner. In essence, love is the outrageous grace of God for the undeserving. That is why Paul declares "nothing in all creation will ever be able to separate us from the love of God that is revealed in Christ Jesus our Lord."

Examining our understanding of the grace of God, we are confronted by one of the most familiar parables in the entire Bible, the parable of the lost son, sometimes known as the prodigal son. However, before proceeding with the story told by Jesus in Luke 15:11–32, we must read the sections of Scripture both preceding and following our text if we are to understand what the Holy Spirit is attempting to convey to the heart.

First, take note of the two brief parables preceding it: the parable of the lost sheep and the parable of the lost coin. These parables speak of something lost, and then the joy of finding it. In merging them with the parable of the lost son, we learn about the grace of God. Some would say that the parable of the lost son demonstrates how human beings differ from inanimate objects (coins) and animals (sheep). Some infer it shows that people have free will and must make morally responsible choices. Others maintain that the parable shows that the boy had to come crawling back on his knees to be forgiven, that he had to repent before coming back home. It is true that all three stories speak of something lost. It is also true that all three stories emphasize the finder's joy. And it is also true the lost son returned home of his own free will. But the central focus of the story is not about a lost son; it is about the Father's love.

In verse 20 we are told, "And while he was still a long way off, his father saw him coming. Filled with love and compassion, he ran to his son, embraced him, and kissed him." When the son tries to repent, the father interrupts his prepared speech, anxious to get the celebration underway. So, what we learn amid our joy is: grace is unfair.

This is the hardest lesson to learn about grace. It is unreasonable to expect a man or woman to forgive the terrible things done to them because he or she apologizes sometime later. It is unreasonable to love someone who has done horrible things contrary to the moral society in which we live. However, it is clear that in the Scriptures the worse a person felt about himself or herself, the more likely they saw Jesus as a refuge.

Is it indeed true that people stay away from the church today because it is condemning? The down-and-out, who flocked to Jesus, when he lived on earth, no longer feel welcome among his followers. What has happened? Has the church lost that gift? The more I pondered this question, the more I felt drawn to one word as the key. All that follows uncoils from that one word: grace.

Is it any wonder that people have such difficulty in understanding grace? Try to reconcile the attitude of many in the church today with a God who is outrageously joyful when we return home like the lost son. Many people leave home searching for grace. They try everything else and finally, as a last resort, they try the church but find little grace there. However, they keep coming back to the church because they find grace nowhere else. Here we learn that Jesus's death on the cross was the embodiment of grace.

When I now think about God, I hold up the image of the lovesick father, which is miles away from the stern, condemning, self-clean monarch many portray. I think of Jesus's depiction of the waiting father, heartsick, abused, yet wanting above all else to forgive and begin anew, to announce with joy, "Your brother was dead and has come back to life! He was lost, but now is found!" (v. 32). Should we also not love the poor, the suffering, the persecuted, and the lost just as God does? God sees no undesirables, neither should we. By his example, Jesus challenged us to look at the world through grace-healed eyes. Instead of the message "no undesirables allowed," Jesus proclaimed: "In God's kingdom there are no undesirables," only those who receive his grace through faith in him. Into the heart of God comes compassion without reason, mercy without judgment, love without condition, acceptance without separation, and grace without walls. This is his description of the outrageous joy of the Father.

If one is despondent, in despair, in pain, in bondage to sin—if you have lost hope, feel tired, weary, lonely and alone—Jesus will say, "Quick, fit him with sandals of mercy and grace. Quick, put the robe of grace on him." Yes, put it on the one who comes. What joy for the Father to throw that great mantle of grace over a repentant sinner. What a joy to hear Christ say, "You are the beloved of the Father. You are a child of the King, an heir of God, and coheir with me." You are a child of the outrageous Father in heaven. Consequently, grace means that there is nothing we can do to make God love us more—and grace also means there is nothing we can do to make God love us less. Grace is assurance that God already loves us as much as an infinite God can love. The most outrageous act in all of human history was this Father sending his son to die for the sins of the world, and offering his life as a free gift—it's the outrageous love of an outrageous God. The songwriter exclaims with unfettered joy:

The love of God is greater far than tongue or pen can ever tell / It goes beyond the highest star, and reaches to the lowest hell / The guilty pair, bowed down with care, God gave His Son to win / His erring child He reconciled, and pardoned from his sin. Oh, love of God, how rich and pure! How measureless and strong! / It shall forevermore endure—the saints' and angels' song.[3]

NINETEEN

INDWELLING PRESENCE

"For God wanted them to know that the riches and glory of Christ are for you Gentiles, too. And this is the secret: Christ lives in you. This gives you assurance of sharing his glory."

(Colossians 1:27)

A young boy went running into his house and exclaimed to his mother, "Mother! Mother! I am six feet tall!"

"What makes you say that?" his mother asked.

"I used my shoe to measure me," he told her, "and I was six shoes tall."

The mother replied, "But son, your shoe is not a foot long."

"It has to be, mom," he said, "'cause my foot's in it!"

The young boy was mistaken about the standard he had used in measuring his height. To be sure, there are many different standards used to measure different things. For many, accuracy is of the utmost importance, while in others it is not as critical. For instance, in the manufacture of components for the space shuttle, accuracy to the standards is vital. On the other hand, if I build a storage shelf in the garage for odds and ends, 1/16th of an inch off is not as important.

Often people establish their standard for something, although there may already be an accepted norm. Someone may say, "It's freezing outside!" when the actual temperature maybe reads 36 degrees and not 32 degrees. When you drive the speed limit, how many people pass you? Thus, certain standards are recognized and accepted, while others are subject to the desire of the individual.

In much the same way, the world is filled with many different spiritual standards. If you were asked the question, "How do you know that you have been born again?," those who respond would certainly have different criteria as to why they responded in a certain way: they feel it in their heart, they believe in God, they obey the gospel, they go to church, they're a good person. Unfortunately, like the little boy in the story, many such standards are flawed. Paul would respond by saying, "The reason I know that I am born again is 'It is no longer I who live, but Christ lives in me' (Galatians 2:20)." So, the answer to the question, "How do you know that you have been born again?" is clear. Christ has taken up residence in our earthly body. We are no longer alone, for Christ lives in us.

One of the greatest doctrines of the Christian faith is the mind-blowing reality that the Lord Jesus Christ indwells a believer. Paul would say, for example, "But even before I was born, God chose me and called me by his marvelous grace. Then it pleased him to reveal his Son to me" (Galatians 1:15–16). Elsewhere he said, "As surely as the truth of Christ is *in me*" (2 Corinthians 11:10, emphasis added). And in 2 Corinthians 13:3 he said, "Christ speaks through me." He also commanded, "Keep putting into practice all you learned and received from me—everything you heard from me and saw me doing. Then the God of peace will be with you" (Philippians 4:9).

Further, one of the most comforting realities of life in Christ is also one of its greatest mysteries: "And this is the secret: Christ lives in you. This gives you assurance of sharing his glory" (Colossians 1:27). The truth is, Jesus indwells every believer through the Holy Spirit. Thus, as Paul told the churches of Galatia, "It is no longer I who live, but Christ lives in me" (Galatians 2:20). In addition, Romans 8:9 cautions, "remember that those who do not have the Spirit of Christ living in them do not belong to him at all." In my book *Almost Persuaded, Now to Believe*, I noted,

> The reality is that we are brand new people on the inside because the Holy Spirit has given us new life, and we are not the same anymore. As Christians we are not merely made over, improved in character, rehabilitated, or reformed— we are re-created, i.e., new creations, now living in vital union with Christ. In 2 Corinthians 5:17, we are assured, "What this means is that those who become Christians become new persons. They are not the same anymore, for the old life is gone. A new life is begun!" Receiving Christ as Lord of your life is the beginning of life with Christ, but you must continue to follow his leadership by being rooted, built up, and strengthened in the faith. No longer living to please yourself, rather, spending your life pleasing Christ. [1]

Consequently, we learn that the Holy Spirit is our power for living. He is the same Spirit of Christ who dwelled in Paul and also indwells all true believers. It means that God, in his plan to bestow himself into us, was embodied in Christ "For in Christ lives all the fullness of God in a human body" (Colossians 2:9). And Christ, through the means of his death and resurrection, became a life-giving Spirit: "'The first man, Adam, became a living person.' But the last Adam—that is, Christ—is a life-giving Spirit" (1 Corinthians 15:45). Because of that, he can enter into us: "And Christ lives within you, so even though your body will die because of sin, the

Spirit gives you life because you have been made right with God" (Romans 8:10). In the believers' experience, the Spirit in you is Christ in you.

So, as one embraces the truth of a living Savior's presence within you, and the more you become accessible to Christ, the more he can take over so that your Christian walk becomes vibrant and effective! We read in Philippians 4:13, "For I can do everything through Christ, who gives me strength." Therefore, we should be able to say with Paul, in practice as well as in theory, "Christ lives in me." But one may ask, "Why do we keep failing, even in our best efforts to live the Christian life?" A person can refuse to steal, lie, or use drugs and alcohol. A person can indeed try to be sinless, but that is still you, that is trying to live the Christian life on your own. However, no one other than Jesus can live the Christian life—for the simple reason that he *is* the Christian life! And only he can live it in our lives as well.

Once we have trusted in Jesus, we are strengthened by the Holy Spirit so that we can both enjoy a relationship with Christ and live for him. The role of the Holy Spirit mediates Christ's presence to us, and this experience takes place in the inner being, the nonmaterial part of us that makes decisions and relates to others—the seat of our affections, the site of our decisions, and the source of our feeling of identity. The Apostle John says in his first epistle, "Our actions will show that we belong to the truth, so we will be confident when we stand before God. Even if we feel guilty, God is greater than our feelings, and he knows everything" (1 John 3:19–20). This being true, it is the indwelling of the Holy Spirit in us that conforms us to the will of Christ.

Several years ago, a very dear friend of mine confided to me that at one time he was so enraged with another man that he felt like he was prone to commit murder. Two of his daughters had been physically abused by their uncle when they visited his house to play with their cousin. His deeds were exposed when the girls told another young girl, who revealed the information to her parents; the man was confronted and admitted his guilt. My friend confessed to me that upon finding out about what had happened he was so incensed that he thought such a criminal act on his daughter's innocence deserved severe punishment. He then called the man's home to make sure he was home, as he intended to confront him face to face. On the way there in the car, his wife asked him, "What are you going to do?" He replied, "I don't know. I am so angry right now that I feel like killing him."

As my friend related what transpired, he explained, "When we arrived at his home, the man's wife said he was out but would be arriving soon." My wife and I sat on a sofa directly across from where he would be seated when he came home. Upon coming in the door, he sat down next to his wife, with his head seemingly bowed in remorse. From that moment there was a silence that seemed like an eternity. My friend said, "I could only glare at him with righteous indignation, but suddenly something astonishing happened right before my very eyes. I seemed frozen in time as I watched my spirit leave my body and go over to him. The man's lips began to move and I will never forget what he said, 'How could you love me after what I have done?'" My friend said, at that moment, "I realized that the Holy Spirit living in me had offered grace where I had apportioned judgment for his sin." God had, in that divine moment demonstrated that "It is no longer I who live, but Christ lives in me."

Therefore, the world will know the love of Jesus as the presence of the Holy Spirit is daily manifested in your life. John says in his gospel (14:21), "Those who accept my commandments and obey them are the ones who love me. And because they love me, my Father will love them. And I will love them and reveal myself to each of them." The question is, what does Jesus mean when he says

I will "reveal myself to each of them"? In several other translations the word "manifest" is used. To reveal means to uncover something unknown and to see with clarity something that was previously a mystery. The word "manifest" means to "shine, or break forth." When something is manifest it is evident, apparent, plain, open, clearly visible to the understanding, not obscure or difficult to be seen or understood. Therefore, God reveals himself to us through his Word and the person of Jesus Christ. Consequently, we are to become an instrument or channel that radiates Christ's presence for all to see.

My question is, why do so few believers today manifest the presence of Jesus in their lives? Why do so many church members lack the understanding that the Holy Spirit's presence is, in reality, the life of Jesus? Could it be because experiencing the presence of Jesus in a church is not so much a corporate matter as some suppose but rather an individual one, where one must be willing and available to receive the divine presence of Christ? The church often prays, "O Lord, send us your presence, send us your Spirit, come among us, fall upon us, and reveal yourself to us!" Many seem to have the idea that God's presence is like an invisible smoke that God sprays into the atmosphere, like the Old Testament glory-cloud, so filling the temple that the priests could not stand to minister.

However, Paul reminds us in 1 Corinthians 6:19, "Don't you realize that your body is the temple of the Holy Spirit, who lives in you and was given to you by God? You do not belong to yourself." Our bodies are the temple of the Lord and if his glory comes, it must appear in our hearts and fill our bodies. Christ does not inhabit buildings or a certain atmosphere; he does not come because of a certain amount of noise or feeling; he does not arrive simply because we have spent a designated amount of time preparing for him; he does not come because of a certain tradition. No! He comes and is manifested through yielded, obedient, sanctified bodies, which are his temples. Every member is a temple and remains personally responsible to obey God and to be available as an instrument of his presence.

A person may complain about what is not happening in their church, or how dry and lifeless the worship is, but unless the life of Christ is truly manifest in their selves they are part of the problem. How audacious it is to sit among the saints of God who radiate his glory and never seek his divine presence. How risky it is to be among those to whom Jesus reveals himself so powerfully and not be changed! How perilous it is to ignore the ugliness of sin in one's life! How tragic for one to sit Sunday after Sunday in God's presence and not see their great need for Christ!

In Luke's gospel Jesus says, "Then you will say, 'But we ate and drank with you, and you taught in our streets.' And he will reply, 'I tell you, I don't know you or where you come from. Get away from me, all you who do evil'" (Luke 13:26–27). Some perfectly respectable people claiming allegiance to Christ will miss the Kingdom of God because they are not true followers. Many will admit they sat in Jesus's presence and heard the good news about his death, burial, and resurrection, but they were not changed.

It is not enough for one to merely eat in the presence of Christ. It is not enough to merely claim his name and fail to allow his life to be manifest in you. It is not enough to sit under convicting sermons and never respond to his word. We must be changed and purified by being with him. We must have a desire in our hearts to obey him and walk blameless before him. We must have a deep hunger in our souls for the things of God. We must want all secrets to be exposed, and all hidden things to be confessed in our lives. We must want to be as much like Jesus as is possible for a human being on this earth. We must want to be rescued from the power of Satan forever. We must want the Holy Spirit to do in us what God alone can do.

I may be wrong, but my thought is there are many today who have little knowledge of who the Holy Spirit is and what his role is in manifesting the presence of Jesus in a believer's life. Previously we noted that Jesus said, "because they love me, my Father will love them. And I will love them and reveal myself to each of them" (John 14:21). Further in verses 24–26, Jesus explains,

> What I am telling you is from the Father who sent me. I am telling you these things now while I am still with you. But when the Father sends the Advocate as my representative— that is, the Holy Spirit—he will teach you everything and will remind you of everything I have told you.

In assuring the disciples of the blessings that would follow his return to the Father, Jesus had not specifically mentioned the Holy Spirit. Now he explains that he would soon be leaving them, but that he would not desert them. He would send the Holy Spirit as the Advocate, Counselor, Helper, to guide, instruct and strengthen them. Although people, in general, would see him no longer, his disciples would, in a sense, continue to see him. They would see and know him spiritually, because he would dwell within them, giving them deeper insight through the testimony of the Holy Spirit.

Many people acknowledge the efficacious work of Jesus Christ on the cross, and we believe he came to save us. We believe he abides in us, and we know his presence, but do we acknowledge the work and ministry of the Holy Spirit within us? Do we question seriously why the Holy Spirit has been given to us? Do we approach the Scriptures and ask prayerfully, "Holy Spirit, the Bible says you were sent to me as a gift from my heavenly Father. The Word says you have taken up residence in me. Please tell me, please reveal to me—why have you come? What is your eternal purpose? What are you trying to accomplish in me?"

The eternal purpose of the Holy Spirit in us is to bring us home to Jesus Christ as his eternal, spotless bride. Paul says the Spirit has come "to make her holy and clean, washed by the cleansing of God's Word. He did this to present her to himself as a glorious church without a spot or wrinkle or any other blemish. Instead, she will be holy and without fault" (Ephesians 5:26–27).

The eternal purpose of the Holy Spirit commences according to Jesus in John's gospel (16:8): "And when he comes, he will convict the world of its sin, and God's righteousness, and of the coming judgment." He then says in verse 14, "He will bring me glory by telling you whatever he receives from me." The Spirit comes to open Jesus to us, to show us the beauty of his holiness, and to make him known. If you were to tell me today that you have been born again and that you are chosen in Christ and that you love him, might I ask, "By what standard do you make that claim?" According to the Scriptures, the standard is clear: "Those who say they live in God should live their lives as Jesus did" (1 John 2:6).

Do you have a broken heart for Jesus? Is he the lover of your soul? Is your love for him growing and consuming your heart? Do you have a burning hunger more than ever to please him, to follow him wherever he may lead? Are you resigned to the guidance, comfort, strength, and obedience of the Holy Spirit in your daily walk? The Holy Spirit has one message, one divine purpose: to manifest Jesus to the church so that we will fall in love with him. The Spirit brings us into Christ's presence as a foretaste of our inheritance. The apostle Paul says,

And when you believed in Christ, he identified you as his own by giving you the Holy Spirit, whom he promised long ago. The Spirit is God's guarantee that he will give us the

302   A Wonder-Filled Life

inheritance he promised and that he has purchased us to be his people. He did this so we would praise and glorify him. (Ephesians 1:13–14)

Paul is describing people who are especially marked by the work of the Holy Spirit, who has produced in them a distinguishing mark, a glorious inner work, something supernatural that has changed them forever. He is describing once ordinary men and women, in whom it is readily seen that "They have been with Jesus." There is the story in Acts 3 about a lame man as Peter and John were going to the temple for prayer.

> As they approached the Temple, a man lame from birth was being carried in. Each day he was put beside the Temple gate, the one called the Beautiful Gate, so he could beg from the people going into the Temple. When he saw Peter and John about to enter, he asked them for some money.
>
> Peter and John looked at him intently, and Peter said, "Look at us!" (vv. 2–4)

In other words, "look and see Christ in us"—and when they got the man's attention they spoke those liberating words, "In the name of Jesus Christ the Nazarene, get up and walk!" (v. 5). They helped him to his feet, and for the first time in his life, he not only walked but went into the temple courts leaping and praising God. Despite the healing, the religious officials were furious because the name of Jesus was still being proclaimed. They thought they had done away with Jesus, and that the crucifixion had ended this sect; but here were these annoying disciples of the Nazarene still preaching about him. Words, ideas, philosophies, might contradict their viewpoints—but a miraculously changed man? What could they say? What could they do about it? Everyone had known the lame man for years as he sat by the temple gate asking for money, and now they could see the change.

People may have known what you were before, but after you claim to be born again there ought to be a definite change that will cause others to ask questions: When did it take place? How did it happen? Who or what changed you? One of the greatest arguments for the Christian faith is a transformed life. The life that becomes like Jesus Christ is a question the world cannot answer, and yet the answer is clear. In the narrative, John speaks of the courage and boldness of Peter and John, and we read about the change in Peter's life after he denied Jesus, but even more, we are pointed to the lame man who had been healed. What a tremendous testimony for Christ's healing power. What a confirmation this is of Christ's life resident in Peter and John. The question is, how did Peter and John get that way? Why are not Christians today able to speak with that same life-changing boldness and power?

The answer is simple. It's so plain that even the religious rulers recognized it, and "were amazed when they saw the boldness of Peter and John, for they could see that they were ordinary men with no special training in the Scriptures. They also recognized them as men who had been with Jesus" (Acts 4:13). God can communicate life and power to you through the Lord Jesus Christ; and when you live, act, and speak according to God's Holy Word, what you do and say will testify to the power of God, and people will then realize that you have been with Jesus.

These disciples of Jesus were not moved by threat or hardship or trial. They were unshakable; they were steadfast. We are reminded, "don't look at the troubles we can see now; rather, we fix our gaze on things that cannot be seen. For the things we see now will soon be gone, but the things we cannot see will last forever" (2 Corinthians

4:18). When believers sing, every song is an offer of praise. When they pray, every word is given unction by the Spirit. When they worship, every thought is centered on their risen Lord, and their hearts cry out, "Come quickly, Lord Jesus."

The question is, what happened to change them? What did the Holy Spirit do in the lives of these believers? What is it that marks people and seals them as God's eternal possession? What does one need to do today so that the life of Jesus will be manifest in them? How can we experience everything that God has prepared for us?

First, you must approach him, just as you are, with nothing in your hand. You must acknowledge your utter disregard for sin and your need for forgiveness and mercy. You must desire to have the veil removed from your eyes and long for his holiness, and for purity to be unfolded in you. You must yield your heart to his love and thirst for his presence to flood your life. You must be open for his life to be formed in you by the Holy Spirit while realizing, "This is supernatural. This is a work from above. This isn't me—this is God's Spirit working in me." All this is possible because the Spirit of God delights in pulling back the veil to give us insight into what is to come. Paul confirms this in 2 Corinthians 3:16–18:

> But whenever someone turns to the Lord, the veil is taken away. For the Lord is the Spirit, and wherever the Spirit of the Lord is, there is freedom. So all of us who have had that veil removed can see and reflect the glory of the Lord. And the Lord—who is the Spirit—makes us more and more like him as we are changed into his glorious image.

In the past few years God has impressed upon my heart the need for his people to bear his image. One might ask, exactly what does it mean to bear the Image of Christ in our lives? What are the pieces of evidence that reveal Jesus? First, there is love for him and obedience to his every command. I have been in churches where I have not sensed or experienced the real presence of Jesus in Mass meetings or worship because the people exhibited no true self-denial or repentance. If people are not living in obedience to God, in truth they could not be loving him. Surely Jesus will not manifest himself to those who say they love him but do not bow to his will and obey.

On the other hand, wherever you find visible manifestations of Jesus breaking forth among God's people, there is manifested a deep, piercing, conviction of sin. Whenever holy vessels embody the living presence of Jesus, and his holy presence bursts forth from obedient, humble, and grateful hearts, the person who harbors sin in his or her life will do one of two things: either fall and confess, or try to run and hide. Wherever you find the presence of Jesus you will find God's people manifesting the power to destroy sin. The awesome, manifest presence of God is like a hurricane that blows away desire, wickedness, and immorality; melts down hardness; and deepens the sense of the sinfulness of sin. The evidence of the presence of Jesus is that God's people manifest a spirit of holiness. They have a spirit that automatically draws them to the light, and they say," I want all hidden things to be brought out! I want to be as much like Jesus as possible for a human being on this earth"; and their testimony is, "I'm being changed." Consequently, when the presence of Jesus is manifest God's people share the Lord's burden. When the presence of Jesus is manifest, God opens his heart and shows himself to the alcoholics, addicts, prostitutes, the lonely, depressed, abused, a suffering world.

Finally, whenever you find the revealed presence of Jesus, God's people manifest an exuberant and exceeding joy. "You have shown me the way of life, and you will fill me with the joy of your presence" (Acts 2:28). Joy comes when one knows that death could not hold Jesus—and because it could not hold him, it cannot hold us. Joy comes when we know that the Lord is at our right hand in all our troubles, and know that he is beside us at all times. Joy is not needing to know *how*, but knowing *who*. Joy is knowing that we will rise to new life in a new body, in a new world. Joy comes because the Holy Spirit floods us with his presence. Joy comes when the presence of Jesus is so revealed in us that our family, friends, acquaintances, and yes, even our enemies take note and realize, "They have been with Jesus."

John writes in his first epistle, "Dear friends, we are already God's children, but he has not yet shown us what we will be like when Christ appears." But the joy comes in knowing, "that we will be like him, for we will see him as he really is" (1 John 3:2). If you have a hunger for Jesus alone—all of Jesus, more of Jesus, and only Jesus—you will surely experience the visible manifestation of his presence; for he says, "Those who accept my commandments and obey them are the ones who love me. And because they love me, my Father will love them. And I will love them and reveal myself to each of them" (John 14:21).

TWENTY

BEHOLDING

"So all of us who have had that veil removed can see and reflect the glory of the Lord. And the Lord—who is the Spirit—makes us more and more like him as we are changed into his glorious image."

(2 Corinthians 3:18).

In concluding this book, I am reminded of how much music has impacted my life and helped shape my journey of faith in Jesus Christ on my way to healing and wholeness. I recall the words of the song my parents used to sing to me when an infant: "Jesus loves me, this I know / for the Bible tells me so / Little ones to him belong / they are weak, but he is strong. / Yes, Jesus loves me! Yes, Jesus loves me! Yes, Jesus loves me! The Bible tells me so."[1]

I remember it to this day, but when I reached the age of maturity and realized that my sin had condemned me to hell, I heard the song that caused many people to come streaming down from the balconies at a Billy Graham crusade: "Just as I am, without one plea / But that Thy blood was shed for me / And that Thou bid'st

308 A Wonder-Filled Life

me come to Thee / Oh, Lamb of God, I come, I come."[2] This was a turning point in my life, because shortly after I attended a revival and gave my death to Christ in exchange for his life and at that moment I testified,

> I have decided to follow Jesus. I have decided to follow Jesus. I have decided to follow Jesus / No turning back, no turning back / The world behind me, the cross before me / The world behind me, the cross before me / The world behind me, the cross before me / No turning back, no turning back.[3]

Earlier I mentioned my first hearing of the song "At Calvary" and how it affected my life and focused me to focus my every thought on Jesus's death on the cross:

> Years I spent in vanity and pride / Caring not my Lord was crucified / Knowing not it was for me He died / On Calvary / Mercy there was great and grace was free / Pardon there was multiplied to me / There my burdened soul found liberty / At Calvary. / By God's Word at last my sin, I learned / Then I trembled at the law I'd spurned / 'Til my guilty soul imploring turned / To Calvary.[4]

And now in the closing years of my journey to Christlikeness, there is no lack of focus on Jesus. My worship today has been greatly enriched by the fact that I have discovered the song that testifies of my present-day worship, "I Exalt Thee."

> For Thou, o Lord, art high above all the earth / Thou art exalted far above all gods / For Thou, o Lord, art high above all the earth / Thou art exalted far above all gods / I exalt Thee, I exalt Thee / I exalt Thee, o Lord / I exalt Thee, I exalt Thee / I exalt Thee, o Lord.[5]

In my memoir *The Top of the Stairs* I wrote:

[O]ne morning during my worship time, I was listening to
music and heard the song, "I Exalt Thee." God took that
moment to remind me that in my eighty-seven years of life
on this earth I had experienced moments of sadness and joy,
laughing and weeping, spiritual perceptions and insights, a
still small voice, waves pounding the beach, brilliant sunsets, and music in rain. I had always thanked him for these
experiences. What was different about what I was now going
through? I then recalled my answer to a previous question,
Have I resolved my view of life after death? Without hesitation, I knew in my heart that nothing had changed in how I
felt about dying, because nothing had changed in how I felt
about Jesus. I now saw the same things I'd seen when I first
met him in the canes and crutches at the top of the stairs.[5]

I then felt I could face my remaining years with expectancy
and joy, so I turned to the song that presently has such an effect
on my life that every time I hear it, my reaction is somewhat like
the prophet Ezekiel when he encountered the glory of the Lord:
"When I saw it, I fell face down on the ground" (Ezekiel 1:28).
That is how I feel when I hear the song "We Shall Behold Him." I
can only bow in worship, tears streaming down my face, as I now
await the Lord Jesus Christ, the Lamb upon the throne.

In this book, I have attempted to set out the sum and substance
of my life in the body over these glorious years because of the love
of God in Jesus Christ. In that time I have grown to love, admire,
and worship the Lord Jesus Christ. While many theologians more
learned and far wiser than myself have decided to use their time
probing our end in the Apostle John's vision on the Isle of Patmos,
as told in the book of Revelation, I have decided to simply spend

310   A Wonder-Filled Life

my time beholding the Lamb of God until I see him face to face. To that end I find Jesus Christ embedded on almost every page of the book of Revelation. Instead of studying eschatology as end-time prophecy, I am grateful that I have discovered Revelation as the greatest book of worship known to mankind because it is, in essence, a book of beholding, beginning with John's testimony:

> I, John, am your brother and your partner in suffering and God's Kingdom and in the patient endurance to which Jesus calls us. I was exiled to the island of Patmos for preaching the word of God and for my testimony about Jesus. It was the Lord's Day, and I was worshiping in the Spirit. Suddenly, I heard behind me a loud voice like a trumpet blast. It said, "Write in a book everything you see and send it to the seven churches in the cities of Ephesus, Smyrna, Pergamum, Thyatira, Sardis, Philadelphia, and Laodicea." (Revelation 1:9–11)

The book of Revelation is the last book in the Bible and is most noted for its concern with last things: death and the end of this present age, life in the age to come, the coming of Christ to gather up his church, Christ's final victory over evil, and the reality of eternal life with him. It concludes with the promise of Christ's soon return (22:6–21) and John's ardent prayer that has been echoed by Christians thru the centuries (22:20): "Amen! Come, Lord Jesus!" The book commences with the Apostle John caught up into heaven, where he sees a vision of God Almighty on his throne. Following this, he is given specific messages from Jesus to the seven churches in Asia. Then we hear of a murderous beast who hates all believers, because they look like their father. It introduces the woman giving birth to Jesus and the Devil's attempts to abort the birth. It speaks of the old covenant, of Israel giving birth to new Israel; and it concludes with God's ultimate triumph over sin and evil and the picture of a new heaven and a new earth.

The key to the entire book is found in chapter 14, with the appearance of the Lamb of God who takes away the sin of the world. Jesus Christ is the central person in Revelation. He gives it validity, he gives it reality, and he gives it compulsion. Visible or invisible, he is at the center of every vision.

The purpose and theme of the Apostle John's writing is to present to the church a book about beholding the Lord Jesus Christ's triumphal return. References to the Lord Jesus Christ abound throughout Revelation: 1:1, 8, 10, 12-18; 4:2–3; 5:1, 11–14; 6:1; 7:9–12; 8:1–4; 9:1; 10:1; 12:1–4, 10–11; 13:8; 14:1–3; 15:1, 3–4; 16:15; 17:6, 14; 18:1; 19:11–16; 20:1, 4–5, 11; 21:1–7; 22:1–7, 16–21. Beholding means to see, to look, to gaze upon. However, many of us satisfy ourselves with just little glimpses of God, and deceive ourselves into thinking that is all God is. True praise and adoration bows before the vastness of God's glory and beholds the Lord, high and lifted up, where one can see the heavens opened and hear the seraphim crying, "Holy, holy, holy is the Lord Almighty." While some people worship idols, only the Creator God is worthy of praise.

Earlier in this book, I talked about Ezekiel's vision of the people's sin and wickedness in the temple. In the one place their spiritual leaders should have been teaching God's truth, they were teaching lies. So God chose to abandon his temple and leave them to their destructive behavior. As he departed the temple, his glory stopped over the Mount of Olives, to the east of Jerusalem, and not one person tried to stop him before leaving the city. But now, the Lord's glory returns to the temple:

> After this, the man brought me back around to the east gateway. Suddenly, the glory of the God of Israel appeared from

the east. The sound of his coming was like the roar of rushing waters, and the whole landscape shone with his glory. This vision was just like the others I had seen, first by the Kebar River and then when he came to destroy Jerusalem. I fell face down on the ground. And the glory of the Lord came into the Temple through the east gateway. (Ezekiel 43:1–4)

Once God returns to the temple he declares, "And this is the basic law of the Temple: absolute holiness! The entire top of the mountain where the Temple is built is holy. Yes, this is the basic law of the Temple" (v. 12). God is holy, perfect, and blameless. And just as God is holy, so we are to be holy. "Give the following instructions to the entire community of Israel. You must be holy because I, the Lord your God, am holy" (Leviticus 19:2). Peter adds, "But now you must be holy in everything you do, just as God who chose you is holy" (1 Peter 1:15). People are holy when they are devoted to God and separated from sin. Thus, we must understand the concept of holiness so that we may progress in our Christian growth. In my book *On Holy Ground* I note:

> The desire to be holy as God is holy appears to have been replaced with a self-absorbed desire for love, wealth, happiness, and success. Whatever the reasons, God's Word to "be holy as I am holy" cannot and will not go away. It cannot be displaced from its origin nor is there any worthy substitute for it.[7]

Some theologians, in describing God, have used the phrase "wholly other," meaning that God is not one of us, nor is he like us; he is beyond anything we could even imagine. Greater than we can comprehend, more magnificent than we could ever describe. Good beyond description, powerful beyond description, holy beyond description. Thus, when Isaiah heard the angels singing of God, "Holy, holy, holy is the Lord Almighty; the whole earth is filled with his glory!," he learned what God is like—his complete independence of this world, and his involvement with humanity by choice.

This, then, is our invitation to express God's greatness, majesty, strength, and honor while looking for ways to extend his kingdom. There is something about being in the presence of God. When we see him, he opens our eyes and we fall on our faces before him in worship. And through our worship, we come to see things as God sees them. The songwriter says:

O soul, are you weary and troubled? / No light in the darkness you see? There's light for a look at the Savior / And life more abundant and free / Turn your eyes upon Jesus / Look full in His wonderful face / And the things of earth will grow strangely dim / In the light of His glory and grace.[8]

There is probably no greater illustration of God-exalting worship than that recorded by John in Revelation 7:9–12:

After this I saw a vast crowd, too great to count, from every nation and tribe and people and language, standing in front of the throne and before the Lamb. They were clothed in white robes and held palm branches in their hands. And they were shouting with a great roar,

"Salvation comes from our God who sits on the throne and from the Lamb!"

And all the angels were standing around the throne and the elders and the four living beings. And they fell before the throne with their faces to the ground and worshiped God. They sang,

"Amen! Blessing and glory and wisdom and thanksgiving and honor and power and strength belong to our God forever and ever! Amen."

The crowd in heaven praises God, saying that salvation comes from him and the Lamb. Salvation from sin's penalty can come only through Jesus Christ. Is this not a reason to praise and worship God? Paul writes in Philippians 2:9–11,

Therefore, God elevated him to the place of highest honor and gave him the name above all other names, that at the name of Jesus every knee should bow, in heaven and on earth and under the earth, and every tongue declare that Jesus Christ is Lord, to the glory of God the Father.

God is one substance shared by three independent persons. In the case of the Son, it is even more important that we grasp this fact. In Genesis, the first book of the Bible, God says: "Let us make human beings in our image, to be like us. . . . So God created human beings in his own image. In the image of God he created them; male and female he created them" (1:26–27). You see here a mixture of plural and singular pronouns. Who is God referring to saying "Let us" or "in our image"? The Genesis account begins (v. 1), "In the beginning, God created the heavens and the earth." The Scripture records there was God the Father, God the Word Spoken, and the Spirit of God "hovering over the surface of the waters" (v. 2).

John, in the prologue of his gospel (1:1), concurs: "In the beginning, the Word already existed. The Word was with God, and the Word was God." He then goes on to say this very word "became human and made his home among us" (v. 14). He was full of unfailing love and faithfulness. Paul further explains in

Romans 8:3 that because the sin of Adam was imputed to all mankind, and since

> The law of Moses was unable to save us because of the weakness of our sinful nature. So God did what the law could not do. He sent his own Son in a body like the bodies we sinners have. And in that body, God declared an end to sin's control over us by giving his Son as a sacrifice for our sins.

Because Jesus came into the world, Satan—who deceived God's creations into sin— would now be in mortal combat with Jesus for the lives of God's people. In Genesis 3:15 God declared, "I will cause hostility between you and the woman, and between your offspring and her offspring. He will strike your head." Because Jesus would strike a fatal blow to Satan's head, the victory is already won.

Revelation is the greatest book of worship for this present hour, with its main focus on the divine inhabitant who resides far above the words of the text, the God who declares himself: "I am the Alpha and the Omega—the Beginning and the End" (21:6a).

After John announced in his gospel that "the Word became human and made his home among us," he wanted us to know that we could know God fully because Jesus was the perfect expression of God in a human form: "And we have seen his glory, the glory of the Father's one and only Son." Many contemporary believers, for the most part, feel rather secure in their knowledge of Christ, citing that "Jesus died on the cross to save us from our sins and if we accept him into our hearts we will receive new birth and live forever with him." However, if this is the extent of our relationship with Christ we have failed to understand and apprehend the true glory of his being. The apostle Paul says of Jesus, "Though he was God, he did not think of equality with God as something to cling to" (Philippians 2:6). Further, Paul notes, "in Christ lives all the fullness of God in a human body" (Colossians 2:9). John, in the opening verse of his first epistle, declares:

> We proclaim to you the one who existed from the beginning, whom we have heard and seen. We saw him with our own eyes and touched him with our own hands. He is the Word of life.

Jesus is God's only and unique Son—with the emphasis on "unique." When Jesus was born, God became a man. He was not part man and part God; he was completely human and completely divine. Before Jesus, people could only know of God. After Jesus's death and bodily resurrection people could know God personally, because he is the perfect expression of God in human form. In Hebrews 1:1–3 the writer declares:

> Long ago God spoke many times and in many ways to our ancestors through the prophets. And now in these final days, he has spoken to us through his Son. God promised everything to the Son as an inheritance, and through the Son, he created the universe. The Son radiates God's own glory and expresses the very character of God, and he sustains everything by the mighty power of his command. When he had cleansed us from our sins, he sat down in the place of honor at the right hand of the majestic God in heaven.

This is one of the strongest statements about the divine nature of Christ found anywhere in the Bible. Not only is Jesus the exact representation of God, but he is God himself—the very God who spoke in Old Testament times. He is eternal; he is the full revelation of God in a human body. He was with the Father in creating the world. He is supreme over all creation, including the spirit world.

Thus, he is the final revelation of God, and here in these verses we find a series of seven powerful statements.

First, "God promised everything to the Son as an inheritance." Heir is a title of dignity, which shows that Christ has the supreme place in all the universe and the highest place in heaven. As Paul writes, "Therefore, God elevated him to the place of highest honor and gave him the name above all other names" (Philippians 2:9). This did not mark some new dignity for Christ, but simply marked his reentry to his rightful place.

The second truth about the Son is that through him, God "made the universe and everything in it." This statement preserves the truth of John 1:1–3:

> In the beginning, the Word already existed. The Word was with God, and the Word was God. He existed in the beginning with God. God created everything through him, and nothing was created except through him.

The third truth, "The Son radiates God's own glory," means that Jesus is the reflection of God himself—that through him we can apprehend the revelation of God's majesty. "Everything about him expresses the very character of God" is the fourth assertion about the Son. Jesus said in John 14:9, "Anyone who has seen me has seen the Father!" The fifth statement is that Jesus "sustains the universe by the mighty power of his command." Here "sustains" does not mean holding up as a dead weight; he enters the world he created and carries it along toward fulfillment of the divine plan.

When we come to the next statement, "When he had cleansed us from our sins," we come to the heart of the matter. Sin is, was, and always will be the great problem. Sin is the power that deceives and leads people to destruction. It is the power that causes

318   A Wonder-Filled Life

people to turn a deaf ear to God's word—and it is so lethal that its influence and activity can be ended only by death. Therefore, this final statement by the writer leads us to the final revelation that "When he had cleansed us from our sins, he sat down in the place of honor at the right hand of the majestic God of heaven."

Most of us would simply acknowledge that Jesus's death on the cross saved us, and that we are now right with God. This is the essence of the gospel, and all who bear the name of Christ have accepted this truth for their lives. However, if this is the extent of our relationship with Christ, we have failed to understand and apprehend the true glory of his being. Jesus's death accomplished much more. He made atonement for our sins, meaning his death removed God's wrath toward us. He put away sin so that God remembers our sin no more. He bore our sin, taking it upon himself. He offered sacrifice for sins. He made himself an offering for sin and brought about remission and forgiveness of sin. It is clear from all this that Jesus accomplished a many-sided salvation.

Thus, Jesus Christ is *prima causa* (the first cause), the origin and source of all being, who sheds his glory upon us, which causes us to esteem him most excellent, to exalt him most high, and to behold him in all his glory. That is why the song "We Shall Behold Him" has become my song in glory:

> The sky shall unfold / Preparing His entrance / The stars shall applaud Him / With thunders of praise / The sweet light in His eyes shall enhance those awaiting / And we shall behold Him / Then face to face. . . .

> And the angels shall sound / The shout of His coming / And the sleeping shall rise from / Their slumbering place / And those who remain shall be changed in a moment / And we shall behold Him / Then face to face / We shall

behold Him / Oh yes, we shall behold Him / Face to face in all of His Glory / We shall behold Him / Oh yes, we shall behold Him / Face to face my Savior and Lord / And we shall behold Him Our Savior and Lord! / Savior and Lord! [9]

It's encouraging to know that a vision of the Son is yet for today, even though the church is much like in the time of Samuel: "Now in those days messages from the Lord were very rare, and visions were quite uncommon" (1 Samuel 3:1). Messages and visions from God are rare today because God doesn't give visions in an atmosphere of sin and rebellion and indifference to his word.

Let me tell you what must happen to see a vision of the Son. First, surrender your heart to the Lord. Then, have a sincere desire to know him, and spend much time with him sitting at his feet learning of him. Then, concentrate everything on him until one day you realize nothing else matters but Jesus. Then you won't be satisfied until you see what Isaiah, Jeremiah, Ezekiel, Elisha, Stephen, and John saw. Then God will say, "Come up here, and I will show you what must happen after this" (Revelation 4:1). And then you will behold the Son of God, Jesus Christ, the Lamb upon the throne. It had been sixty years since John had last seen the Lord, but now in his vision in Revelation, he beholds Jesus the glorified Son of God:

Then as I looked, I saw a door standing open in heaven, and the same voice I had heard before spoke to me like a trumpet blast. The voice said, "Come up here, and I will show you what must happen after this." And instantly I was in the Spirit, and I saw a throne in heaven and someone sitting on it. The one sitting on the throne was as brilliant as gemstones—like jasper and carnelian. And the glow of

320   A Wonder-Filled Life

an emerald circled his throne like a rainbow. Twenty-four thrones surrounded him, and twenty-four elders sat on them. They were all clothed in white and had gold crowns on their heads. . . . Day after day and night after night they keep on saying, "Holy, holy, holy is the Lord God, the Almighty—the one who always was, who is, and who is still to come." (Revelation 4:1–4, 8)

John further testifies:

Then I saw a scroll in the right hand of the one who was sitting on the throne. There was writing on the inside and the outside of the scroll, and it was sealed with seven seals. And I saw a strong angel, who shouted with a loud voice: "Who is worthy to break the seals on this scroll and open it?" But no one in heaven or on earth or under the earth was able to open the scroll and read it.

Then I began to weep bitterly because no one was found worthy to open the scroll and read it. But one of the twenty-four elders said to me, "Stop weeping! Look, the Lion of the tribe of Judah, the heir to David's throne, has won the victory. He is worthy to open the scroll and its seven seals." (5:1–5)

Now close your eyes for a moment and listen to the Apostle John while receiving the revelation from Jesus Christ:

Then I looked again, and I heard the voices of thousands and millions of angels around the throne and of the living beings and the elders. And they sang in a mighty chorus:

"Worthy is the Lamb who was slaughtered—to receive power and riches and wisdom and strength and honor and glory and blessing."

And then I heard every creature in heaven and on earth and under the earth and in the sea. They sang:

"Blessing and honor and glory and power belong to the one sitting on the throne and to the Lamb forever and ever."

And the four living beings said, "Amen!" And the twenty-four elders fell down and worshiped the Lamb. (vv. 11–14)

And so we too join in singing to the Lord, exalting God for who he is and what he has done. Amen! We shall behold him!

The Spirit and the bride say, "Come." Let anyone who hears this say, "Come." Let anyone who is thirsty, "Come." Let anyone who desires drink freely from the water of life. (Revelation 22:17)

Amen! And we who have seen the Lord say: Amen! We who have a vision of the Son now cry: Amen! Amen! Amen! *Come, Lord Jesus*!

ENDNOTES

SECTION I

Chapter One

1. Manning, B. (2010). *A glimpse of Jesus: The stranger to self-hatred.* HarperCollins.

2. McClure, J. A. (2008). *Almost persuaded, now to believe* (pp. 196–197). Tate Pub.

3. Graham, B. (2016, January 28). "In the world, but not of it." Decision, https://decisionmagazine.com/in-world-not-of-it.

4. Wallace, B. J. W. (2021, March 16). "Christian worldview: What does it mean to be 'in the world' but not 'of the world'?" Cold-Case Christianity, https://coldcasechristianity.com/writings/christian-worldview-what-does-it-mean-to-be-in-the-world-but-not-of-the-world.

5. McDowell, B. (2015, December 14). "The paradox of story: Spirituality is rooted in earthiness." Norway Avenue Church of Christ. http://norwayave.org/bill-mcdowell/2015/12/14/the-paradox-of-story-spirality-is-rooted-in-earthiness.

6. Ibid.

7. Ibid.

Chapter Two

1. Livingstone, M. (2021, May 3). "Worshiptainment: Heretical methods are as bad as heretical messages." ChurchPlants, https://churchplants.com/articles/11330-worshiptainment-why-heretical-methods-are-as-dangerous-as-heretical-messages.html. Mike Livingstone is an editor of Bible study materials at LifeWay Christian Resources.

2. Ibid.

3. Quoted in McClure, J. A. (2006). In *Can these bones live?: The miraculous story of what can happen to a church that follows God's vision* (p. 34). Tate Pub.

4. Dalton, K. (2020, March 31). "Who is Tommy John and why is the surgery named after him?" Sportscasting, https://www.sportscasting.com/who-is-tommy-john-and-why-is-the-surgery-named-after-him.

5. Yancey, P. (1995). *The Jesus I never knew* (p. 122).. Zondervan.

6. Hall, E. M. (1865). "I hear the Savior say, thy strength indeed is small." https://hymnary.org/text/i_hear_the_savior_say_thy_strength_indee. Public domain.

Chapter Three

1. Newell, W. R. (1893). "At Calvary." https://www.hymnal.net/en/hymn/h/342. Public domain.

2. Edersheim, A. (1954). *Jesus the MESSIAH: Being an abridged edition of* The life and times of Jesus the messiah. Eerdmans.

3. Lucado, M. (2009). *No wonder they call him the savior* (p. 11–12). Thomas Nelson.

Chapter Four

1. Lucado, M. (2012). *Gentle thunder: Hearing God through the storm* (p. 83). Thomas Nelson.

2. Sheen, F. J. (n.d.). "Quotes from Bishop Sheen." http://archbishopfultonsheencentre.com/Quotes.html.

3. Surber, C. (2010, June 17). "The Lord's servant." Sermon Central, https://www.sermoncentral.com/sermons/the-lord-s-servant-chris-surber-sermon-on-jesus-christ-147730.

Chapter Five

1. N.a. (2004). *NLT life application study Bible* (endnote 1 John 2:15). Tyndale House.

2. Bausch, W. J. (2015). *Storytelling: Imagination and faith* (p. 173). Clear Faith Publishing LLC.

3. McClure. *Can these bones live?* (p. 59–60).

4. Miller, C. (2000). *Into the depths of God: Where eyes see the invisible, ears hear the inaudible, and minds conceive the inconceivable* (p. 15). Bethany House.

Chapter Six

1. Schmitt, M., and S. Schmitt. (2011, September 11). *On fishing for men by Paul Harvey.* https://mikeandsus.org/2011/09/11/on-fishing-for-men-by-paul-harvey.

2. McMillen, S. I. (1984). *None of these diseases* (p. 113). Pickering.

Chapter Seven

1. Bausch. *Storytelling* (p. 66).

2. McClure, J. A. (2010). *The crimson thread of the Bible: Unlocking the mystery of the Bible* (pp. 115–116). Deep River Books.

3. Liddell, E. (n.d.). "Eric Liddell quotes." Goodreads, https://www.goodreads.com/author/quotes/802465.Eric_Liddell.

4. Bausch. *Storytelling* (p. 115).

5. Lemmel, H. H. (1922). "Turn your eyes upon Jesus." Public domain.

Chapter Eight

1. *NLT life application study Bible* (endnote Heb. 1:3).

2. Beveridge, W. (n.d.). *The theological works of William Beveridge.* 12 vols. Logos Bible Software. https://www.logos.com/product/37542/the-theological-works-of-william-beveridge.

3. Martin, W. C. (1901). "The name of Jesus is so sweet." Public domain.

Chapter Nine

1. McClure, J. A. (2016). *Made for glory: In the image and likeness of God* (p. 38). Deep River Books.

Chapter Ten

1. McDowell, B. (2015, December 13). "A mofif for living." Norway Avenue Church of Christ. http://norwayave.org/bill-mcdowell/2015/12/13/a-mofif-for-living.

2. Quoted in Robinson, H. (2021). *"Putting first things first."* Bible.org. December 3, 2021. https://bible.org/illustration/putting-first-things-first.

3. Foster, R. J. (2018). *Celebration of discipline: The path to spiritual growth* (p. 87). Harper One.

4. Wikipedia. "The creation (Haydn)." https://en.wikipedia.org/wiki/The_Creation_(Haydn). Accessed July 12, 2021.

SECTION II

Chapter Eleven

1. McClure, J. A. (2020). *The top of the stairs: A spiritual memoir* (p. 273). Deep River Books.

2. Miller, C. (1998). *The unchained soul* (p. xiv). Bethany House.

3. Ibid.

Chapter Twelve

1. Fritz, P. (2001, September 19). "A certain medieval monk announced he would be . . ." Sermon Central. https://www.sermoncentral.

com/sermon-illustrations/9160/a-certain-medieval-monk-announced-he-would-be-by-paul-fritz.

2. Miller. *Into the depths of God* (p. 15).

Chapter Fourteen

1. Miller. *Into the depths of God* (p. 15).

2. Elliott, C. (1835). "Just as I am." Public domain.

Chapter Fifteen

1. Graham. "In the world, but not of it."

2. "Des." (2019, June 29). *The magical city*. Whitfords Anglican Community Church, https://whitfords.perth.anglican.org/parish-blog/the-magical-city.

3. McClure, J. (2018). *Are you Jesus?* (p. 48, 49). Deep River Books.

4. Gershwin, G., Jepson, H., Chorus, & Smallens, A. (1934). "Summertime." Public domain.

5. McClure. *Are you Jesus?* (p. 49–50).

Chapter Sixteen

1. McClure, J. A. (2006). *Can these bones live?: The miraculous story of what can happen to a church that follows God's vision.* (pp. 191–192). Tate Pub.

Chapter Seventeen

1. Tozer, A. W. (2001). *The knowledge of the holy, and, the pursuit of God* (p. vii). Family Christian Press.

2. Wikipedia. "Billy Brae." https://en.wikipedia.org/wiki/Billy_Brae. Accessed October 26, 2020.

Chapter Eighteen

1. McClure, J. A. (2008). *Almost persuaded, now to believe* (p. 31). Tate Pub.

2. Yancey. *The Jesus I never knew.*

3. Lehman, F. M. (1917). "The Love of God." Public domain.

Chapter Nineteen

1. McClure. *Almost persuaded, now to believe* (p. 182).

Chapter Twenty

1. Warner, A. B., and Bradbury, W. B. (1860). "Yes, Jesus loves me." Public domain.

2. Elliott, C. (1835). "Just as I am." Public domain.

3. Jensen, W. (n.d.). "I have decided to follow Jesus." Public domain.

4. Newell. "At Calvary." Public domain.

5. Sanchez, P. (1975). "I exalt thee." https://mojim.com/usy137030x1x5.htm.

6. McClure. *The top of the stairs* (p. 273).

7. McClure, J. A. (2017). *On holy ground.* (p. 27–28). Deep River Books.

8. Lemmel. "Turn your eyes upon Jesus."

9. Rambo, D. (1984). "We shall behold him." http://www.lyricson-demand.com/d/dottierambolyrics/weshallbeholdhimlyrics.html.

Contact Joshua A. McClure

Email: sharethevision31@gmail.com

Website
www.joshuaamcclure.net

Social
Facebook: https://www.facebook.com/joshua.mcclure.961/
LinkedIn: jamministry
Twitter: Joshua A. McClure (@Jalvinm) / Twitter
YouTube: https://www.youtube.com/channel/
UCQczEBpPsiyYtRAgWHJPuAA/videos
or https://rb.gy/0lzm6o

Mail
PO Box 304
Bradford, RI 02808